A solitary immersion
into the flow of a timeless way,
and the people and stories found along it.

Go Slow
Plan Little
Walk Forever

Go Slow
Plan Little
Walk Forever

Along the Camino de Santiago
and Beyond

Jerry Meyer

ISBN eBook: 978-1-7346172-6-9
ISBN print book: 978-1-7346172-5-2

Distributed in print by Lulu.
Available from www.lulu.com.
Distributed in print and eBook by Amazon Kindle Direct
  Publishing.
Available on Amazon.

Cover author designed on *Canva*.
Author photo; taking a rest at Carrefour du Puits du Roi
  March 27th, 2017.
Maps inspired by Jason, and thanks to: d-maps.com
  https://d-maps.com/continent.php?num_con=5&lang=en
Text illustrations are snapshots converted by author.
Frontispiece; on ridge of the prehistoric grave, above Bermeo.

Editorial guidance from K. Daniel, A. Beeson, K. Beeth and
  I. Garcia.
Typeface: Garamond.

For my father and mother, Jerry and Patricia,
who first set me on the path.

OVERALL ROUTE

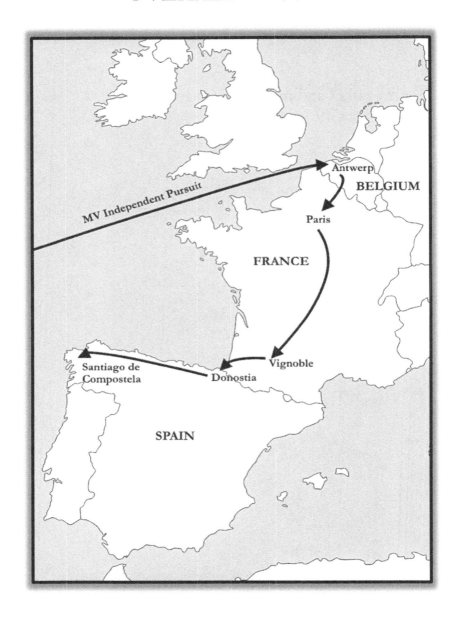

CONTENTS

PREFACE

It is only in the last century that we started riding in mechanical contraptions for most of our locomotive needs. The remaining walking we still do, at least in industrialized societies, has been reduced to connecting between different forms of transport, be it to elevator or airplane. Mustn't this have a profound effect on our state of being? Mustn't it conflict with our very nature?

What would it be like to stop all that riding and start walking again, day after day, week upon week, sky over your crown, ground under your soles? What would it do to you besides give you sore feet?

In 2017 I set off on the Camino de Santiago, first by ship from the United States, then by foot from Antwerp, Belgium. Nearly four months underway. What follows is an account of that journey. It's an account of the Way itself and the people along it. It's an account of what such a walk might do to you.

This book is a sharing, not a guide. For what is the point of a guide to something so mutable? Even referring to the walk as *the Camino* is misleading, for the Camino is not a singular thing. Not only are the possibilities of the route nearly endless, but the effects of the Camino are unique to each person. It depends on what you've brought along with you. It depends on how willing you are to observe what you encounter.

I have written this during the pandemic. I was fortunate to have place, time and wherewithal. Through the writing I could immerse in activities the pandemic had banished from routine life: traveling, engaging strangers, opening homes, a touch, a kiss. As joyful as these memories are, they are tempered with the realization that many of the small establishments I patronized, and even some of the people I met, may not have survived.

Revisiting the days along the Camino made clear how these basic interactions are so elemental to our humanity, and how their restriction leaves us wanting. Walking, too, is elemental to our humanity. It's where we come from. Ironically, it's not the pandemic that has taken walking away. It's how we choose to structure our modern lives.

Along the Camino I was reminded daily of people's essential decency, of our willingness to help a stranger. And within me the Camino tapped a forgotten reservoir of gratitude for the most basic things; for water, for a place to sleep, for a kind word.

I have been fortunate to reconnect with some of the people I met along the Way, particularly in Spain, and they have helped me tell their stories more fully. This has been a delight. Their openhearted sharing reassured we are never alone with our personal burdens; however heavy they may feel. Some of their comments are the result of follow-up conversations. Otherwise, quotations throughout the text should be recognized as my best approximations.

Regarding the history of the Camino de Santiago? I confess I knew nothing of it before a few years ago. Basically, the Camino is a pilgrimage that originated in the early 800s to a Christian shrine of the apostle James, now a cathedral surrounded by the city of Santiago de Compostela in Galicia, Spain. The pilgrimage grew in popularity during the Middle Ages, attracting pilgrims from all over Europe. But the flow has waxed and waned over the centuries with political instability, war and pestilence. The last couple of decades have seen a resurgence, with over 300,000 people reaching Santiago in 2017, the year I walked. There's a lot of easily accessible, interesting history on the Camino and the region, so I'll leave it to your level of curiosity. But in my view the Camino is not merely a series of places, or a special church, or a particular road. And it's not something of the past. While it is a great tradition, the most important element of the Camino de Santiago's history is the lived experience.

Why did I go? To walk over the Earth, to escape routine, to clear the mind. At least that is what I told myself initially, and anyone else who asked, because everyone asks. You have to articulate *something*, right? It can't just be impulse! Of course it can, even if that's unsettling to ourselves, and to others. The deep-down motivation is harder to know. There's something about the Camino that once it touches you, it reels you in. It pulls at those elemental things we tend to forget or keep hidden. You may never know exactly what the spirit of the Camino has fixed itself upon within you, but the pull is tangible.

The Camino is not something to be finished. If anything, it is a venue for the struggle of heart and mind to make sense of one's life. Frankly, you can only get so much by reading about it. The Camino has to be traveled. We ultimately have to step outside ourselves, outside our normal lives, if we are to understand anything about them. If by reading this you are inspired to set off, or reinspired to do it again, I couldn't ask for more.

All that walking, day after day, week upon week? It removes the top of your head. What will pour out? What will flow in?

Why don't you go and see?

Jerry Meyer
South Carolina, January 2022

Faith is patience with mystery.
-Richard Rohr

Compostelagenootschap 1

There is no color. Clouds spread to blot out any trace of the coming sunset. Shops are closed. The adjacent church imposing and locked. There is no one on the streets of Grimbergen, no lights visible in buildings. Where is everyone?

I stand in front of the large door and wait. Is this even the monastery, the abbey? I resist the urge to buzz again. Had I pressed the right button? I'd expected a giant iron knocker, not this intercom panel that looks like it belongs on an apartment building. I can't even tell if it is working. If no one comes I'll have to retrace my steps to the edge of town and find Neo – "Like the movie," he said about his name – and take up the offer of his camper van parked in the drive of his parents' home. It had looked cramped.

Even if someone comes, will they let me stay in the abbey? Do they do that? Neo said he didn't think so. Can I even make myself understood?

My shoulders ache, my hips are tender, and my feet are swollen. And I can still feel the effects of yesterday's dehydration. Only the second day walking and I am poleaxed. At the convent in Lier this morning Sister Liliane said, "Please take our greetings to the Abbot and the brothers," but even she wasn't sure about rooms.

Well, maybe carrying her greeting will boost my chances. The monks will know I'd stayed in the convent, so I'm not a complete unknown presenting myself unannounced in shorts and jacket and a too heavy backpack.

But someone will first have to open the door.

Two nights before, the man who came to register me and collect the €7 at the St. Julianus Gasthuys in Antwerp said, "You are the first pilgrim of the season." He was genial, but so general with his directions that when he left me in the empty hostel, I still had no clear sense of the best route out of the city the next morning.

"Good luck. And drop the key through the slot when you leave."

Antwerp was my first night in Europe, having arrived in its

busy port early that morning. Here I was setting off on this thing generally called *the Camino*, but it was still more concept to me than clarity. I still had no idea where I should go tomorrow. And they didn't even refer to it as the Camino here. It was the *Jacobsweg*.

Fortunately, Rean & Jo unexpectedly arrived.

I may have been the first pilgrim to sign the guest book this season, but Rean and Jo had been underway for a week. A Dutch couple in their late sixties, they had stepped out of home in Etten-Leur, Netherlands and were walking the *Jacobsweg* all the way to Santiago, Spain.

Jo's mother had recently passed away, and he was a cancer survivor.

"We have thought about doing the *Jacobsweg* for a long time," Jo told me, "but to leave our home for four or five months, with my parents living, it was not possible. First working, then caring for my mother, Rean's cancer. This is our first chance. Maybe only chance."

They were well-organized and modestly kitted; sturdy shoes, trekking poles, medium-sized backpacks with water bladders, comfortable clothes. Each had a large white scallop shell attached to their pack, the traditional symbol of the Camino de Santiago, and Rean kept an icon of Sint Jacob in the plastic map pouch around his neck. They carried a stuffed toy from their only grandchild, and a small-sized hometown flag. And a mini-solar panel for charging their phone.

When I said I didn't know exactly where I was heading the next day, they offered I could come along with them to Lier.

"Lier?"

"We will stay in the convent there."

I didn't hesitate to accept, but standing there in the tidy little pilgrim rest house, second thoughts ricocheted around my head: A convent, how am I allowed to stay in a convent as a single male? Shouldn't we be heading south, not east? Won't this couple, 15 years my senior, be walking too slow? Isn't 20km a bit short?

But I had enough sense to know their week underway made them wiser than me about such things. I was well aware there was a lot I didn't know about walking the Camino de Santiago, even very basic things like how to find the way, where to stay, what to carry, expenses. And on top of these, there were more complex issues to navigate like language, customs and culture.

I had only heard about the Camino a few years before and only started poking around online for information in January, two months earlier. I knew I wanted to get from Antwerp to Santiago, but the day-to-day specifics of that were still vague.

To my surprise I'd found the internet somewhat lacking in the concrete details I sought. But the problem wasn't the internet. It was my preconception. I was imagining the Camino as something discreet, like the Appalachian Trail. Something with a clear start and finish, and well-defined points in-between. Something knowable, clearly enumerable. I kept trying to force the Camino into this mold, but it wouldn't fit. If I had been starting off on one of the well-worn paths in Spain or further south in France, it would have been something closer to this. It would have been only a matter of ordering the right guidebook and setting forth. But here, further afield, things were not as apparent, at least to me. I later came to understand this amorphousness is part of the essence of the Camino.

Fortunately, I had stumbled onto the website of the Vlaams Compostelagenootschap, the unpronounceable Flemish organiza-tion for assisting pilgrims. Through the miracle of cut and paste translation Mia, a kind and patient woman, told me how to avail this guesthouse when I arrived in Antwerp. She also reassured me there was a way, the Via Brabantica, that would carry me into the part of France where I was aiming. The gentleman who signed me in earlier, having been alerted by Mia, offered me a booklet describing the Via Brabantica. It was in Flemish, but I knew it would come in handy, even if I couldn't understand most of it. I just needed to get going in the right direction.

The arrival of Rean & Jo could not have been more fortuitous, as if the Vlaams Compostelagenootschap was looking out for me. Whatever their direction, whatever their speed, whatever distance and destination, I knew I was lucky to have them to follow.

The next morning Rean & Jo led the way through Antwerp's

busy streets, consulting their guide and pointing out the occasional waymark. Waymarks, right, I had read about them, small indicators to mark the pilgrim's path. But even when pointed out, and Jo usually saw them first, I had a hard time seeing them. These were round blue and yellow stickers or plaques, about the size of an orange, with a stylized yellow scallop pointing in the direction of travel. In the city they tended to be affixed above eye level on utility poles, unnoticed by the stream of everyday pedestrians. Without Rean & Jo's help, I don't think I would have ever noticed one.

Once we left the city proper, the way wound through suburbs, parks, garden plots, fields and pasture, mostly shadeless and sunny. We peeled down to shirtsleeves early. The way was densely

inhabited, but I never saw a place to refill my water bottle, neither spigot nor shop. I rationed the 40 ounces, but that amount was wholly inadequate. Rean & Jo seemed to have carried plenty in their bladders. I felt embarrassed to ask them, but in retrospect I know they would have done everything to make sure I supplemented my water. It would have probably been as simple as one of them pointing toward an obvious source, a source I couldn't discern because all I could see around me was one big unfamiliar landscape.

"Here, a salt tablet, take it," said Rean at a late afternoon stop in rare shade.

My official first day on the *Jacobsweg, la Compostelle, le Chemin, el Camino*, the Way of Saint James, whatever it was called, and I was sunburned and dehydrated. My surf hat was in the bottom of my pack waiting for Spain, underneath all the warm clothes I'd brought for enduring the cold spring weather of northern Europe. I could feel my forehead radiating heat. O ye of overflowing hubris, I thought, recalling the gross overestimation of my walking capacity the night before. And where did this weather come from? It was supposed to be cold and rainy! Clearly my distress was more

4

apparent than I thought. I'd never had a salt tablet. It was a ridiculous, old-fashioned thing. I didn't even know they still existed. But Rean thought I needed one. I did. Sucking on it boosted me just enough to make the threshold of the convent in decent form.

I spent a night of constantly drinking water and peeing and riding a bunk that felt like it was at sea. The consensus the next morning was that Grimbergen, at 30km, might be a little far for a day, but the sisters said there was a famous abbey there. The home of Grimbergen Beer, I wondered? It sounded interesting so I thought I would try – I had already forgotten the first day's lesson about overestimating my capabilities.

But I'd learned my lesson about water and gulped prodigiously before setting out. Consequently, I needed to duck into the woods shortly outside of Lier. Good, I thought, I'm definitely better hydrated today.

Deeper in, the sounds of leaves crunching, movement – deer, homeless? A young woman with a large green backpack appeared. A huge backpack, way larger than mine, and she was almost half my size.

"Hello."

"Hallo."

"Were you camping back there?"

"No, I had to use the toilet. I spent the night in town."

So our bladders were in sync, and it turned out she was walking the Camino too.

Rebecca had also stepped off from home and was walking all the way to Santiago. The Dutch, I would come to learn, had a reputation as the hardiest of pilgrims, even more so than the Germans who were known to slog through the middle of winter for fun. But the Dutch were modest in their vigor, with simple attire and basic equipment. To walk from home to Spain seemed the most natural of things. Rebecca was in her early 20s, on a gap year before university, and resided farther north than Rean & Jo. She walked at a rapid pace, in spite of her pack, which contained camping gear, which mine did not, and weighed 20kg, to my 15kg. I kept up, enjoying her company. She exuded enthusiasm, curiosity, openness and confidence.

We passed shaggy horses as big as American bison, shaggy ponies, shaggy chickens even. She wondered why I chose to turn certain ways on some of the forest trails. I didn't understand what she meant until I realized she was not looking for waymarks. "How did you get this far without knowing about the waymarks?"

"I don't know," she shrugged and laughed. The day after I'd learned how to spot waymarks from Rean & Jo, here I was passing it on to another pilgrim, as if I were the expert.

Rebecca's hometown radio station had done a feature and was following her progress. While traversing the Netherlands people would slow their cars to wish her well, but this had stopped once she crossed into Belgium.

"I want to be in Taizé for Easter."

"Where? Taizé? What's Taizé?"

"It's a kind of spiritual center, lots of young people from all over, lots of singing, great vibe. It's near Lyon."

Why did I know nothing of such things?

Our water finished by mid-morning, Rebecca suggested we duck into a petrol station. The friendly cashier, Sumeet from Nepal, filled our bottles and gave us coffee and pastry. So that's how it works, I thought. We covered the 16km to Mechelen in about four hours – what would turn out to be the standard Camino pace: 4kph – and followed brass scallop shells inlaid in the sidewalk to the central Grote Markt. There we sat on the warm paving stones, eating our simple lunches and airing our feet in the sun. People filled the cafés on this perfect day, conversing, dining, drinking, smoking. Tour groups, student fieldtrips and practical bicycles crisscrossed the wide plaza. Children bursting with energy shouted and played. Rebecca applied white Vaseline to her raw blisters. She said she had a twin.

"We are very close, but complete opposites. She's very social, loves the city life. And she has blonde hair and blue eyes. Fake nails and makeup!" she laughed.

I couldn't imagine.

From here Rebecca would head in a more easterly direction. Mechelen would be the evening halt for Rean & Jo, then they too would follow a more easterly route into France. I was heading south, through Brussels and then southwest to Paris where I had friends. After these three sturdy folk my first two days, I wouldn't glimpse another pilgrim for a month, and that south of Paris.

But where would I stay tonight? I refilled my water at the public restrooms then, fortified, strode across the Belgian countryside, direction Grimbergen.

Those large brass scallop shells I remember embedded in the sidewalk of Mechelen? Maybe it wasn't Mechelen, but I would come upon them in a number of towns and cities along the way. Ignored by most passersby, they were like a secret, reassuring signal to we pilgrims that, regardless of the everyday swirl around us, we were heading in the right direction.

Though Sister Liliane in Lier asked me to carry the convent's greetings, what I'd really hoped for in the morning was that she would call to see if it was even possible for me to stay in the abbey. But maybe nun telephoning monk was a no-no and I was just grateful we had been welcomed into the convent in the first place. I didn't want to be pushy. Plus, at that moment, I wasn't even sure I'd reach Grimbergen.

Yes, I admit I was somewhat apprehensive about where I'd end up for my second night. But at the same time something told me the Camino is not something to get too caught up in organizing; it's something you enter into and do. I'd end up somewhere. It would all work out.

And here I am at the threshold of Abdij Grimbergen, somewhat surprised at having come all the way. Getting chilled, instead of pulsing with heat, and having to rely on myself, instead of my capable Dutch escorts.

I wonder if I should buzz again?

All afternoon I'd been repeating the simple French phrases for just this moment. But am I even in the part of Belgium where they speak French? No, this is still Flanders, but maybe I'm near enough to Brussels?

I hear the bolt slide.

My heart jumps.

The door slowly swings open, hinges creaking appropriately.

Filling the doorway is a towering man clad in white vestments. It's completely dark behind him. He says nothing.

« Je suis un pèlerin. Je voudrais une chambre pour un nuit. »

The figure's silence continues as he regards me. I'm 6'3", maybe I am down a step, but the apparition in white looms over me. Then he leans backward to get a better view.

Has he understood what I said?

That was it, the only two lines I had. Maybe they only speak Flemish here? Were my two sentences of spoken French really that bad? Was it presumptuous and rude to use French?

After endless moments he says, "You want a room?"

"Yes. Oui!" I blurt.

More moments pass. What is he thinking?

He steps backwards, "Come."

Through doors, up and down stairs, along corridors and cloister. Past the dining hall where I can hear behind the stained glass the clink of the monks' cutlery but no conversation and for one hopeful instant I think we'll enter directly for a nourishing bowl of steaming stew and fresh bread, but no. Up more stairs, a pause for a moment while the robed gentleman disappears then reappears with a thick ring of keys. Higher and higher toward the farthest corner of the abbey, along a dim hall of portraits, to the uppermost floor, not another soul to be seen. Fresh white linens from an armoire, he makes the bed, a sleigh-style bed of heavy wood from a time when people were notably shorter.

My own private cozy room. From standing uncertainly at the door to this, in a span of ten minutes. He asks me what time I'd like breakfast.

Breakfast? "Um, eight, *huit?*"
He nods.

Not long after I was sitting in the bar area of the only open restaurant in town, guided there by a mix of French and English from the monk. Fortunately, the directions weren't much more than go down the back stairs, follow the lane and you'll run into it.

I had said farewell to Rean & Jo at breakfast with the sisters in Lier. I was indebted to this kind, practical couple. They'd taken me along, shown me how to pick out the waymarks that were invisible to my uninitiated eye, and made sure I had a place to sleep at the end of my first day. Mia and the Vlaams Compostelagenootschap had welcomed me, then these two had given me direction. I felt officially underway.

The chair was low, soft and comfortable. I was sunk into it, feeling relief and a heavy sleepiness settling over me. I'd taken soup, bread and a single glass of the most delicious house wine ever. It was all I could eat.

I ached at various places.

Coming from the shower earlier I missed a low step in the unlit corridor of the abbey and fell like a tree. Left forearm and shin nicely bruised. Fortunately, no one was there to see or hear as I lay splayed sans towel.

From the walking my left calf was spiked, and my right thigh felt paddled. Both feet were aflame. A touch of sunstroke? Why was my surf hat still in the bottom of my pack? Why all this sunshine? I covered roughly 30km today. Not too difficult, but definitely not too easy. When my sister asked before I left the US how far I thought I'd walk, I told her I hoped to work up to 50km a day. What did I imagine myself to be? Half that was testing me. Sure, the first three days would be the worst, as Rean said; body incredulous, asking what are you doing, walking all day, carrying this thing on your back? But 50km?

I've got to unload at least 5kg in Paris, I thought. Do I really need the sweater, the second pair of trousers, the second long sleeve shirt, the rain pants? What else had I stuffed in there in my overenthusiastic preparation? The pack's too heavy.

I thought of Rebecca, camped in a farmer's field, putting Vaseline on her blisters. Her heavy pack. Tougher than I.

Surrounded by animated diners and drinkers I was alone yet happy, in spite of my bodily aches. I felt connected to them and boosted by their enjoyment.

But I was ready for the sleigh bed and its over-soft mattress. When I made to get going, I realized I couldn't raise my arms to pull on my jacket. Then I realized I couldn't stand. I had paid the bill but couldn't rise from the chair. I had so relaxed, then stiffened, I was nearly paralyzed. And the single glass of wine had made me lightheaded. People will think I'm drunk when I try to get up. I'll lose my balance, pitch onto another table, twirl into the bar as I struggle to put on my jacket. What a scene. I had to laugh. With much contortion, and trying not to draw too much attention, I wiggled into the jacket while still seated. Then, with all the focus I could muster, I got myself up and out of the crowded lounge without upsetting anyone's drinks.

The next challenge was finding the right entrance to the abbey, remembering the door code, and locating the room. The old building was a labyrinth of silent corridors and stairs, but ultimately I found the sleigh bed.

The next morning it took even longer to find the room where the monk said I'd take breakfast. I had almost given up when I opened a random door and there found a table set for one. Me? I sat. Some moments later he appeared, as if he'd been watching all along, waiting, knowing better than I that I'd finally get here. He was dressed in regular clothes, and with the morning light and my more settled disposition, he didn't look as imposing. He had strikingly pale, but unguarded eyes. Probably older than my 53 years, but his skin was smooth and fresh.

"Tea," I answered, and he served me.

As I finished the breakfast he reappeared and asked if I needed anything else, or any assistance.

No, I said, and took the opportunity to pass Sister Liliane's greeting to the Abbot and all the monks. He nodded in recognition.

« *Combien ?* » How much do I owe?

He looked as if he didn't understand, so I reached into my pocket for Euros.

"No," he shook his head.

No? Ah, maybe it's donation, like yesterday at the convent. "A donation then?" I had no idea of the word in French, but he understood and shook his head again. "Really, I would like to make a donation. I mean, you took me in last night, breakfast, everything."

In careful English he said, "Remember us in your prayers on your way to Santiago."

It was such an unexpected, non-transactional answer, I felt it physically.

While I'd been having a hard time envisioning the way to Santiago, the monk's request reminded me the Way was more of a state of mind than any particular road. There instantly formed a place in my heart for this gracious gentleman and his brothers.

Heading back to collect my things from the room, I found myself in the long hall of oil paintings. I could see in the daylight that these were portraits of the abbots. I'm not sure if every one of them starting from the 12th century was there, but there were many. I came to the last one, the most recent abbot, and was stopped.

I peered more closely. No, it can't be. The figure looked just like the man who had opened the door, made my bed, served me breakfast. I was incredulous. It can't be.

But it was. There he was, the same gentleman who asked me to keep the monks in my prayers, wearing the same white vestments in which he'd swung wide the door.

On my way out, backpack buckled in place, I looked around to find this gentleman, to thank him, to, well, just see him one more time. Maybe ask him to pass my thanks to the Abbot and see what he said. But there was no one. I had glimpsed only the shadow of one other figure since entering the monastery the day before. I let myself out.

Prelude at Sea 2

The high tension lines sang in the strong wind, an eerie low tone over the open landscape. Gone were the sunny skies of the first two days. A high grey layer muted the atmosphere. The wind was cold, flapping my wool trousers and pulling the steam from the mounds of compost piled along agricultural fields. This must be the outer margins of the low pressure system they spoke about on ship, before I disembarked. They were expecting heavy going on the return across the North Atlantic. If the wind was already this sustained in the middle of Belgium, I could only imagine its force at sea.

As I had contemplated walking the Camino, one of the most vexing questions was where to start. If I lived in Europe the answer would have been obvious. Just start from home, like Rean & Jo, and Rebecca. But coming from the United States the choice wasn't as straightforward. So where? Somewhere in Spain? Or the popular Saint-Jean-Pied-de-Port, just over the frontier in France, on the north slope of the Pyrenees? From my friends' in Paris? All options seemed too random, lacking the gravitas of launching a pilgrimage. And they all involved getting on an airplane, which also seemed somehow inadequate to the moment. Might as well fly straight to Santiago, right?

Why not a ship? The container ports of Charleston, South Carolina, and Wilmington, North Carolina were close, and I had been through both before. I checked schedules. There was a vessel open to passengers departing Wilmington in early March bound for Antwerp, Belgium.

Antwerpen, Anvers, Antwerp. That sounded like a reasonable place to start the Camino, neither notable nor obscure, and quite practical – it's where the ship would deposit its cargo. What was another 200 pounds?

"So, you do not like aeroplanes?" It was the second mate standing at the top of the gangway.

I recognized him too. He had been the third mate on a previous voyage. It was good to see a familiar face. It's always with a little trepidation that I board these container ships. Crewed by only 20-25, each is already very busy with their duties. They receive no extra compensation for managing a passenger. At best a passenger is a welcome distraction, but they could just as easily be a nuisance. At least the second could vouch I wouldn't be disruptive.

It actually turned out to be one of my most pleasant crossings personnel-wise. (Weather-wise was another story.) The crew were Filipinos, some from the Visayas and northern Mindanao where I'd spent time. There was an Indian deck cadet, from a part of the world where I had a long association. The officers were mostly Eastern European. The captain and chief mate were Romanians, and I credit them for fostering the good harmony that was apparent on board. I'd found Romanians to be the most genial in my limited sampling of transatlantic container ships. They possessed the right balance of skill, humor and interpersonal ease.

But why a ship at all? They're obviously slower than an aeroplane, and more expensive than an economy ticket. Not only is a flight convenient, but it can also be a wonder; the roiling clouds, the lingering dawns, the deep hues of space, the sparkle of stars that seem that much closer. It's only from an airplane that I've seen the Arctic's icebergs and fireworks over Paris. My fantasy aircraft has a transparent fuselage. Can you imagine being completely enveloped by sky and cloud, by shooting stars and Milky Way?

We're all well acquainted with the grinding hassles of air travel. But what bothers me most is how disconnected it feels. In spite of being cheek by jowl, how many of us really talk with each other? Despite winging through the sky, how many of us sense the exhilaration? We merely endure, counting hours and minutes, ears plugged and eyes locked into the panopticon of inflight entertainment. We are relieved when it's all over. So instead of moments of wonder, flights are mostly blank spots in our lives.

The small port of Wilmington has the largest onsite refrigerated warehouse on the East Coast, according to the port's business director. Among other cargo: flash-frozen salmon arriving from Chile to be brined and smoked domestically; Smithfield pork products heading to China, passing the corn coming in to fatten it. The port's new pelletizers are operational too, turning loads of wood waste into biofuel – though I can't help but wonder how reasonable it is to turn so-called southeastern forest "waste" into fuel for European furnaces. And sweet potatoes! Containers and containers of sweet potatoes heading to England. I had no idea of this fondness.

Though now overshadowed by other East Coast ports, Wilmington played an important role for independence during the American Revolution and was a key base for the Confederacy during much of the Civil War. The city also has the unique honor of being the site of the only successful coup d'état in the United States, when, in 1898, reactionary whites overthrew the legally elected mixed-race local government by violence.

Such local texture doesn't readily present itself in the rush to get to the airport two hours in advance of departure.

When the ship made the sweeping S-turn to leave the Cape Fear River and enter the Atlantic Ocean, it began to animate. Like a plane lifting off from the runway, it too enters its natural element. I was asleep by then, but the new sound and movement woke me. The stretching, popping and flexing. The fuller three-dimensional motion. The *Independent Pursuit* transformed from a large container ship looming over a riverine landscape to a tiny refuge in a vast ocean wilderness. The reassuring bursts of the lighthouse faded off our stern, leaving only blackness with no clear boundary between sea and sky.

While the ship responded to the deeper energy of the ocean, its steel sighing with pleasure, I was trying to adjust to the new, slightly disorienting sway in everything. Overlooked in port; the grabrails in all the passageways, the raised edges on the front of every shelf, the handholds in the heads, the heavy levers and hooks for the hatches, the brass butterfly nuts for the portholes, the latches for drawers, the boxes for condiments on the mess tables. They were all reminders of the dynamic of constant motion.

"When there is a problem on the bridge, there is a big red button. They push it to call the engine room so we can save them," laughed the chief engineer, a wiry, chain-smoking Montenegran.

"You are the heart, but we are the brains," retorted the chief mate, tapping his head.

It was the traditional US departure barbeque, the first day out of Wilmington; sausage, pork belly – what the Filipinos call *liempo* – and squid, Beck's and a nip of homemade Romanian plum brandy. It marked the ending of the circuit and a return toward home port. They were able to grill on deck in the lee, but the weather was steadily worsening, and we ate inside the crew's mess. Everyone seemed relaxed and in good spirits, and the Filipinos had setup karaoke for later.

The increased jostling through that second night became more urgent during the next days as the wind climbed from Force 6, to 7, to 8. We would ride the Gulf Stream north, tracing the eastward bend of North America and follow the great circle route across the North Atlantic toward Europe, all the while staying well south of the "outer iceberg limit" and trying to avoid the worst of the stalking low-pressure systems. The forward life rings and life rafts had been taken in so they wouldn't be stripped away by high waves, and no one was allowed forward. There were swirling snow flurries somewhere off the Mid-Atlantic States.

Everything was in constant movement. The massive engine in the bowels sent a hum and vibration through the whole superstructure. Every surface. It was inescapable, from the deck under your feet to your mattress to the glass on the mess table. But at least it was consistent. In contrast the motion caused by the sea state was unpredictable, at least to me. There was no rest from it. In the shower, try raising a foot to wash. For toilet, try standing to pee. You moved while in bed, eating, sitting, standing, walking. Everywhere, all the time, asleep or awake.

Bunks are laid stem to stern with the trim of the ship, and everyone sleeps head forward with the natural rise and fall of the bow. But when the seas are coming abeam, or astern, lying in bed is more like a ride at the fair. In medium seas I normally adopt the "starfish" – on back, head between pillows, arms and legs wide for stability. In heavier seas, which most of this voyage was, I sleep in the "wedge" – on side, upper hand jammed between mattress and bulkhead to keep from being tossed backward off the bunk, knee and foot pressed against the bulkhead to guard against being thrown in that direction, other foot against footboard, head pillowed against headboard. It's not very restful, but it works.

Walking is either skittering lightly down a passage, touching grabrails to control momentum, or feeling like you're being pressed into the deck as the ship rolls in the opposite direction, legs twice their normal weight.

Dining requires a heightened state of vigilance. On a previous voyage I just managed to simultaneously catch a runaway bottle of ketchup, stop my plate from sliding off the table's edge, and keep my chair and myself from flipping over backward. I was more tuned this crossing, but the winds would peak at Force 10, the strongest I'd ever encountered. For anxiety-tinged amusement, I'd watch the inclinometer on the bridge to see how far past 15 degrees the ship would roll.

"You are lucky. This is good weather for winter in the North Atlantic," the captain laughed.

As a passenger on a container ship there is nothing organized for your entertainment. Mealtimes are really the only event. They loomed larger with each passing day and gave structure to the hours. I checked the clock regularly even though I soon felt continuously stuffed. Meat-heavy stuffed. German meat-heavy: endless *Wurst*, smoked meats, lots of *Schwein Fleisch*. Toothpicks were a pleasure in which to linger.

Normally I'd spend time on the bow. About midship you leave the sound and vibration of the powerplant behind and it's only the wind and sluice of the ocean along the hull. You can forget you're in a relentlessly chugging iron cog of global commerce. On an earlier voyage I pointed my binoculars at a random spot on the horizon, somewhere south of Nantucket, and caught a whale breaching. Seven times in sequence. Massive walls of white water erupting silently from the becalmed surface. I knew that would never happen to me again, but there wasn't even the chance to try – the weather made going forward too risky for most of this crossing.

A few times I went to the tiny gym in an effort to work off the torpor brought on by the heavy diet and never-ending movement. Lifting free weights was too hazardous. A headstand inconceivable. I found the stationary bike the best option because you had something to grab onto that wasn't going anywhere – it was bolted to the deck. Yet it was like a giddy ride at the amusement park, the porthole in front of it swinging between foaming sea and grey sky as the ship rolled over and back.

On my first voyage I picked up two exhausted storm petrels from the cold steel deck and brought them into my cabin to recover in the warm darkness of a cupboard. "It's no use, they never survive," the German officer had said during my orientation, gesturing at a songbird too depleted to flee us we clambered around the flying bridge. Perhaps he'd sensed my sympathies. But these two storm petrels were reassuring company during that first crossing, if smelly. At the end of the voyage, they flew from my palm into the wind, hopefully restored enough to endure. But it was too lashing outside to even look for the creatures this time.

Reading was no diversion either, much less a pleasure. A friend had given me Paul Johnson's *A History of Christianity*. It looked dense. Felt dense. Too dense for casual reading in a pitching, yawing and rolling cabin. But my friend was a history buff and his recommendations were always good. And I guess he thought the book appropriately themed given I was off on an historically Christian pilgrimage, so I gave it a try, jumping around and reading in short stretches. It was like reading in the back of a car on a mountain road and quickly made me queasy. But even with my limited perusal a couple of points reached out from across the centuries. First was considering the Crusades as Europe's first colonial impulse, driven by burgeoning population and increased food and land needs. Clearly the tide is coming back in on that today, as the burgeoning and stressed populations in former colonies seek better opportunities in Europe. I imagine climate change will only accelerate the trend. The other was about the official torture of suspected witches. Priests, or Church functionaries, I can't remember which, had written to their superiors asking permission to stop using torture on the women they were interrogating. They explained the women were confessing to anything, just to get the torture to end. The torture *didn't work*. I couldn't help but think of the United States justifying its use of torture in the first years of the so-called War on Terror. If only there had been a student of Church history in the National Security hierarchy, our country could have avoided this moral turpitude, if only for practical reasons. But then again, maybe it wouldn't have mattered. Torture has never been about extracting the truth, has it?

I knew the book must be full of more thought-provoking facts, but the sea state was against me. I'd leave the weighty volume at the Gasthuys in Antwerp, for other pilgrims to peruse.

Was it time for lunch yet? Was it the designated day for laundry? Could I shave?

In more reasonable weather there'd be an abandon ship drill, where at the blaring alarm we'd don lifejackets and helmets, grab our immersion suits, and make for the assembly point.

"This is the assembly point. Whatever happens, come here. Nothing will happen. But in case, we must be prepared."

Then we'd load into a lifeboat dangling from davits over foaming sea, or, if so equipped, into the escape pod, a bright orange, bullet-shaped encapsulated lifeboat stocked with two weeks of provisions and fixed to a steep ramp aimed off the stern. I cannot conceive of being sealed inside, strapped into our seats, releasing the cable and plunging into the sea. Ship listing, on fire, in heavy seas, at night. Still, there is a sense of having some  agency in the face of disaster, unlike on an airliner where your utter helplessness courses just below the surface of every wobble of turbulence.

These are the kind of things you think about with so much idle time in a strange environment.

What else? Something less macabre. The engine room. Not really a room but more of a complex. I always found the engineers good-humored, salt-of-the-earth fellows, the sole exception a taciturn Russian on a previous cruise. Maybe it's the nature of their hands-on, reality-based worlds. They delight in sharing their hidden space; hot, shockingly loud, bright, and full of potential hazards. Main engine two stories tall, boiler, diesel generators, heaters, filters, separators, compressors, tanks, desalinator, pipes and ductwork, ladders and grates and gangways. The heated fuel-oil is injected at high pressure with a double pulse, almost like a heartbeat, the rapid clack/clack so intense you can feel it in the air. Operations produce approximately one ton of sludge a day, offloaded every two months in Antwerp.

"In China and Africa they pay you for it."

Tools for fixing and fabricating. A control room of innumerable dials, panels, gauges, buttons and switches. And, incongruously, a bin of walnut shells used for decarbonizing the turbines. The wrinkled shells seemed out of place, relics from an alien world of soft earth and quiet groves.

The one advantage of the engine room is that it is relatively stable, being at or below the waterline. Back where the glistening propellor shaft spins, you can press your hand on the steel skin of the hull and feel the cold of the ocean inches away.

In spite of all the running machinery, the whole compartment was immaculately clean. Not a speck of excess oil, not a whiff of exhaust, nary a neglected spill. There was constant vigilance for fire, the ship's greatest hazard.

These sailors, spending months below decks keeping their ships running safely, are a separate breed. The chief smoked almost continuously and never wore hearing protectors. And he spoke so passionately of the beauty of Montenegro, I believe I'll have to go one day. I didn't think to ask him how long it took, once ashore, for the sound to leave his bones. Maybe it never does.

Getting to the engine compartment takes an invitation and the visit is more of a tour. It's different for the bridge. Once you demonstrate you are not going to be disruptive, you can visit at any time and stay as long as you want. It's where I spent most of my time outside my cabin, especially since the bow was off limits.

The bridge is expansive, and from its vantage point you get a sense of the ship's purpose. The cacophony and power of the engine room is refined into course and speed and the smooth running of a multitude of systems. Gyroscopic compasses indicate bearing. Redundant GPS systems provide location and other data. The autopilot guides the ship, easily adjusted with the twist of thumb and forefinger. Position is plotted on the paper charts spread on the map table, though a newer, fully automated system is being introduced. A barometer scratches its readings on a rotating drum of paper for easy visualization of trends. Large radars reveal nothing at either short or long range. The radios are on, but silent. The bow seems to heave in slow motion, the ocean exploding silently beyond water-

streaked glass. Hundreds of dull red containers, lashed in their computer-plotted locations, stretch forward among three grey cranes.

"I prefer the midnight watch," she said, "so peaceful, and I am responsible for making sure that everything runs safely, so that everyone can sleep soundly." She was the second mate on a previous voyage, the only woman I'd encountered. She'd been a teacher, then, at 42, decided she wanted to join the merchant marine.

Each of the three mates stand two, four-hour watches a 24-hour period. During the three night watches the officer on duty is accompanied by a crew member or deck cadet. This second person roams the sleeping ship checking for fire. I don't think the engine compartment is manned at night. But all the sensors are wired to alarm panels throughout the ship. On another voyage they seemed to go off constantly – I was in a small cabin next to the second engineer and could hear the shrill beeping through the wall all night.

"Oh that's a terrible ship," the chief mate said to me when I told him about it. "Was in a German yard during the crisis. Financing kept running out, so they kept cutting corners. It changed owners some times. The finishing work is terrible. I did two contracts on it. Never again. The captain called out to me through the wall, he didn't need to use the phone!"

In contrast that ship, the *Independent Pursuit*, had just come out of drydock and had a completely new paint job.

"We touch it up in every port," said the third mate, "like when you have a new car."

"But it is like makeup on a woman," said the chief, "what is important is on the inside, and how do you know?" he laughed. "No, this is a good ship. Chinese yard. Well-built."

The chief mate had one child, an eight-year-old boy who it was clear he missed very much. When he flew into Bucharest after a contract, his wife and son came to meet him and drive back to Constanta together. But when he left, he left by himself, saying goodbye at their apartment door. Though he was always ready for the sea after several months on land, saying goodbye to his family was the hardest part of his work. Better to keep it quick. He knew his wife carried the extra burden of single parenting while he was on a contract, and he worried about the time away from his son. He tried to make it up when he was back, "to have a father's influence," but it was a hard balance. He and his wife finally relented and got their son a kitten for his birthday. The boy was so happy he cried.

For the Filipino crew the terms are starker. Their contracts last nine months. And back in the Philippines they are at the mercy of the manpower agency as to when and whether they get another job. Because of this uncertainty, many try to reup and stay at sea, in order to maintain an income.

From the bridge in better weather I'd seen spouts and the slick backs of surfacing whales. Also bounding megapods of common and Atlantic white-sided dolphin. Schools of flying fish sparking from the surface, and the occasional giant jellyfish tumbled by our passing. And, in the Gulf Stream, drifting islands of yellow sargassum concealing their communities of turtles, fish and crabs. But in this weather only one creature remained visible - the shearwater. These large, solitary birds constantly skimmed the surface searching for prey. It seemed incongruous, seeing a bird so far from land, hundreds if not thousands of miles. What did they think, riding the wind and ragged swells day after day? Where did they go at night?

The sense of isolation always strikes me powerfully. In spite of the amount of global maritime traffic, the ocean was always empty around us. Maybe tuning the radar to a more distant range you'd pick up a single blip, another vessel on another course to another destination – this information was available with a click. But it wasn't company. Staring from the cabin porthole at night at the wake that hung like a luminous contrail, it was easy to feel the pull of another force, a voice that said, "Come." If you went over the rail that was it, oblivion. No one would know. You'd sink 10,000ft to the bottom. What would you see on the way down? What would you find when you got there? This was the pull of a force we prudently keep at bay in our everyday lives. But here, in the raw North Atlantic, it comes close.

The captain had used discretionary funds to purchase a Krups espresso machine for the bridge, a highlight of the days. While the navigation charts were shifting to the electronic system, the logbook was still done by hand: details of weather, sea state and other observations. It was amazing to see how far north the warm waters of the Gulf Stream reached, and then how they'd break into eddies, the water temperature sometimes varying wildly hour to hour. Icy cold wind tore steam from expanses of warm ocean surface, just like the wind whipped the steam from the compost heaps as I walked toward Brussels.

There were customs onboard: Always a salutation when entering or departing the bridge. This was especially important at night in low light, so the watch knew if someone was present. Likewise, always a "Good appetite" when entering or leaving the mess, to which all those present would respond, every time. Each person had a designated place at one of the tables for the entire voyage.

There were vestiges of times past in cabin designations: *Purser* – no need to carry large sums onboard; *Supercargo* – loading and unloading is precisely computed by the shipping company; *Owners Cabin* – how many owners elected to travel on a working container ship? It was the echoes of these obsolete positions which made room for the possibility of passengers. That and the thin margins in the container business, where even a hundred extra dollars of income a day made a difference.

For while the experience of being a passenger on a container ship is potentially much richer than on an airplane, the business is just as cutthroat. The pressure is intense in cargo handling. At the time, each lift of a container cost an average of $100, which is why the loading/unloading for the various ports on a circuit is so exactingly calculated. And fuel consumption is another critical area. The ships could easily travel faster, say 18-23 knots depending on conditions, shaving as much as three days off the Atlantic crossing, but they ran notably slower to reduce consumption.

"The rough running cost of a vessel this size is $5,000 a day, not including consumption," the chief told me. And these small vessels (2,500 TEU) are under pricing pressure from the larger classes of vessels which reach up to almost 15,000 TEU. There is significant over-capacity in the industry, which is part of the reason crew sizes continue to shrink, and more costly employees are replaced by less expensive ones, e.g., Western Europeans by Eastern Europeans, Eastern Europeans by Asians.

While the tyranny of the clock falls harshly on the plane passenger, it is felt mightily by the container ship crew. The captain has to ensure he brings the ship across the ocean to arrive at a precise spot and time to rendezvous with the pilot boat, or he risks losing his slot and causing a cascade of problems in port. The chief mate has to ensure cargo operations run as quickly and as smoothly as possible - extra time alongside the quay means extra costs. The chief engineer is required to be on duty in the engine room if there is a harbor pilot on the bridge guiding the vessel. If it's a long passage, and there's maintenance needed once in port, he can be up for two days straight before they're back running at sea. While some of the crew are off duty during parts of port operations, by and large everyone is exhausted by the time operations are finished. "And in Asia it's terrible, sometimes two port calls a day. These long crossings are preferable. At least we can take care of the ship," one of the officers told me.

"There are no seamen anymore," the chief engineer said. "Now it's all rush, rush, rush." His first ship was a bulker out of England. "Eight-month contract. But we had long stays in port. You got to know a place, some people. It was a different feeling. And, in the evenings, we'd all meet in the lounge. Have a drink, play cards, talk. Now everyone goes back to the cabin, watches videos and goes to sleep."

"Twenty-five years ago, in the Asia ports, vendors piled aboard, spread their wares on the poop," someone else told me. "It was an instant bazaar. Trinkets, food. And of course girls. Now we can't even leave the ship. Only security and procedure. In your country, if there is time, all we do is take the van to Walmart."

The ship is momentarily steady, a notable pause that portends not a settled sea, but even greater movement to come. We wobble, then dip to starboard. She comes back up gathering momentum and goes further over to port, the skeleton popping and creaking loudly, and we simultaneously pitch forward, the ocean foaming in the empty space beneath the fat, round stern, the propeller straining. Then we  hurl back to starboard, faster and deeper, the whole ship groaning with effort, bellowing into the night. I'm wedged into the bunk, sleepless. I feel as if I'm on an intergalactic rocket ship hurtling through space, aglow with interstellar turbulence. I regain my bearings looking out the porthole where bands of clouds leach light from a weak moon. The sky is like water.

Water. Everywhere. It's easy to imagine other worlds completely covered in water, teeming with their own life. Where are they? Are they imagining us? What will it be like to finally meet?

I see the hand on the clock advance an hour, as if by its own volition. Who is it that moves the hand in each clock aboard, five or six times during the crossing? The second mate from the bridge, of course, to smoothly sync the ship's time with the destination. Or no, maybe it's the spirit of one who slipped voicelessly overboard, to be carried eternally in the Gulf Stream. *"Faster, faster, come and find me!"* when the ship is chasing the current. *"Slow, slow, do not sweep me by,"* when the ship heads west against the flow and time. Such are the thoughts during the long, bounding nights.

Even though the deep rolling could be unnerving, at least I could feel it coming. Worse was the sudden shocking jolt, both felt and heard, as if a giant sledge had struck the hull. It didn't happen often, but it set my pulse quickening when it did, especially alone in the cabin. What must be the force of such a wave?

The salad, like the moon, is a pale affair: iceberg lettuce, tomatoes a drained orange color, red-rimmed dimes of radish, translucent onion slices, watery bell pepper. Was that a bit of carrot? But with crumbled blue cheese and olive oil, not bad. "Good appetite." Schnitzel and a soup of spareribs.

There were rainbows in every direction this morning, colored stairways to bunches of low grey clouds. Is purple always on the inside of the curve?

The third mate, from Madeira, had worked in retail almost 10 years but always knew he wanted the sea. He had known his wife since secondary school. They'd been together for 13 years, married the last three of them. They decided to go to sea school together.

"There are only a few other women with the line, I could almost name them," he said. Mostly Germans. The line began to recruit other nationalities, starting with the Philippines.

"There were fights, one captain divorced. It was a disaster," he laughed. "They ended the initiative after only one year."

"If half the crew are women," said the chief mate, "then no problem. Everything will be normal. But if only a few, it changes everything. It's like you have a needle in your leg. It bothers you. At first we are all polite, gentlemen. We sit, have a glass of wine, then excuse ourselves. But she is with you for the whole contract. For four months, working beside you. Sweating. The barriers are broken down. So now instead you have three glasses of wine. Every man has a little lion inside!"

Porcupine Abyssal, Pendragon Escarpment – some of the enchanting names to be found on the paper chart.

The chief makes rabbit roast for dinner.

The captain borrows my magazines, among them a report on hate from the Southern Poverty Law Center.

"America is finished," is his conclusion. "Would you like an espresso?"

This ship, the pumping engine, the unforgiving steel everywhere, the impossible timetables. The human beings, soft, vulnerable, replaceable. Serving market forces. What is this system we've created but now enslaves us?

Sitting on the bridge, beside a small tree potted in a five-gallon Mobil bucket, the sea navy and streaked, peaks foaming and whipped, sun brightening the rust red containers and grey cranes, the ship rolling smoothly and deep, the second mate tending the navigation, maybe remembering his fiancé at home in Poland in their new apartment studying for her PhD, and I am enveloped by tranquility.

While this sea crossing might seem extraneous to walking the Camino, it was integral for me. It served to pull me out of my comfortable patterns and it thrust the raw power of nature in front of me. The voyage was enlivening, and a kind of deep preparation. I think that's why I felt that sense of tranquility on the bridge. I sensed I was underway, even before the first waymark.

Mia, of the Vlaams Compostelagenootschap, had finished one of her first emails, *"You are on your way already, for this periode is also an important part of your route!"* She was right. I had conceived of the Camino as a trip. But its extent was greater than mere dates and places.

Likewise, when I first imagined walking the Camino, I only wondered how it may affect me. But already more interesting to me was how my walking might affect others. A pilgrimage has to be about interaction, right? The meditation group at our church back home helped me first consider this. At the last session before I sailed, each member offered a random bead, which I strung along with a small, purplish scallop shell I'd found on the local beach. I tied this to the left shoulder strap of my pack. And our priest asked me to carry something for him.

They are all here with me now, I thought, on this ship, participating, even before I realized I'd begun. For where is the beginning, and end, of a pilgrimage? The voyage, a stripping away of independence and control, traded for uncertainty, vulnerability and dependency. The ship and crew were playing an important part in getting underway. Just as Mia had. Just as Nancy and Jill and Denise and Rick and Sue and Amy and Dottie and Leda and Wil had. Just as had those first intimations I heard from people I didn't know of this incomprehensible thing called the Camino de Santiago.

The weather improved this morning, as we neared England, allowing me to catch the full moon setting. We would cross the SECA (Special Emissions Control Area), where vessels are required to switch to low sulphur fuel, this afternoon. The charts indicated we were passing from 4,000m of water to 100m. I knew what that sudden depth change suggested and made my way to the bow, feeling the excitement in my chest. Sea state was 5 with a steady rolling to 15 degrees starboard and there was quite a bit of travel in the bow. I leaned against the cold steel of the forecastle rail, sun bright but wind cutting.

Though I'm looking for it, my eye registers the small explosions on the surface before I comprehend. They're here, they've come! Dozens and dozens of dolphins charging headlong for the bow of the *Independent Pursuit*. Bounding from the rolling surface, flying outstretched through the air, plunging in. I wave and shout, the grin on my face pulling to pure joy. They crowd the bulbous bow, riding the underwater wave, pumping, coasting, coming up for air, their breathing audible. Some roll on their sides, turning their white bellies toward me. I am convinced they see me, leaning out as far as I dare, still waving, calling. One peels away, disappearing in a flash, to be replaced by another. They must hear our ships at great distance. They must know the ones that are best for surfing. What a grand way to have some fun.

Sunday lunch: steak with garlic butter and parsley, *frites*, sautéed mushrooms and a bottle of white wine for each table – a small glass to mark the safe return to home waters. And Sunday is special for another reason. It's ice cream day in the merchant marine! Three heaping scoops of chocolate, vanilla and strawberry, with sauces and whipped cream.

Sunday supper not as special: a buffet of chicken salad, sweaty deviled eggs of chicken salad, shiny pink rolled ham slices, two dishes of oily fish with onion, one in red sauce the other yellow. I choose yellow and the second mate says, "Good luck." There are sausages wrapped in bacon. The only vegetable is a dumpling stuffed with sauerkraut.

The final approach is an eight-hour sequence of three pilots guiding the ship through the dark and congested English Channel, then up the Schelde River, and finally negotiating the narrow locks to the ship's berth. The captain stays on the bridge for the whole sequence, as he always does when there's a pilot aboard. I was there for a lot of the passage and at some point, maybe entering the river, looked up to see we were on a collision course with an MSC container ship closing from the port side.

Doesn't anyone see this? Captain, chief mate, pilot, helmsman, they all seem quite at ease, oblivious even. I stand up. Really, should I point out we are about to have a catastrophe?

Seven zero, the pilot gives a command to the helmsman.

Seven zero, the helmsman echoes the bearing, adjusting a wheel that looks like it belongs on a go-kart.

Thank you.

We're going 16kts, which at that point feels like 70mph.

Eight zero.

Eight zero.

Thank you.

We're being pulled toward the MSC vessel, as if magnetized.

Nine zero.

Nine zero.

Thank you.

We are swinging through a hard, 50-degree starboard turn. The MSC lettering looms larger and larger.

One, one zero.

One, one zero.

Thank you.

The hatch to the port bridge wing swings open from the force of the turn and I am tilted outside. We close rapidly on the MSC vessel. Soon I'll be able to leap to it.

The turn completes and we stabilize.

Ever so slowly we pull away, leaving the MSC ship to follow off our quarter. The dark bulk of a car carrier looms ahead.

The passing shore looks like a city of sparkling topaz. It's covered by the lighted pipes and pumps and towers and tanks of a vast bunkering complex. Its hazard is the antithesis of the wild darkness of the North Atlantic.

Where are those dolphin now?

Albert 3

Albert refused to get in the van. We spent over an hour in the drizzle and mud, encouraging, cajoling and threatening to no avail. Albert's mother was already resting comfortably inside, dry and warm and snacking. Jean would lay a trail of dried corn up the ramp into the back of the black van. Albert would snuffle them up, but as he got higher, he became more wary, keeping his hindleg extended as far back as possible. We had blocked off the sides of the ramp as best we could. Albert would extend for just one more grain, reaching with his snout, his rear cloven hoof quivering as it lifted slightly. At Jean's signal we'd charge Albert's hindquarters to shove him inside. But with a squeal and explosion of pure muscle, Albert would backpedal and wheel, scatter us and splash off through the yard to hunker down in his mud wallow and await our next move. This game went on for an hour. Jean suggested a firm smack with a stave the next time we got him up the ramp, but Albert's keeper demurred. Albert, of course, prevailed.

Albert (the "t" is silent, it being a French speaking part of Belgium) was a good-sized, fuzzy, charcoal-grey pig. He was a rescue pig, as was his mother in the van, as were the four dogs, two of them enormous and shaggy, filling the vehicle with their steamy breath. As were the goats, pigeons, cats and a parakeet who had already gone in the first load. Jean and Jeanne's neighbor, the good shepherd of all these strays, was moving to the Pays Basque in southwestern France, near Bayonne. It registered vaguely that I too might pass through that part of the world in a month or two, but being so fresh on *le Chemin*, the next days were hard enough to imagine, much less somewhere so distant.

"Well, I think I must be going. It'll soon be dark, and the drive will take all night. Let him stay. He'll get lonely. I'll come back for him in three weeks." She predicted his homesickness for the menagerie would be stronger than his tie to the sty. "And any of the pigeons who are still here."

She couldn't extricate the van from the tight lane along Jean & Jeanne's property and asked if I'd do it. I eyed the hounds inside – they had barked ferociously at me two hours earlier as I emerged from the woods to enter Braine-le-Château.

When I opened the door they stopped panting and perked up, but the woman assured me they wouldn't bite. She didn't claim they were friendly. If the one in the passenger seat clamped onto my forearm, I didn't know what I'd do. I spotted a couple of rabbits maintaining a low profile in the footwell.

Jean & Jeanne (pronounced exactly the same to my ear) were in their late 70s. Ten years earlier they had stepped out of the house with their dog and walked to Santiago, 2,450km. They mostly camped. It took four and a half months. I had found their name in the Flemish guide to the Via Brabantica. They spoke not a word of English, but somehow I made myself understood when I called the day before from Brussels – *pèlerin, demain, une nuit, possible*? Jeanne was very patient on the phone.

Leaving Brussels in the morning the weather had turned cold and drizzly, what I expected of northern Europe this time of year. The way was wet, sometimes muddy, and the forest was splashed with yellow daffodils. Actually, I'm not sure if they were daffodils, but they were yellow and lovely against the dark forest bottom. On open ground the wind buffeted me. So strong I leaned against its heavy, pressing force. The voice of the high-tension wires rose an octave. This must be the core of the big low pressure that had blown in the North Atlantic. I wondered how the *Independent Pursuit* and crew were doing, now well on their way back to the US. Steam whipped from mounds of hay and manure.

In Buizingen, about halfway here, there was a fair. I stopped in a crowded bar to warm up and took a late morning coffee. All the patrons were speaking Flemish, so I ordered in English. Language seemed a patchwork in this area. Sometimes sounding French, sometimes sounding Dutch. The communities mixed, like the warm eddies of the Gulf Stream in the cold North Atlantic.

Geese hissed at me as I left Buizingen, and my sudden appearance set horses galloping in a quiet pasture. This was good walking. Mostly over the earth, rather than along roads, which my feet appreciated. Somewhere along the way I crossed the invisible line between Flanders and Wallonia, hence the very French name Braine-le-Château.

When I knocked on Jean & Jeanne's door late that afternoon, my first private house, I wasn't sure what to expect. But they couldn't have been more open and welcoming. There was a place for my wet and muddy gear, and they showed me to their children's bedroom upstairs, which had a large, torn Michelin map on the wall highlighting their walk to Santiago. There was a chicken in the pot, and fresh bread and a bottle of red wine on the small kitchen table. They gave me a clean towel, showed me the shower and toilet downstairs, which were separate rooms, a typical configuration I'd find in these older homes. Jeanne offered the use of their washing machine. A Jack Russell dashed around with a ball in his mouth but wouldn't give it up. Imagine how happy his predecessor had been, accompanying Jean & Jeanne week after week outside, every day new sights and sounds and smells. And for me, the sensations of being in a home, the kitchen aroma, the intimacy of things, was powerful and lovely. Upon returning from Santiago, Jean & Jeanne opened their home to pilgrims. While only three or four passed this way a year, they welcomed whomever called.

After the contest with Albert, Jeanne showed me her gardening, and Jean showed me the garage and mimed driving while repeating the word *camion* until I understood he had been a truck driver. He had a ready, mischievous grin, laughed often, and seemed full of energy. Jeanne was quieter but showed high cheeks and dimpled eyes when she smiled. Very patiently she helped me understand a friend of theirs, Michèle, who spoke English and had also walked *le Chemin*, would come over later. She was eager to speak with me, a fellow *pèlerin*. The image of the beautiful Michèle eager to meet perked me right up.

Alas Michèle turned out to be Michel – like Jean & Jeanne, pronounced exactly the same to my ear – a gregarious, friendly fellow who joined us for dessert in the cozy kitchen. To say walking was his passion was an understatement. Michel was a peripatetic, long-distance walking fanatic. He had walked to Santiago several times, and back. And back! It made sense. You had to return. Not so long ago pilgrims didn't have a flight to hop on and whisk them home. Santiago was only halfway. Not embracing this was like thinking your summit attempt of Everest was successful when you stood on top – it was the return that completed the journey, and it could be even more challenging.

"Yes, you lose the way a lot. The markers are all on the other side of things, so you are always turning around to try and find them."

And I think he said he'd walked from Rome to Santiago, or was it Santiago to Rome?

"Farms, they are my favorite place to stay. The farmers are always happy to give you a place to sleep, the barn, sometimes the house. Maybe a meal and a shower too. For the next walk, I'd like to go to Jerusalem."

Jesus. My feet hurt just thinking about it.

Michel gave me his mobile number, in case I ever needed on-the-spot translation.

The next morning after a hearty breakfast and ready to depart I asked, « *Combien ?* »

« *Non, non, non,* » said Jean, waving his long hands, hands shaped from years on the steering wheel.

I fished Euros from my pocket. Maybe he didn't understand what I was asking.

« *Non,* » he held up those hands. Jeanne shook her head, smiling.

All this hospitality in their humble home, and they absolutely refused to take anything for it.

What is this Way I am upon?

They had walked their Camino ten years before, and they haven't stopped giving back. This source of immense gratitude was still beyond my comprehension.

I pinballed across the Belgian countryside toward the French frontier. Looking back, I don't have much recollection of these initial days, this first week of I didn't know how many more to come. The more pavement I avoided, the better my feet felt at the end of the day, I remember that. My backpack was too heavy, that was also obvious. It was an Osprey, with a 45–50-liter capacity, and I would come to love it. But I had naïvely stuffed it full. My shoulders would ache by early afternoon. My body was adjusting to the new reality of steady walking, and I ended these first days spent. I'd wake fresh in the mornings but wondered if I could keep it up. In hindsight I was probably a little more anxious those first days than I admitted; about my physical capacity, about water, about the way, about where I'd stay, about how to interact. But with each step, with each encounter, I was gaining confidence and becoming more comfortable with the uncertainties.

I had been to Europe before, mostly short stays in major cities, the exact circumstances long faded away. Mostly for work, these visits are unmemorable. Though I have spent many years living and traveling abroad, it was primarily in South Asia, the Middle East and Africa. Europe was essentially new territory for me. Especially the Europe of small towns and villages and countryside. The languages, the customs, they were almost as strange to me as those on the Arabian Peninsula had once been. Somewhere during those last days in Belgium, I watched a group of men and boys dressed like jesters march along an empty road, accompanied by drums, bagpipes and two tubas. They were passing out blood oranges, so sweet and tart I wish I had asked for more.

I say Europe, which is an overgeneralization of a very diverse landmass. This walk for me would only touch Belgium, France and Spain. Again, as if those three names satisfactorily described the people living within their borders. Even in small Belgium the mix of language was a reminder of the diversity at hand, and how little I really knew about these places. My perplexity must have been plain on my face, for in Ittre a woman broke from a group of day-hikers.

"You are walking the Camino?" she asked me in English, touching my forearm.

I nodded.

"You're going to be okay."

Her spontaneous warm words touched something inside me, and I almost teared up. She had walked the Camino in Spain. Somehow, she just knew to come speak to me.

Later; « *Vous êtes Jeff ?* » a woman in a car stopped.

When people get my name wrong, they usually call me by my brother's name, even if they don't know I have a brother. Even in Belgium.

"Jerry," I smiled.

It was Michel's wife, on her way somewhere. I must have been the only *pèlerin* in the area. She guessed it was me and stopped to say hi and see if I needed anything.

People were like that in Belgium. Further on in Seneffe a tradesman with a bucket of tools guided me to the correct doorbell of an unmarked house that took travelers. The host there, though he had no room, invited me in and called the only other place in town to see if her sole room was free. This kind woman waited for me in the path that ran along the canal, prepared an enormous dinner and washed my clothes, and the next morning sent me off with another hearty breakfast, like Jean & Jeanne. They knew what a pilgrim needed here.

The last full day in Belgium, at a café in Estinnes-au-Mont, the young people behind the bar filled my water and pulled out their smartphones to find the only option for me to overnight between there and France. A strikingly beautiful young woman, probably beautiful in the way of Rebecca's twin sister, called the place in Croix-lez-Rouveroy.

"She is not open for the season yet, but she will take you."

The wind stayed heavy those last days in Belgium, the atmosphere wet and grey. But Belgium warmed me. Reassured me. Along the quiet ways roosters crowed and hens clucked, the sounds of things tended, of living, of sustenance. The rocking of the beds at night, as if still at sea, had subsided. And finally, on the last evening in Belgium, I didn't feel completely spent. My body was becoming conditioned.

Strolling into Croix-lez-Rouveroy, feeling good, I thought I'd try out Michel's farmhouse technique.

« *Il est Américain,* » one old man said to the other after I'd approached them.

« *C'est un petit village,* » he nodded thoughtfully, then whistled through his teeth. « *Tout est fermé.* »

« *La France ! C'est à tout juste quatre kilomètres.* »

I didn't need to understand all they said to know there was no offer of accommodation coming. Clearly I'd need to work on the farmhouse pitch. But Giselle was expecting me at her *gîte* in the village. She drove me to a small market since there was none in Croix-lez-Rouveroy, then took off to watch *Moonlight* with a friend at a theater in Mons. But not before firing up the heater on my side of the house and feeding a bag of wood pellets into it. I wondered if they had been shipped out of Wilmington.

BRUSSELS to PARIS

Settling into France 4

Though the border was unmarked, the differences between this part of northern France and neighboring Belgium soon became apparent. First and foremost, markings for the Way all but disappeared. I learned later that maintaining waymarks is done by local organizations of Camino enthusiasts, like the Vlaams Compostelagenootschap. So even though the Via Brabantica carried on to Saint-Quentin, it wasn't as well marked in France as it had been in Belgium. Yellow paint stripes, apparently a Camino standard, did show up, but the first official marker I noticed was red and white instead of blue and yellow. Its scallop still pointed the way with the hinge of the shell, the umbo. I'd cross areas where they did just the opposite, using the fan of the ribs toward the ventral edge to indicate direction. Finding a shell indicating straight-ahead sometimes was the only way to be certain which orientation was being used. I spent long moments over the weeks in front of some waymarks trying to interpret what they were saying.

In online searching pre-trip, no specific pilgrim accommodation had appeared in France until Compèigne, two thirds of the way from the frontier to Paris. While the Belgians I'd encountered were attuned and eager to help, the French in these parts seemed less sensitive to the blunderings of a single *pèlerin* along *le Chemin de Saint Jacques*. I called ahead to a *gîte* in Mariolles, thinking I might make it that far the first day in France, but the woman made certain I understood there was no pilgrim discount and that she certainly would not be cooking. Well.

And a few days later at Hôtel Le France in Ham – the only place in town and I'd had to wait until 6:00 p.m. for it to open – the manager sniffed when I asked if there might be an electric kettle for the room. They were not impressed with my pilgrimage visage. They had a fine *gastronomique* restaurant. I ordered *truite* in almond sauce as a nod to the trout farm I'd walked past. But the bed rocked like a bunk on the *Independent Pursuit*. So there.

To be fair, these were the only two even slightest points of friction I encountered during the walk across France, and you can see how minor they are. I found no truth to the notion that the French are somehow predisposed to be rude to visitors/travelers, particularly those who don't speak French or speak it poorly. My day-to-day experience was just the opposite. If anything, it would be my alien manner that was responsible for any irritation.

After the dispiriting phone exchange with the *gîte* in Mariolles, I turned around and walked back to the center of Aulnoye-Aymeries for my first night in France. The only *hôtel* I could find had been swankily refurbished – the room had black walls, black curtains and a black bedspread. But the young co-owner cut me a discount and threw in breakfast, though he asked me to wait until the businessmen ate their fill.

It had taken about a week to get to the French frontier from Antwerp, and it would take a little more than a week to reach Paris from there. I crossed the frontier at tiny Vieux Reng, noted only  because of its sign and dominating central church. Half of the nights to Paris I'd have to stay in *hôtels*, because of the general absence of infrastructure geared toward *pèlerins*. If I had followed Rean & Jo and Rebecca further east, my guess is Camino accommodation would have been more available. From what I had read, the regular routes in France started south of Paris; in Tours, Vézelay, Le Puy-en-Velay and somewhere near the Mediterranean. In fact, Rean & Jo and Rebecca would ultimately connect with the route starting in Vézelay. I didn't realize it then, but eventually I'd bump into all these Ways, my path more arbitrary than fixed.

The Belgian countryside seemed wealthier than what I was now passing through. In general, there had been better homes, nicer cars, and the agricultural land was composed of smaller holdings, but well-tended, with more horses and livestock, including deer. And the clucking chickens. Besides the gritty urban splash of Maubeuge the first day in France, the countryside was turning to wide croplands. Many fields looked only brown, tilled and harrowed, but others sprouted a monoculture of something I didn't recognize. It had tough green leaves that were bitter and smelled vaguely of old broccoli water.

There would usually be a giant tractor in view raising a cloud of dust, or, on the far edge of a field, a small white *utilitaire*, the ubiquitous farm vehicle of France – kind of a cross between panel van and mini station wagon – but I rarely encountered people in the countryside. Hedgerows were trimmed, but most were without foliage, like many of the trees, spring having yet to burst. Once, when a tractor passed close, I raised my hand in an eager wave, but the man was absorbed in his smartphone, the tractor on autopilot.

Jean Louis, a friend who grew up on a farm in the Béarn, in southwestern France, later recounted to me what agricultural life was like when he was a boy:

"I born in 1953 in a little farm of south of France, in a time the majority of the farms were little farms doing polyculture of cereal, vine, cows, and porks and pigs, and maraichage, and I saw the agriculture who has been practiced during centuries. And I see, I saw, I watch the beginning of the tractors who arrive in the fields. As I was a child, my father, who was a very hard country man, use me to work in the fields as a, very young. I begin to work with him at six years old, seven years old. So my brain has a good memory of this, this moment. It, I was, how can I say? It was the beginning of the mechanization in the agriculture. My father was a, he, ah he was a warrior, and he was introducing, he was the first in introducing the first tractor, the first TV, the first machines. For one side the traditional old agriculture, on the other side, the new agriculture: mécanisation, productivism, technique and technologie. It was after war and Europe was in a conflict between the Russian model and the American model. Marshall Plan, and the American way of producing. He was a warrior, because he was the first in the area turning into the modernity and it was necessary to have a strong

determination for that. So I could watch and see that.

"All the country mans around were using cows and horses to work in the fields. When the tractor were arriving it has been a progress. It was easier to work and I remember when the little tractors begin to work in the fields, the soil was so alive that it was plenty of worms and bees and insects. When the tractor was opening le sillon, there was hundred thousand of worms falling down in the trail. Plenty of birds were arriving to eat the worms. There was all, of course the hens, chickens, ducks, but crows and all kinds of little birds. And they were eating quantity of worms. I remember very clearly too, when I enter in a field before cutting the grass for the hay, it was the same. The fields were full of insects. Big quantity of insects. And when I enter it was a music of sounds of insects, millions of insects in the fields. Butterflies, and all kinds. And now, 50 years after, or 60 years after, when a tractor is preparing the soil for planting corn or maize there's a big tractor with a big charrue, very big charrue, opening the soil there is nobody, nobody, no birds, no worms. The soils are, are pretty dead. Dead. Sixty years ago it was like a boat on the sea with the birds waiting for the fish. And now, it's a desert. The soils are dying with the use of pesticides, les herbicides, les engrais, since 40- or 60-years using pesticides now they are, the soils are compact. Hard and the air don't enter on the soil. The water is running on the soil, ça fait des innôdations, floods. When I was child, I used to work in the field, from six to 18, 20 years old, so that I remember this period and the change. The change.

"Wild animals like birds or rabbits were used to eat in the farms. The people were living with their own production and hunting and killing animals to eat. My mother was telling me, oh, can you bring me three grives, four five grives for the meal. And, I don't know the word in English. Little birds. I took the gun and I was, I went in the first tree. I was waiting maybe 20 minutes and I was killing four or five birds to prepare for the meal. That was the life. That was the life. Now the, this biodiversity, is falling down."

There were no birds following the tractors I was seeing. No parade of insects. No cascade of worms. Only dust. Jean Louis's vivid imagery begs a broader question about modern human culture: All our unbridled technology, our efficiency and "progress", is it making us richer, or, like the monoculture I was walking through, denuding us? Is everything in reality *falling down*?

Massive wind turbines loomed in the distances, or sometimes right on top of me, and the blade tips made a colossal sound while spinning. Cairns with crosses dotted isolated places, usually along a dirt road outside a small village. I couldn't tell if they were memorials, or of some other significance, but each one was different. Whenever I crossed one, I couldn't help but pause. And with the presidential election approaching, sometimes even the smallest places had a wall where the slew of candidate posters were plastered neatly, one alongside the other.

The farmhouses looked more like the fortresses they must have once functioned as; house, kitchen, barn, stable, workshop all one large squarish structure with few external windows, arranged around a central yard that at least at one time must have contained a well. I had seen a few farmsteads like this the further south I got in Belgium, but they seemed more common here. These large, isolated compounds usually sat on higher ground in the open landscape, silhouetted by massive trees. When I happened to pass alongside one, dogs as fittingly large would throw themselves against gates I prayed would hold, barking wildly and gnashing their teeth. At some places they were chained, which only animated them further. But I couldn't blame them – a stranger approaching their territory with staff in hand? They did their jobs exceedingly well. Michel didn't mention the dogs but hats off to him for getting by them. I wasn't hearing the intimate cluck of chickens anymore. Only tractors, dogs and wind.

Another thing that struck me in this part of France were the sites relating to the World Wars. There was no need to seek them out. They popped up regularly. Wilfred Owen, perhaps England's greatest poet of World War I, killed at 25, a week before Armistice.

He was buried in Ors. I found myself walking the canal where he and his men were cut down.

If in some smothering dreams, you too could pace
Behind the wagon that we flung him in,
And watch the white eyes writhing in his face,
His hanging face, like a devil's sick of sin,
  (from Owen's *Dolce et Decorum est*)

The Somme River, famous for its World War I carnage. Small, placid and meandering. I filled my water at the source. This is it, this pleasant, peaceful thing?

I walked over bridges men killed and died for.

Near the E.Leclerc *hypermarché* south of Ham, where I filled water and bought apples and cheese for lunch; two tidy cemeteries, side by side, one German, one British. Nearly 2,000 young men interred, some nameless.

Gun emplacements, bunkers, fortifications, some used in both world wars, crouched and crumbling. Some overgrown. All with a dank blackness inside, ghosts of forces awaiting reanimation.

There is one site I would have sought had I been skirting Paris further east. A plot really, in the beautiful, well-tended Oise-Aisne American Cemetery. It's the hidden Plot E where over 90 American soldiers are buried in graves marked only with numbers. They represent nearly all the soldiers executed in theater for crimes committed during World War II. Most by hanging. Information on Plot E is not readily available, but I'd read the vast majority of the executed were Black. How can it be that Blacks, while only a small percentage of men who served, represent the majority of soldiers deserving death and an anonymous grave for their crimes? Was this true? Later I consulted World War II enlistment records in the National Archives, using serial numbers. Of the 76 I could find, 61 listed race as *Negro*.

The weather had lifted since leaving Belgium. It was cool and partly cloudy, white clouds in a soft blue sky, with a heavier carpet of grey sometimes sliding through. There was more road walking than my feet liked, but maybe that reflected the limitations of the Flemish guide combined with my utter unfamiliarity with the topography. I'd expected, once the Via Brabantica terminated in Saint-Quentin and I picked up the GR 655, it would be more trail walking, but it wasn't always the case.

The GR, or Grande Randonnée, is an extensive network of marked walking routes in Western Europe, especially France. I'd be on and off them regularly, and sometimes they were synonymous with sections of *le Chemin*. Apparently, the GR 655 starts in Vieux Reng, where I'd crossed into France, and continues to Tours where it blends with the Way from there. A GR is distinguished by red and white markings, which I saw frequently. But often I wasn't sure which GR they were indicating. The markings weren't only on trails. Many times they followed small roads. You could wander a lifetime following them.

The short stretch between Landrecies and Ors was my favorite during these first days in France. A little over an hour, I came upon only one other person. It was a single track of firm grass along the Sambre à l'Oise canal. There were coots and ducks and wheeling hawks. And some sort of shy muskrat/beaver/nutria type who'd plop into the water from the bank and disappear when my footfalls disturbed him. This was the same canal Wilfred Owen had died fighting to cross.

But even away from roads, eventually there'd be the faint sound of an engine in the distance. There was no escaping it; the land is plowed, the trees are planted, and the water is canalized. Everything is tended for us. There was no wilderness expanse in the sense of a dominating non-human dynamic, not in this part of Western Europe. It was a full anthroposcape, which I suppose is where the whole world is heading.

The next day, pounding pavement, I passed the Le Creuset factory in Fresnoy-le-Grand. Excellent cookware, though I can only afford their kettle, made in China.

Cafés seemed to serve more *bière* than coffee. Maybe that was because – and this is really my only complaint about France – the standard of coffee/espresso is so dismal. Basically watery, and brown in flavor. But still I was grateful when I found a café. The majority of the small towns and villages through which I passed had zero commercial establishments, nowhere to stop for refreshment. And I mean refreshment in its most sincere sense; to refresh a fatigued body. When setting out for the day I'd have to make sure to have a baguette, fruit, *fromage* and maybe *saucisson* in the top of the pack, because there was a good chance there'd be nowhere to buy anything all day. I have passed a good number of days walking and pedaling in the Himalaya. A place for refreshment always seemed within reach: a glass of tea, a plate of food. The scale there still matched traveling under your own locomotion. In Europe, like the United States, the scale has long shifted to accommodate the private automobile. Having nothing for 30km is hardly a concern for a driver. On foot that's your whole day.

I was even having a hard time finding places to fill water, which is less optional than a mediocre coffee.

In contrast to the coffee, the bread in the *boulangeries* (bakeries) was consistently wonderful. Not because it was a fancy gourmet product, but because it was so simple and fresh. Maybe like everyday espresso is in Italy. I'd heard the French regulate what can go into a traditional baguette, limiting it to four basic ingredients. Perhaps this explained why they were so good, everywhere.

The *boulangeries* were operating before the sun was up and I sought them out, sometimes locating them the evening before to be sure of a fresh loaf. But neither were there bakeries in every village and small town anymore. Much later I'd stumble upon a bread vending machine, a practical if unhappy solution to the disappearing *boulangeries*. After a bit of whirring and clunking, a fresh loaf would drop out. The sleeve bags were on the side. These loaves were quite good, stocked fresh daily by a regional baker, the timings posted.

The beauty of an actual *boulangerie* though is you could also get a croissant. Sometimes an almond croissant. But you couldn't get a coffee. In Maroilles, a well-appointed village famous for its *fromage*, I'd stopped at my first café in France. The gentleman served me *un café*, filled my water bottle and went back to wiping the counter and watching TV. The woman was busier. At the cash register she was constantly serving those who were playing *loterie*, or *loto*. A couple of tables were occupied by these people, watching the TV, picking numbers, talking, checking their numbers, drinking coffee. The prize could be over a million euros, each week. At the bar there was a lone fellow drinking a slow *bière*. I ate the croissant I'd brought with me and no one seemed to mind. I'd run into this scene over and over through France.

Coming into Le Cateau-Cambrésis for my second night I was a little put off. After the hours in the countryside, including the fine stretch to Ors, the town felt overly large and sprawling. Disjointed, cacophonous, its energy banged against mine.

As I was trudging a narrow strip of sidewalk along a road, a passing woman asked, « *Vous faites le Chemin de Saint Jacques ?* » I saw she was smiling. My shoulders untensed. Her simple engagement penetrated the barrier I was unconsciously raising, resetting my mood. It was I who determined how I felt, she reminded me, not the surroundings. Be grateful.

I reproduce her sentence above as if I heard it in its entirety, each word in its place. In reality I only comprehended "*Sanzhaq*", but it was enough to know what she was asking. « *Oui,* » I smiled in return.

Sometimes someone referred to the Camino as *la Compostelle*, but mostly the French called it *le Chemin*. I knew this, but still couldn't *hear* it. And I tried to use *le Chemin*, but no one could *hear* me. It took me a long time to figure out my horrific pronunciation was not only incomprehensible, but also impeding my comprehension. I was pronouncing it *lay shameen*. (Even now I cringe.) The spoken reality is closer to *luh shimah*, the word endings open and soft. The full French sentences I render in these chapters? In the moment I only understood them in pieces, aided by cues, context and assumption. But like "*Sanzhaq*", or Saint Jack, this was usually enough.

I soon found my way to the Office de Tourisme, where the friendly and helpful Angelique, the *hôtesse d'accueil tourisme*, spent over an hour calling around trying to arrange accommodation for me. These government tourist offices, when they were available, turned out to be great resources. The women staffing them were always eager to help, knowledgeable, understood what a *pèlerin* might be looking for, and usually spoke the loveliest English. She also booked the next night for me, in Saint-Quentin, a larger place with too many options for me to figure out.

« *D'accord,* » Angelique said, locking the door, "wait here. *À dix-huit heures trente*, Mireille will come to take you with her car."

And promptly at 6:30 p.m. Mireille pulled up in her small red car and drove me through narrow streets to her flat. A satisfying meal, a TV gameshow, clothes washed, and a clean bed. The only challenge was negotiating the wooden stairs with my stiff legs for the middle of the night pee.

Such were the typical scenarios.

The Michelin ZOOM France series road maps were a great help. While I generally followed marked ways, the maps' broaader scale helped me keep the surroundings in perspective. I'd cut away and discard the parts I didn't need, which made them easier to handle, but also because every ounce of weight made a difference. Weight was the reason I didn't carry an extra bottle of water even though I was still having problems finding it. I also only kept the pages I'd need to get to Paris from the GR 655 guide I'd bought, a surprisingly heavy little book.

An elderly woman in Saint-Quentin heard me asking for maps in the *librairie* and caught me in the street.

"You are walking the *Compostelle*?" She was bent. Her bottom teeth were crossed. Her wispy yellow hair perfectly coiffed. She was neatly attired, and her eyes sparkled like jewels.

"I walked it eight years ago. There is freedom on the Camino!" She said this was such force I was caught off guard – another person who had been deeply touched by their experience on the Camino.

What is your story, what made you so passionate about this Way? But she was gone before I could collect myself.

Her enthusiasm was welcome. I'd walked 45km to Saint-Quentin from Le Cateau-Cambrésis the day before, my longest till that point. My daily average had been creeping up, from 25km to 30-35km, so I thought I'd see how I did closer to 50km. It had taken 11 hours, right at the 4kph average. (Though you actually walk a little faster, this pace includes all your stopping.) My feet and calves were still pulsating the next morning. Fortunately, *ibuprofen* is the same word in French. But it had been a good day. Hunters popping off on field edges, gently rolling terrain, the menthol scent of evergreens, and finally, the reassuring scratch of hens and a cock's crow.

I was enjoying the steady pace and constant movement. It was almost hypnotizing. And this is a pilgrimage right, not a vacation? I'm doing this to go, not linger. I may not know exactly what has compelled me on this walking, but I know I have to let the Camino unspool and see what comes of it. I wasn't fixated on getting to Santiago. In fact, I was wary of a fixed, overarching "goal" coming to dominate my thinking. Just go and see, I reminded myself.

Thank you for this body. Thank you for this fitness. Thank you for this health. I know it is unearned and passing. But thank you. This was the little prayer of thanks I'd taken to saying to the Great Whomever, in those moments when it struck me how fortunate I was.

In Vaux-Andigny the barmaid comped my coffee. A man in a passing car somewhere flicked his lights and waved. Three days further south, in Le Plessis-Brion, the *boulangère* smiled with eyes the color of meadows.

Small moments, passing instances, but each one renewing, propelling me on, tapping into the invisible undercurrent that runs through *le Chemin*. I'd forget, feel completely isolated, alone in my paces, content to be alone even, but then the smile, the wave, the comment, the kind gesture and I was reminded that being alone is a self-imposed state of mind. While this part of France was not as attuned to pilgrims as my passage in Belgium, it was far from being inhospitable.

"Pilgrims are dirty. Carriers of disease. Strangers of uncertain manner. That's why you find many pilgrim houses on *rue Lazare*, Lazarus. It's where traditionally centers were established in the saint's name, to care for lepers, on the outskirts of town. Groups of pilgrims were equally feared. They were kept at a distance."

This background might explain why the pilgrim facility at the Abbaye d'Ourscamp was a musty, unswept bunkroom outside the abbey precincts. The hope of repeating the cozy room and antique sleigh bed of Abdij Grimbergen vanished in the dingy light. The monk who showed me here had been perfunctory, reluctant to linger in the stale air. Granted the abbey was busy hosting a weekend retreat for 30 engaged couples, so there were other things to attend. The event piqued my interest, and I was looking forward to meeting some of these young hopefuls and hearing what they imagined for their coming lives. But even though I had gotten all cleaned up and made myself as presentable as possible, it was not to be. While a great clatter of nuptial bonhomie rose from the dining hall, I was directed to a small room where I ate alone. That would have been fine had the abbey been empty, but with so many others so near, it felt a little bit like punishment. Later I was permitted in the church for vespers, but not encouraged to mingle. Ah well, a little taste of rejection to leaven things.

Taking the sun early the next morning the same monk in brown robes popped out from a big wooden door. "You do not want breakfast?" he said with some irritation.

"Yes," I said, that's why I'm sitting here waiting for eight o'clock I didn't add.

"You are late." Testy, aren't we?

My single place was set with a large white bowl, and I anticipated a steaming mound of porridge; the perfect fuel to get me to Compiègne. I waited. The din from the couples next door was even more animated. It must have been a good night.

"You do not want coffee?"

I was happy the monk came back to check on me, just for the interaction. Poor fellow seemed to be on his own.

"Tea," I said, and a cup appeared but no porridge. Maybe they ran out because I was late? Well, it was bread and butter and confiture, good enough.

After arriving at the abbey yesterday afternoon, I called the number for the first official *gîte des pèlerins* I'd found in France – in Compiègne, where I was headed after a night in the abbey lazaretto. It rang in the Office de Tourisme.

« *Je suis désolé, mais le gîte est fermé,* » said the *hôtesse* sympathetically.

She tried to explain something else, but I couldn't understand. I knew *fermé* though. It meant closed. She gave me a phone number, which was also difficult because the French say the numbers in tens, not single digits. But she was patient, and I was finally able to read it back to her correctly. I think she was trying to tell me it was possible the *refuge des pèlerins* had just opened. The person at this number would know for sure.

I practiced my *Je suis pèlerin*, I would like a room for one night, and dialed.

"Well you can't," answered a voice in English before I could finish. "It's closed."

Before my shoulders drooped further in self-pity, he added, "You'll just have to stay with us."

Seamus (he had some Irish in his recent past) and his wife Claire, a retired nurse, had walked the Camino together. "In seven stages over nine years, from Le Puy." Now they open their home, an apartment in a *banlieue* not far from central Compiègne, to stray *pèlerins* when the *refuge* is closed.

"In the winter," Seamus explained, "we use the *refuge* as an overflow shelter for the homeless. It'll probably open for pilgrims next week. It's still early in the season. You are the first to pass through." The *refuge* was located on Rue Saint-Lazare.

Seamus collected me in front of the Office de Tourisme where I'd been sitting on the steps fingering the string of beads from the meditation group. We drove through the forest to the fairy tale castle, Château de Pierrefonds, for a *bière* in the sunshine. Yesterday it had been grunting pelotons of men in skintight, bright cycling attire. Today, a Sunday, it was rumbling motorcycles of doughier physiques clad in black leather.

It had been an easier walk to Compiègne from the abbey than I expected, thanks to Seamus. When I told him the evening before I was basically relying on the GR 655, local Michelin map and *Chemin* markings when I saw them, he recommended a different way, essentially following the Oise canal. "It's shorter, more direct, and better walking." When I told him I didn't have a smartphone to receive email, he didn't hesitate. "I'll drive up."

Despite my protests, he did, and passed a mimeographed draft of directions through the fence of the abbey, the grounds having been locked for the evening. I can't remember now if these directions were in French or English, but they got me there. I don't

recall much about the route. The Oise is a large canal, but it was quiet. Barges were moored, not underway, some clearly converted into floating homes, others still meant to earn a living. I do remember, when nearing Compiègne, coming across a menagerie of exotic animals munching buckets of food, including a Bactrian camel and a bovine of enormous horns, perhaps an Ankole-Watusi?. These creatures were the forced laborers of *le cirque*, which apparently was in town. I never liked the circus as a kid. I think it was an unarticulated sense of the coercion lurking just below the surface of everything; behind the clown makeup, in the eyes of the animals, and especially in the aggressive barking of the ringmasters. Fun at the expense of others is no fun at all. It never felt right to my kid-self. Even now it's the same.

In the sun at Pierrefonds Seamus shared the background on the route as leathered bikers admired each other's rides. The local association was mapping out a new way for the region, from Saint-Quentin to Paris. It was going to be more direct than the GR 655, which, like the nature of most Grande Randonneés, could spend a lot of time meandering through historic and scenic areas. This new way was meant for pilgrim travel, and they were calling it *le Chemin* Estelle, named for a girl in his daughter's class who had died of cancer at 18 years old.

"I didn't know her personally, or the family, but we went to the funeral out of solidarity. She knew she was terminally ill, and she had chosen all the songs and readings for her service. It was, it was all so beautiful and powerful. I came to know her through her selections. We were all overwhelmed. And so, when the association was deciding what to call our new Way, we thought of her. It's a way to remember someone so lovely and wise. Estelle, part of *Compostelle*, it fit naturally."

While walking it had been just another set of directions for me. Now, hearing Seamus, the Way took on meaning, felt animated. I was touched to have been able to walk part of Estelle's *chemin*. It was like feeling part of the legend that had pilgrims following the stars of the Milky Way to Santiago. You are not alone. You are sharing in something greater, even transcendent.

On the way back to their flat Seamus pointed out the Royallieu-Compiègne. "The great shame of France." It functioned as an internment camp during World War II, from where French Jews were shipped to Nazi concentration camps during the Vichy regime. "We've only really acknowledged this history in recent years. It is not something we like to admit about ourselves." I had no idea this site was in Compiègne.

Claire had prepared a welcome meal, which we shared in their galley kitchen. I loved the fresh beet/apple salad, but the real highlight for me was…ice cream! I hadn't had ice cream since that Sunday aboard the *Independent Pursuit*. I unashamedly accepted seconds, though manners kept me from going for thirds.

It turns out I had been late for breakfast at Abbaye d'Ourscamp because France set its clocks forward one hour as I slept in the stale *refuge*. (Saturday, March 25th, 2017). Seamus enlightened me to the time change. It would take me a bit longer to realize my empty porridge bowl was actually a big coffee cup, into which you dipped your day-old baguette. That seemed a good use for mediocre coffee, though not very appetizing.

Seamus pointed me toward Senlis.

I was only a few days out of Paris now, but both Compiègne

and Senlis enjoyed large tracts of nearby forest, a welcome change from the agricultural landscape. Some of these lands were the remains of royal preserves. In la Fôret de Compiègne, the deserted trail passed through le Carrefour du Puits du Roi, the crossroads of the King's well. Trails went off in all directions. These multi-spoked carrefours were typical in the forests, and you had to pay attention to which track you took.

In the forest past Senlis, following the GR 12, there were ancient *chaussée* markers of heavy, grey stone, stained by centuries of moss. On their face the chiseled distance and royal insignia were weatherworn and fading. I was just one more in the flow of people who had passed this way for, what, 1,000 years, more?

At other places signs warned of galloping horses, and sometimes I could hear the muffled thud of their beating hooves. I crossed those sandy expanses carefully. Being run down by a

charging stallion would do you in as sure as if it were a speeding truck.

Inevitably I'd also have to cross the pulsing arteries of mechanized life. Standing on the bridge over the A1 motorway, the noise and motion of tractor trailers and automobiles was intense. I felt sympathy for the drivers urging their vehicles along, knowing what that felt like. Coming upon a TGV line I waited on the overpass for the next train. It came speeding like an arrow, silent and invisible. Then when it passed beneath, it was like the world exploded.

Senlis was a pleasant, midsize town and Seamus suggested I stay at the Monastère des Clarisses. What a contrast to Abbaye d'Ourscamp. The sisters' *refuge des pèlerins* was also empty, but it was clean and bright with a well-appointed kitchen, and even a couple of private rooms. Their chapel touched me most. The sisters were Poor Clares, an order founded by Clare of Assisi in the 13th century, in the Franciscan tradition. I sat in the chapel for evening and morning prayer. It is a simple, unadorned structure that looks into the garden. If I recall correctly, the *monastère* was only established a decade before, when seven nuns relocated from Paris. I think all seven sisters were present, in their grey habits, and they sang their prayers in unaccompanied voice. That was it. There was no other ritual or ceremony that I witnessed. No priest, no choir, no bells and incense.

Across France great hulking churches stand in the center of towns, even in some of the smallest villages, and sometimes alone in the countryside. While the soaring architecture is meant to evoke the grandeur of God, you can't help but notice the sense of temporal power, wealth and hierarchy they would have exuded in their heyday. But the once pervasive Catholic Church in France, having become so corrupted, has had its resources and influence steadily stripped, sometimes violently, beginning with the  French Revolution in 1789. So much so that most of the churches I was passing were owned by the state.

"Do you have a knife?" the receptionist asks me. I didn't think she meant my Swiss army knife with the indispensable corkscrew, so I gesture to my adjustable trekking pole.

« Eh bien, » she says seriously, "when you hear about something happening in Paris, something bad, they mean Sarcelles, even when they don't say it. Don't get lost. Stay on the main roads."

I was spending the night in Écouen, just north of Paris. Cities aren't designed to be approached on foot, to state something obvious but not normally considered by most of us. It had been a circuitous route getting to Écouen, dodging Paris' supporting infrastructure.

Early in the day, standing on a rise overlooking Fontenay-en-Parisis, trying to get a sense of the approach to the metro area, a small thunderstorm materialized, like some kind of herald. It was the tiniest, most compact thunderstorm I had ever seen, in a sky of very few clouds. I realized it was coming straight for me, a heavy black curtain of rain hanging under it, dragging along. Then it started spitting grand jabs of lightning. I could see them strike the plowed fields stretching below me, feel the crack and jolt. I broke into my best trot, and hauled off down the farm road, pack joggling away, making for the village and trying to get out of open ground. To be incinerated so early in the Camino could only be interpreted as well-deserved divine justice. With relief I made the village and huddled under dripping eaves until it was clear.

For the whole day Senlis-Écouen, multi-engine behemoths climbed out of Charles de Gaulle, groaning like overburdened beasts, heading to points around the globe. I passed under a wide run of high-tension wires, seven gigantic transmission towers like *Transformers*, ready to metamorphose and stomp off to the next battle. Their right-of-way hummed and popped and crackled and sizzled and I scurried through it as quickly as I could. Occasionally the tiniest, most elegant *Transformer* of them all, the Eiffel Tower, would reveal itself on the horizon – I knew I was going in the right direction.

Near Le Mesnil-Aubry the thick sweet smell on the wind reminds me of what, a garbage truck? In the distance; a massive landfill, with backhoes and front-end loaders churning over the Parisian heaps. The flecks of thousands of birds wheel perpetually in the wavering air.

As I cut under the N16 I was startled encountering a woman, walking in the opposite direction. She was one of a few actual people I had seen all day, none walking along roads. Long dark hair, high-heeled, knee-high black boots, black short shorts, and a loose-fitting black blouse that just contained her milky white breasts.

« *Bonjour,* » she says sleepily.

Where on earth have you come from? Regaining my composure, « *Bonjour,* » I reply, and we keep on our ways.

This might have been my favorite thing about French culture, if I can overgeneralize again. Everyone greeted everybody. Children, young people, adults, the elderly, no matter where you were or what you were doing. And, to me at least, the greeting sounded sincere. The exception to this ritual was the over-busy city, obviously. But even there, when you walked into a shop, you offered a « *Bonjour !* », much as we did entering the mess shipboard. At a minimum these salutations serve to connect, to keep the lines between us open when routine threatens to deaden them. I thoroughly enjoyed it.

Écouen was a beautiful village, but there was nowhere in it to stay. I went to the *mairie* (the town hall) in the hopes of finding something informal, but to no avail. The woman there called the church, but no one picked up. A young man in on another matter overheard and offered me a lift to the business motel. Resigned and grateful, I accepted his offer. While it was only a half a kilometer straight-line distance, with the highway and its barricades in between, the directions to walk there were too detailed for me to understand. He dropped me just outside the bright lit compound, surrounded by a high, chain-link fence.

The receptionist gave me a small discount, which I appreciated.

"It's like that," she says, "but here, on this side," she motions behind the motel property, "gypsies. You know the gypsies, yes? Don't go that way. They have guns and cause trouble. They will shoot you." She regards me for a moment. « *Mais un pèlerin sur le chemin comme vous ? Peut-être qu'ils vous laisseront tranquille.* Maybe they will leave you alone."

Lying in bed later, door bolted, the shutter down against the security lights, I can hear the airplanes, the traffic, the guests above me coughing and fiddling. I guess it's easy to be afraid of a place you never go and that's filled with people who don't look like you. Sarcelles can't be *that* bad.

It wasn't. The diciest moment the next morning leaving the motel wasn't gun toting gypsies but jaywalking the highway back to the other side. The notorious *banlieue* of Sarcelles was mostly people at the bus stops, preparing to start their day of work or school. So much for needing the Swiss army knife.

I thought I'd treat myself to a real espresso in Paris. I hadn't had good espresso since Caffènation in Antwerp. So, after following various canals and Rue Saint-Martin to la Tour Saint-

Jacques, I hoofed it to the 11th arrondissement to wait for my friend to finish work. There I found *Thank You My Deer*. It was a slot of a café. I could almost touch opposite walls and was self-conscious trying to tuck my backpack out of the way.

The young woman came out of the kitchen where I could see her working, sleeves rolled and fine sweat on her brow. I ordered, including a delicious looking brownie. I could tell she made everything herself.

The cappuccino and brownie were so well done I ordered another round of goodies. The only two other patrons finished and left.

"You are walking the Camino?" she asks, when she brings me espresso and other delights.

"Yes."

"Oh my god." She opens her arms and I stand up for a wonderful, completely unexpected hug.

"Me too. It saved my life." She had walked from Le Puy after leaving a United Nations job in Geneva, "because of a horrid boss."

Jana, from Slovakia, had started this little café a few years before. She worked 60 hours a week. "But the space is too expensive. I clear maybe 1,000 euros a month. I know it can't go on like this. But it was a dream and I had to try."

I can see the fatigue in her face, the lines, the tension. But I can also sense her enthusiasm and independence. From now on, she would do things on her own terms.

"You decided to do this after you walked to Santiago?"

I had gorged excellent coffee and a variety of her homemade baked goods. Despite of the fat tab and tight margins, she wouldn't accept a cent.

M. et Mme Chenu 5

Five days in Paris, immersed in the companionship of friends and their children, relationships that go back over two decades. That and soaking in Epsom salts, and mind and body and spirit had been renourished. I had lightened my pack by a few kilos, even taking into account the terrine of *porc* handed to me on departure, and walked out of the city with only a wee puddle of fatigue unevaporated. I was ready for the next phase; the vast expanse of France south of Paris.

It was a pleasant, easy exit. Essentially a bicycle/walking path the whole way. No long stretches of busy road lined with auto repair shops like coming in from the north. At a juncture where I was uncertain, a wiry gentleman wordlessly tapped the small scallop shell on my string of beads and pointed the way.

I felt so restored that the second day out of Paris I completely overestimated how far I could walk and found myself late in the afternoon in a place called Boissy-sous-Saint-Yon. I'd thought I could make it to the *presbytère* in Étampes, from where I spent the night before in Vauhallan. But it was after 4:00 p.m., some low clouds had appeared, spitting the occasional drop, and it looked like the track from here entered a tract of forest. Better go ahead and find something, I thought.

There was nowhere obvious in the village center, so I backtracked to a place I'd seen on the outskirts. It turned out to be a combination *gîte* and stable, and it was full. In France, school holidays rotate through different regions so popular spots don't jam up with the whole country on holiday at the same time. Now was the turn of the Paris region, the woman explained, and said they always filled up with families from the city. A young girl trotted around the *manège* on a fine-looking horse. Actually, I was a little bit relieved because once inside I realized it would have been too pricey for me. The woman was helpful and looked up the address and number of another place she knew and gave me directions.

I set off, sure I'd encounter options as I made my way, but there were none. And I was having no luck finding the street she'd told me about. I asked a fellow who pointed the way, but he had been difficult to understand, and I failed again. I drifted back to the center of the *ville*.

Now what?

An older gentleman, with white pressed shirt and white hair, was coming down the lane. I wonder about the subconscious mechanism that helps us evaluate a stranger at a glance. I hadn't had much faith when I queried the previous fellow, but for some reason I felt drawn to this particular gentleman among all the others going about their business.

« Pardon. »

The man takes out his spectacles to look at the name of the street. He begins to explain, then sees I am not comprehending at a useful level.

« Allons-y », and he motions for me to follow.

We head to the other side of the village, which is further than I anticipate. Along the way we come upon two women, one leaning over her garden wall talking to the other outside. They greet Monsieur Celo warmly and a good-humored back and forth begins. He explains my circumstances and the woman leaning over the wall confirms the *gîte* is a little further along.

We find it and peer into the property. It seems quiet.

« Oui, c'est certainement ça. » M. Celo says to me.

There is the main house and a smaller separate structure that looks renovated inside – airy and open-planned, probably catering to a single group of guests. We walk around the corner of the ivy-covered property wall to the main entrance and buzz.

We wait.

Nothing.

When I had called the number earlier, I had gotten a long message which I couldn't understand. I ask M. Celo if he can listen, and I dial the Nokia.

As he listens his eyebrows raise, then he furrows his brow and hands the phone back to me.

« Il est parti à Orléans ! Pendant les vacances ! » he says with some exasperation. Indeed, if you run a *gîte*, shouldn't you be there to offer it to wayward travelers, especially during the holidays?

The woman on the wall had told him of one other place so we set off. But it too is full, like the first place.

"Yes, from Paris," the woman says sympathetically, but she knows of nothing else except the place we have just come from.

We start back toward *centre-ville*. The clouds release a few more drops and a cool breeze passes down the lane. I am concerned for M. Celo in only his white shirtsleeves. We had been at it for the better part of an hour. He is perspiring slightly. This has got to be a lot more walking than he had intended before I accosted him. My poor planning and now I've thrust myself on this gentleman, taken advantage of his sense of social duty.

He is under no obligation to me, yet he persists, leading me somewhere. Should I leg off, release him, head for the forest and bear the consequences of my miscalculation? There is clearly nowhere to stay in this village. But to say thanks and walk away now, won't that be dismissive of M. Celo's efforts up until now?

« Essayons la mairie, » he says, as if detecting my uncertainty. We pick up our pace to get to the *mairie*, the town hall, before its 6:00 p.m. closing. The woman on staff dials a couple of numbers associated with the church, but no one answers.

I need to head off, I think. This is too much for this kind man.

Walking down the stairs in front of the *mairie* he touches my forearm reassuringly, *« Ne vous inquiétez pas, on va vous trouver un endroit pour dormir ce soir ; c'est sûr. »*

I submit. I am completely in his hands now. Suddenly I feel completely at ease.

In front of the *boulangerie* he tells me to wait and motions with his hand to make sure I understand. M. Celo had stepped out for a fresh evening baguette when he ran into me an hour earlier. His brief errand had turned into an open-ended expedition.

« Ma femme doit se demander ce que je fait ! »

As we walk toward his house, he explains his wife recently broke her leg and is in difficult circumstances. Otherwise, he would have offered me a place. We stop by to drop off the baguette, his wife on crutches. He explains who I am and what we're up to.

From the road he calls to his neighbor, a young man listening to rock music we can hear in the street. I can't follow the exchange, but from the body language I'm pretty sure the neighbor basically said, "Sure, he can crash on the sofa." But it seems M. Celo has another possibility in mind.

« *Venez,* » M. Celo says, « *en dernier recours, vous pourrez rester ici, mais j'ai un autre endroit en tête.* »

We continue down the lane to where the village ends in a field of colza, the rapeseed crop I had been walking through since entering northern France two weeks earlier. Now the colza is blooming, transforming the dull, dark green fields to vibrant carpets of tiny yellow flowers.

We turn the corner and stop in front of a house. M. Celo pushes the bell. We wait outside the low wall.

A woman emerges from a side door, atop steps. She is tall and slim, somewhere in her 70s, and wiping her hands on her apron.

« *Oui, bien sûr,* » she says after a brief exchange. Then looking at me, « *Vous avez faim ?* »

« *Oui !* » I exclaim, beaming, not only hungry, but relieved to find such a place for the night, and, almost more so, to release M. Celo of his burden.

Madame Odile Chenu ushered me into the house and set a third place at the kitchen table – dinner was ready. Through the window I could see a serious looking man in the back garden. The sun had broken underneath the clouds and he was taking advantage of its rays as it dipped toward the horizon. I worried he wouldn't take kindly to a stranger suddenly intruding on his evening. He looked even taller than the Abbot of Grimbergen.

When Michel Chenu entered, he towered over me. He even seemed too tall for his own house. And when we shook hands, his enveloped mine, even though mine are quite large. His grip was naturally powerful.

He broke into a smile and welcomed me warmly. I shouldn't have worried. His reaction was like his wife's, "but of course!"

They were farmers. Technically retired, M. Chenu, 80, kept his hand in, doing the paperwork for operations, instead of handling implements and machinery. Maybe he leased out their land? I didn't quite catch the arrangement, but I did seem to be understanding more than I had with Jean & Jeanne. The colza across the road was theirs, I believe, and M. Chenu explained they generally ran four crops on rotation in this region: the rapeseed, wheat, barley, and broad bean.

« Vous trouverez du soja au sud de Pithiviers, et de plus en plus de pommes de terre et de maïs en continuant vers le sud. »

Their two sons had chosen not to follow into the farming business. One was living somewhere else in France, the other in London, married to an English girl, I think. It was to his old room Odile showed me. She gave me a fresh towel and extra quilt, for the night felt quite cold. She let me know I had the whole upstairs to myself.

Who were these people that they could so readily take in a stranger, vouched for by a neighbor who only just met me? How many of us are capable of this? How did I deserve any of this?

I didn't *deserve* this or not. The only thing relevant here was their capacity to give, not my worth for receiving. True giving entails no calculation. Theirs was clearly a life of abundance. I don't mean materially, but in terms of human solidarity.

After a shower I went downstairs to ask if I may use the internet.

« Oui, oui bien sûr. » They were sitting together, a news program on the television. Since I didn't have a smartphone, I was carrying

a small laptop. I used it to access Google Earth to help piece together an idea of the next day's route when needed, to periodically email snapshots back to my parents to let them know all was well, and to study a little French when I had the energy, which wasn't all that often. I know, it wasn't the most efficient arrangement, carrying the laptop and the Nokia feature phone. But I was comfortable with the setup, even with the extra weight. I liked having the bigger keyboard and screen for writing and for looking at imagery and maps. It would take another year and the exasperation of a close friend to finally thrust a smartphone into my life – I admit it's pretty handy.

I asked for the password. They looked at me puzzled. What was the word for password, *clé*, or no, *mot de passe*, right? I tried to rephrase the question.

« Ah, il y a un mot de passe ? On ne savait pas. C'est notre fils qui a tout installé pour nous. Quand on a un problème, on l'appelle. Voulez-vous qu'on lui demande ? »

« Non, non ! » Typical of their generation it was the children who had set up the internet and kept the wireless running. They weren't familiar with the actual arrangements.

The password was probably the long alphanumeric on the back of the router, but it might not be, and I knew if I started down this path I could end up disrupting their evening for the next hour. They would feel compelled to call their son in London to find out the password, disturbing him too. No, it wasn't important. I was more than content to get in bed, glance at the Michelin map, and go to sleep. Étampes, tomorrow's destination, wasn't even that far.

The next morning I was back at the kitchen table, Odile making breakfast. Michel sat across from me pushing around three pills with his thick, calloused finger.

« Un comprimé à soixante, deux à soixante-dix. Maintenant trois à quatre-vingt. Si j'arrive à quatre-vingt-dix, quatre ! » he laughed, and popped them down. Not bad. One pill at 60. Two at 70. Only three at 80. He looked like he'd easily reach 90 for his fourth!

Before leaving, Odile gave me some pears and insisted I take a small *gâteau*. I protested, the generosity already too much, but I relented. I admit I looked a little askance at the *gâteau*. It wasn't a homemade French delicacy, but a packaged, store-bought fruit cake, sealed in cellophane. But later that day, when I opened it under some byway tree feeling peckish, I recognized what a gift Odile had given me. Dense and durable, enhanced with candied fruit, it was the perfect snack. I'd end up buying them regularly along the way, the store brand being just fine for these industrialized cakes. I would lament their eventual reduction in quality and final disappearance from the shelves as I entered Spain.

M. et Mme Chenu stood together in front of their house looking somewhat stiff and serious, reminding me of Grant Wood's American Gothic painting. Michel raised his long arm and waved, his big hand with a weight of its own, like a pendulum. « *Pensez à nous quand vous arriverez à Saint Jacques,* » he called as I closed the gate. And then, with a broad smile and beaming eyes, « *et envoyez-nous une carte postale !* »

Odile poked his ribs and admonished him for the postcard request. He laughed some more, and I couldn't help but smile. Yes, I thought, that's the least I can do, remember you both to Saint James and send you a card from Santiago.

Father Giuseppe **6**

I left Étampes following the la Voie Romaine, a Roman road still in use nearly 2,000 years later, older than the idea of the Camino de Santiago. Who were the others who had walked this way? What burdens had they carried, where had their lives ended up? I'm certain we have much in common.

The road, its current version a course, grey aggregate without markings, was relatively straight. It stretched over a series of deep undulations in the land, disappearing in the distance. I'd close my eyes to see how many steps I could make before drifting into the middle, or off the edge.

Maybe once every 20-30 minutes a vehicle would pass. I'd see the speck of it on the farthest hilltop then it would disappear. After long moments, sometimes so long I thought the vehicle had turned off, it would reappear atop the next closest swell, then dip out of view again. On the nearer hills I could make out the car lift slightly as it crested, the load on the chassis lightening perceptibly before it bore down again. Because of the intervening swales, the vehicle's approach was silent. The ambient sounds were birds, crickets, a breeze and the rustle of grass. But as the vehicle came over the last top, I'd finally be able to hear it. The sound of the motor grew. And grew and grew, as did the hiss of the rubber over the aggregate and the vibration of this block of steel forcing its way through the air. When the vehicle finally slammed past me, the air burst.

None were going especially fast, but the violence of the moment was intense. The driver was cocooned in his steady momentum. Tires humming, music playing, scenery passing, he was oblivious to the shockwave ripping over the landscape, his machine shedding molecules of petroleum products like dandruff.

It was like suddenly having my ears boxed.

Imagine what it feels like to the creatures along the road, or the plants who cannot escape. No ill will on the driver's part. We've all, most of us, been behind the wheel. There's generally no malice in it. The smeared insects. The broken butterflies and birds. The  smashed snakes and frogs and turtles. The squirrels, opossums, armadillos and raccoons. The family pet with her jaws ripped away, legs in spasms. The exquisite fur of a mink in the morning sun. The tattered wing of a raptor fluttering with passing traffic. The dinosaur-old alligators bludgeoned and swelling. The brown eyes of a deer, staring heavenward. A crumpled man in a spreading pool of blood. This is the unsuspecting bycatch of transportation, representing a fraction of what only I've glanced. Multiply these daily collisions billions of times across Earth and maybe you'll have a better feel for the corridors of death sometimes called freeways.

Eventually, in Saclas, I dropped into the upper end of the Juine, a small river that nourished a pleasantly forested meandering valley among the endless croplands. I came across a small, hand-painted sign warning of *vipères*. Snake, I thought incredulously, so many snakes you need a sign? Sure enough, a little further on, one slithered across the path. It was a boggy area where they were growing mâche, a tasty salad green I had only tried recently.

Under a wide tree across from the skeleton of Les Maisons Gillet, I enjoyed an Odile-inspired *gâteau-aux-fruits*. Beware: Though it is spelled the same, *fruits* is pronounced more like "fwee".

Inevitably I emerged back into the agricultural land; yellow colza, green wheat, and brown tilled earth as far as I could see.

Ever since arriving in Paris, except for those spitting clouds in Boissy-sous-Saint-Yon, the weather had been gorgeous. High blue skies, warm sun and cool air. In these beautiful heavens near Autruy-sur-Juine, a pair of Mirage jets performed maneuvers, the roar of their engines blanketing the landscape. In spite of the clear skies, it was hard to pick them, my eyes following the laggard sound as it ripped through the peaceful atmosphere. There! Like a black arrowhead, banking, twisting, rolling, rocketing out of sight again, even now I can feel the force of the thrust in my belly, hear the roar in my ears. It was both exhilarating and irritating. Even a little dispiriting, for after all these amazing machines are engines of war.

As a child, we'd park at the end of the runway of Miami International and watch the aircraft come and go, especially the big ones servicing South America. There was something exciting about it, all that power. Kids love big machines, at least boys typically do. But I remember a woman who did too. When I moved away for my first real job I lived on the flightpath of Washington National. One sleepy weekend afternoon the housewife next door told me she loved it when the airplanes took off upriver. "The sound, it makes me orgasm." Still so innocent, I can't imagine what my expression betrayed in that moment. But my instinct advised caution, like when you encounter a *vipère* sign.

Sunshine, but a cold north wind. I took shelter in the lee of a stand of trees that had escaped the plow because of a wrinkle in the earth. These roads amongst the fields could be awkward walking. The massive treads on tractor tires churned the deep mud which dried into an uneven, gouged surface. They were for machines, not feet. Still, it was better than walking on asphalt.

I had signal and needed to try Father Giuseppe again at the *presbytère* in Bazoches-les-Gallerandes.

Last night, at the *presbytère* in Étampes, I had been taken care of by the very welcoming young Damien, a German I think, but I'm not sure if he was a priest in training, a layperson, or a volunteer. There was a dedicated *refuge des pèlerins* upstairs which I had to myself.

"There were two Frenchmen and a Canadian here yesterday."

They were headed to Orléans, via Angerville, to eventually join the *voie* in Tours. I was aiming for the Loire Valley and had considered Orléans, but the thought of another city so soon after Paris was unappealing. Plus, I intended to head up the Loire River, not down it, and thought I might hit the valley around Sully-sur-Loire, a fairly random selection but it seemed to make sense, at least looking at the Michelin.

Damien thought about this for a moment then said, "I will bring my father, he knows this way." Biological father I think, not a Father father. I was surprised there was some kind of "way".

Damien made to go.

"Wait, do you have a bucket?"

"Ah, what?"

When I arrived, Damien apologetically explained the hot water heater in the shower had stopped working, and "the man will only come tomorrow."

But there was an electric kettle and the cold water still worked. I have taken many a wash by bucket. Half hot and half colds yields plenty for a squat, scrub and rinse. But a bucket, that essential daily item in much of the world, took a good while to find. What I was going to do with it was clearly perplexing, but they were happy to indulge me. Sometimes our conveniences stifle our innate resourcefulness – no hot water doesn't mean you have to wait for the plumber to come to the rescue.

Damien's father had gone to several different places before he found a working copy machine, but he showed up later delighted to give me several pages of faded directions that would help me reach Bazoches and Father Giuseppe, starting with the Roman road.

"He's a very good and generous man, and I am sure you can stay with him." We tried his number several times, but it always went straight to voicemail.

This time, as I sit in the sun sheltered from the wind, he answers.

"*Sì, sì, sì,*" he says, as I try in my kindergarten French to ask if he received the message I left. Then he begins to explain something

that totally loses me. I am pretty sure he is telling me I can stay, but
there is a "but".

« *Je ne comprends pas, désolé.* »
"*¿Habla español?*"
"Not really."
"*Italiano?*"
"No."
„*Sprechen Sie Deutsch?*"
If only I had studied seriously in high school.
"*Português?*"
At this point I laugh.
"I speak five, *cinque. No inglese!*"
« *Je viens ? Ce soir ? Okay ?* »
"Okay, okay, okay!"

This was a long day from Étampes to Father Giuseppe,
somewhere between 35-40kms. But the previous day from Chez
Chenu had been short, less than 20kms, so I felt strong. The final
15kms from Autruy-sur-Juine to Bazoches was wide open
agricultural land. This wasn't a well-traveled *voie*, and I don't recall
many waymarks, but the old directions of Damien's worked.

After the phone call it was basically a straight line, nearly due
south. I could see a church steeple piercing the featureless horizon.
After a while it became apparent I was heading right for it. Once I
realized this I couldn't look away, like sighting land while adrift at
sea. It drew me on, as if by force of gravity. For over an hour the
steeple grew imperceptibly with each step, and then I was there,
Faronville, nothing more than the *église* and a farm compound. This
is the kind of terrain where the church steeple comes into its own.
It stands out in the flat, endless landscape like a beacon, orienting
all who see it.

Water. The gravitational force that drew me directly here was
my hope that I'd find water in the graveyard. I was out and felt
myself wearing down because of it. I had noticed the French were
very serious about visiting and tending ancestral graves. They liked
to keep flowers. Not plastic, but fresh. It was finally dawning on me

that there was a very good chance of finding a water spigot in these graveyards. And how appropriate, water being the source of life.

I sat giving my feet a rest, drinking the cool water. In front of me was a simple family tomb. At the foot was a plaque with the name Louis Vaury. He *disparu* with his infantry regiment, *au Bois des Loges le 5 octobre 1914*. It was easy to guess what the word *disparu* means; disappeared, went missing. M. Vaury vanished in battle, probably along with thousands of others, while his family perhaps prayed here for his safe return. He was 32.

A car pulled up and stopped outside the graveyard wall. A woman got out, opened the back, took a pair of clippers and a bunch of flowers and walked to the other side of the graveyard, stopping at the spigot to fill a pitcher. I quietly got up, shouldered my pack, and moved on.

Bazoches-les-Gallerandes was a small village with a big church at the center, surrounded by the same sea of cropland. I found Father Giuseppe in his office, nearly obscured behind a desk stacked deep with work. He was having a loud conversation on his cellphone in what sounded like Russian but must have, in retrospect, been Portuguese. That concluded, he gave me a warm welcome and took me by the arm into the *presbytère* straight to the kitchen. There, on an ancient cast iron range sat a vat of tomato sauce, simmering away.

He takes a wooden spoon and tests it, licking his beard then nodding with satisfaction. He is making us pasta for dinner. Of course! He is Italian, not French, it dawns on me.

In the old fridge he indicates a six pack of Leffe. They are a convenient, smaller sized bottle – you don't end up with the last, desultory warm swallow characteristic of the standard 12oz. He also points to a plate of *fromage* and several tortes. The pasta sauce smells delicious.

I follow Father Giuseppe up a creaky set of stairs to a sagging landing. There is a washing machine squeezed into the bathroom, which he indicates I am free to use. I will, this being the fourth night out of Paris. I essentially had two sets of clothing I'd switch between. Being wool, they easily endured several days wear in the cool weather. But it was a fresh pair of socks every day, given the primacy of feet to the whole endeavor.

There are nearly a dozen bathrobes hanging in the bathroom. I am free to use these too, Father Giuseppe says. I would try on a few later, but found they were sized for someone notably shorter and rounder. Father Giuseppe shows me the bedroom and then heads back to his stack of work.

I push open the heavy shutters and there, just to the right, is the hulking black roof of the church. The orange orb of the sun is dropping toward the fields. Outside is cold and fresh. Turning back to survey the room a million dust motes hang in the air, caught in the sunbeams. It's like an image from the Hubble Space Telescope.

The bed linen was fresh and tucked, but its very neatness made it notable. The *presbytère* looked as if it had been ransacked.

It was impossible to tell when it had last been swept, and perhaps it had never been vacuumed. Rooms were full of clutter. Furniture was askew. There were piles of clothes upstairs and down. Books were everywhere, stacks of them. Papers and files. Stacks of them too. Pages here and there. Semi-burnt scraps in the fireplace. In the kitchen was a fabulous jumble of ancient moka pots of all sizes. Where did Father Giuseppe sleep? In the room he'd given me? On the sofa? Did he sleep? If there was ever an argument for allowing Catholic priests to marry, this scene was it. Not for the wife to keep house, but to be a partner, someone to share strengths and weaknesses and make something even greater through union. To make sure neither one of you gets overwhelmed. To help make time and space for yourself, both of you.

To be honest, Father Giuseppe seemed unfazed by what looked to me like chaos. He probably knew the exact location of every sock, spoon, paper and book. I got the impression, through the attention he paid me, a passing stranger, he was a sincerely engaged priest. Who had the time to fold laundry when there were parishioners to attend? Father Giuseppe had come late to the priesthood. If I recall, he had been, among other things, a dishwasher and salesman, and maybe worked in the merchant marine. He'd lived in Brazil and seen a good part of the world. He brought his broad experience, and I think his compassion for our struggles and weaknesses, into his current role. I don't know how well he could quote verse, but I sensed he could relate well to people.

When I passed downstairs after showering and settling in and getting the laundry going, Father Giuseppe was at the dining table having a glass of whisky with a parishioner. By the time I returned from a quick run to the local shop, she was gone, and Father Giuseppe had cleared a space at the end of the table and set two plates. The tortes were on the table, a fresh baguette, and a half bottle of Bordeaux. Father Giuseppe indicated it was all for me. He had to go out.

"I'll wait. *Je mange avec vous.* »

« *Non, non, non.* »

He tells me the pasta is ready. You don't leave fresh pasta for later, I know. But really, I think, I can wait on my host. More than that, I *want* to wait on this big-hearted man.

With great patience he helps me understand that the earliest he will be back is 8:00 p.m. But it could be 11:00. He doesn't know. He is going to hear confession at church.

"There is honestly not much to confess here in the countryside," is my rough understanding of what he says, "But still, the old folks, they sometimes have a lot to talk about." He smiles and bids, « *Bonne nuit.* ».

For my part I ate a heap of spaghetti, finished the red, and tried to eat only half of each torte, but the strawberry one, so fresh, I couldn't help it.

The church bells ring out at 5:00 a.m.

Each pilgrim on the Camino carries a passbook, a Carnet de Pèlerin/Credencial del Peregrino, into which you collect a stamp, or *date et cachet/firmas y sellos*, at each night halt. Without the *credencial*, you can't stay in the dedicated pilgrim accommodations, the *refuges des pèlerins* and *albergues de peregrinos*. In my third week of walking, I already had a colorful variety, from simple *hôtel* stamps to ones with the stylized scallop shell of the Camino, the *coquille Saint-Jacques*.

Father Giuseppe's parish stamp stood out for its plainness. A black circle with the church address ringing an empty center.

A parishioner in for coffee teases him about how sad it looks.

"Is that all you have?" he basically says, "look how nice these others are. Even *la poste* would give a better stamp!"

Father Giuseppe retrieves a purple felt-tip and leans over my *credencial* on the dining table. With great concentration he attempts to draw a shell in the blank center, then signs and dates the cachet with a flourish. He picks it up and regards his work at arm's-length.

"What do you think?"

It looks more like a cauliflower than a scallop shell. I tell him I love it.

« *Vous êtes marié ?* » Father Giuseppe asks as he hands me the credential.

"No." I'm not married. Never have been.

« *Célibataire ?* »

"No," I declare, thinking he means celibate. But maybe, I learn later, he just meant single?

But my answer elicits further teasing from the parishioner. « *N'est pas célibataire,* » the parishioner chuckles.

Father Giuseppe sighs and shakes his head, then walks me outside.

« *Bon Camino !* »

Like a scrap of paper caught in gusty updrafts, the kite fluttered upward, then dropped, fluttered then dropped, moving seemingly at random along the fresh green sprouts of wheat. He was white, with black, ink-dipped wingtips. At first glance I had thought him a wind-blown paper or bag, loose in the field. Then, after I realized it was a kite, I thought this must be some kind of mating or territorial display. On a number of occasions the past weeks I'd encountered a small, urgent bird who would flutter vigorously above fence lines, chittering a kind of Euro-electronica. I assumed it was his spring rite. It was the season after all. But the kite's pattern appeared more erratic than ritual.

Then the kite plunged and disappeared. In that moment I realized the act all along was to flush prey. He flapped aloft with a small brown creature, a mouse I suppose, the size of my thumb. A bellyful.

The tuxedoed magpies had been with me all along, from the first days in Belgium, hopping in fields, perching on fences, calling raucously. They must be cousins of the ones that my father and I saw in the western half of the United States, as we drove and camped our way across the continent over a decade before. But the American cousins had had a dash of emerald green, hadn't they?

Great tits too, a surprise for me. Little guys in bare brush and trees, very handsome with their black heads and fat white cheeks, olive and yellow bodies. I associated them with spring in the Himalaya, and here they were in France, which showed how little I knew of their distribution.

A glimpse of these feathered creatures instantly transported me to opposite sides of the globe, conjuring scenes and friends and family. Memories, even longings.

At what point in life do we have a reservoir deep enough for such reveries?

At what point do we stop creating memories and only live in them? Even living the memories of memories barely conceived, like the flash of a bird's wing? Why these associations at all? What's the point, dwelling in the past, remembering other places? That's just it. These are more than transient images. These memories, these sensations, they are part of the present. Their reservoir helps sustain us.

About halfway to Vitry-aux-Loges, the open cropland turned to planted forest. Somewhere in the timberland I followed a road along a lush green pasture. In that pasture a small herd of cows rested, chewing their cuds. Eventually my passing caught their attention. First one, then another, then another, and finally all of them got up and began walking to intercept me along the fence. They were butter colored, hornless, with a shaggy mop between their ears. These were solid, well-muscled animals. They didn't rush, but came steadily, and then walked along with me, maintaining regular spacing one between the other.

When I say butter colored, I don't mean the strong yellow of store-bought, but the paler color of butter made at home. The fence line ended and when the lead cow stopped the rest stopped where they were, keeping their spacing. Before the road disappeared around a bend I stopped and turned. They were still there, watching, their ears tuned towards me. My uncle would later tell me they were *Charolais*, known for their meat. *Charolais. Magpie. Great tit.* These are what we name them.

But what do they name themselves?

What do they name us?

In the afternoon, among the planted pines and greyish white soil, and I am instantly transported to a quiet day in the South Carolina midlands of my youth. It is the aroma of the transpiring pine, the feel of the sandy soil under my tread, how it squeaks as I walk. This was definitely a longing, more than a memory or mere association. A longing for my grandmother, my aunts, for the days before the world became the noisy rush and I joined in, when time moved like the tides, not like the internet, when you knew people, not just your friends.

Such longings can be misleading, for while they contain truth, they obscure much. I wonder why the feeling can be so powerful, yet completely unbidden. Are these longings an admission of mistaken choices, of misplaced priorities in the rush to join the race of life? To win it? Is a longing the recognition of having discarded the wrong things in our haste? Helpless against their manifestation, I let these longings come freely and try to embrace them. They are indeed part of the present reality. Passing from the pines, I let them go, until the next time.

The sky remains cloudless, the magic blue of a soft spring. But in every part of it, no matter where I look, I see a streaking airliner or hanging vapor trail.

Father Giuseppe had called Father Herman to see if he'd be at the *presbytère* in Vitry-aux-Loges – he didn't stay there every night. The answer seemed to be yes, and I had to be there between 4 o'clock and 6 o'clock. Or maybe either before four or after six. Or maybe not at all if he couldn't make it. I wasn't sure.

At some point late morning, as I passed along the main street of a small town, a car pulled alongside me. It was Father Giuseppe. He told me something reassuring about Father Herman, then barreled off to the next parish errand, waving his arm out of the window.

I arrived at 3:30 p.m., that way covering any eventuality. Father Herman arrived at 6:00.

I love language. How *caravan* and *magazine* come from Arabic. How the days of our week come from Roman knowledge of the heavens. How *caucus* comes from Algonquian. How *juggernaut* and *sugar* come from Sanskrit. How *television* came via the French *télévision* from a combination of Latin and Greek. How *coach* (as in the vehicle) comes from the Hungarian village of Kocs, famous at the time for building the fanciest passenger wagons. How a slang word for coffee, *mocha*, is still a dusty, flyblown Red Sea port from where coffee was first exported, before seedlings were stolen and then established in *Java*. How I can find the same word for *table* in Latin America, the Arabian Peninsula, South Asia and the Philippines.

It's easy to imagine walking around the world along trails of languages that constantly cross and interweave, connected by steppingstones of words. While I love language, I don't have a talent for learning them – I'm no polyglot. Part of it is a basic lack of capacity. I struggle. But the other part of it was being conditioned to view languages as separate and distinct entities, rather than the porous modes of expression they are, not only intermingled with each other, but also with so many other ways of communicating. And I've come late to my enthusiasm with language. The one advantage of this more seasoned vantage point is I'm no longer burdened by the illusion of perfection, worried about making mistakes and embarrassing myself. I happily plunge in and don't mind the perplexed looks I sometimes generate, or the "Would you prefer if I speak English?" as I'm stammering. Allegedly the mental stamina and plasticity is not what it would have been in my youth. Nevertheless, it is enough to get me here.

Father Herman joined the minor seminary at 12 years old.

I had no idea there was such a thing.

"Yes," he laughed, "On payday my father gave me a military buzzcut. That's okay when you are seven or eight. The priests had long hair. And they played soccer and did a lot of other fun things for a boy my age." Minor seminary is basically a Catholic boarding school. It provides an education for kids who might want to eventually join the priesthood but may not otherwise have the opportunity.

Father Herman served in Papua New Guinea, studied English in Australia, and had written several books on the history of missionaries in Southeast Asia. There was a possibility he might be posted to the US soon. Normally he stayed in a shared residence with other priests.

"From West Africa," he said, and I think Eastern Europe. I hadn't met any French priests in France so far. True, there had been a French Jesuit in training at the Abbaye Saint-Louis-du-Temple in Vauhallan, that first night out of Paris. But the rest around the dining table were from Cameroon and Haiti. A pink-faced Irish priest ran the show in Étampes, then there was Father Giuseppe of Italy, and now Indonesia.

"It is hard to recruit in France. So there are more of us here from different parts of the world."

Not only had the Catholic Church in France lost most of its property and influence since the French Revolution, it also seemed to have lost its draw as a vocation too.

"But if you go to Sully tomorrow, there is a French priest there. Father Leroy. He is very popular. A well-known cyclist. I will call and see if you can stay there."

In the morning I stripped the bed and showed Father Herman

how the washing machine worked, so he didn't have to take the linens with him. His *cachet* definitely had more character than Father Giuseppe's. In the center was a figure wearing a miter and holding a crozier, the hooked staff of a bishop. In his right hand he must have been holding a chalice, or some other meaningful object, but the quality of the stamp was such that it looked like he was giving his middle finger.

I soon reentered the forest, heading toward the Loire Valley. It was still very much agricultural land, composed of vast plantations

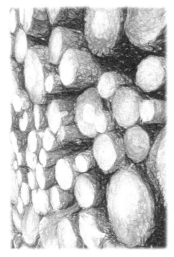

of oak and pine in various stages of growth and harvest. Like the day before leaving Bazoches, I left carrying hand sketches and notes I made from looking at imagery on the laptop. There were no waymarks in these areas that I could find. Yesterday it was mostly stitching together farm roads. Today it is linking forest tracks, connecting from spoked carrefour to carrefour. And this was the only day the whole Camino where I bought an extra bottle of water to carry. It was worth the additional 1.5kg not to run out late morning in countryside that looked unlikely to offer a spigot or someone to give me water, much less a graveyard.

Father Herman had warned me of criminal activity in the *forêt*. I think it was Father Herman. But if not him, then who else would it have been? Maybe I'm thinking of a different stretch of forest. And really, I think the stories were about people leaving their car to go for a hike and returning to find a window smashed. So I wasn't that concerned. Yet, while Rebecca might have plunged right on, I could see why a solo woman might reconsider such long, isolated stretches.

The most consistent company I had this day was a bird I never saw. He sounded like a cuckoo clock that needed winding, a single high to low note, with a long interval in between calls. These lonesome birds marked their broad territories with their calls as I walked through. If I encountered a soul all morning I don't recall. Maybe one car bouncing slowly lowly along. The roads were chalky grey, sometimes crossed by long lines of processionary caterpillars. There were stacks of timber, enormous logs bleeding sap, sparkling and spicing the air.

I was eager to see the famous Loire River Valley, though also a bit wary of its tourist cachet. The Loire is the longest river in France, rising in the Massif Central to the south, flowing north, then making a giant sweeping turn west to finally empty in the *golfe de Gascogne*, or Bay of Biscay. Two Ways start from its banks: the *voie* from Le Puy-en-Velay about 400km upriver from Sully, and the *voie*

from Tours a little over 150km downriver. I didn't expect to find too many tourists this time of year, early April, and thought most of the attractions in any case were further downriver. I'd be heading up. Not as far as Le Puy-en-Velay, but to a point where the *voie* from Vézelay crossed the Loire – about 100km. From there I'd turn right. At least that's how I'd started to envision the route.

Walking over the bridge into Sully-sur-Loire, the high turrets of its storybook castle in the background, two shiny Mercedes sedans came speeding by, flashing their lights and blasting their horns. A wedding party; heavy makeup, rich garments, elaborate headscarves on beautiful, big-featured women, all looking very serious, except for one petite blonde wedged in the backseat smilingly delightedly. Alas, as I walked through the pretty streets there seemed to be more tourists than locals, and I had to include myself among the interlopers. This was the first place where I felt this imbalance. Even Paris didn't feel this way, with its millions of annual visitors. But tourists meant Office de Tourisme and the woman there, once again knowledgeable, helpful and lovely, directed me to the *presbytère*.

The priest doesn't get off his cellphone when he comes out after I ring. He pulls the door behind him, letting me know with his body language I'm not welcome inside.

He motions me impatiently to the Sunday school classroom. There, still on his phone, he points to a bare, musty looking mattress, black cobwebs encrusting one end.

He pulls the phone momentarily away from his ear. « *Fermez les volets la nuit et quittez les lieux vers huit heures.* » I think he just told me to keep the shutters closed and be out by eight. That's it? What about the shower?

« *Douche ?* »

He resumes talking and indicates a spigot on an outside wall.

Really? *Are you always such a douche?* I want to ask.

My luck with *presbytères* had run out. I don't know if he was the famous cycling cleric, but he could have been the finger-flicking likeness used to model the stamp for Vitry-aux-Loges. No, that's too much. How could I judge what pressing business had him in a rush on a beautiful Saturday afternoon? There was plenty of other accommodation available in town, and he was in fact offering free shelter. I had no right to ask for more, and not even that.

The friendly Karim at the 2-star Hôtel Henri IV was happy for my business. His wife, clad in a shiny robe of geometric shapes, nodded her assent to the slight discount. I couldn't help but notice the flash of her manicure as she counted the bills. My room, number 2, was pink, with a padded headboard. The €40 was well outside my budget, but it was a much better deal than the bare mattress on the cold floor.

I needed a break from all the great bread and *fromage*. For a completely different taste, I eyed a joint called Chez Wang, but it was empty and steamy looking. With a nod to Father Giuseppe, I opted for a small Italian place and another good bowl of pasta.

Over the Loire 7

The bright morning sun caught the dew in the grasses fringing the bike path atop the levee. Its sparkling revealed a vast array of spiderwebs, innumerable webs of various sizes, reflecting as if they were encrusted in diamonds. It reminded me of that latticework city of topaz, on the banks of the dark Schelde River. In addition to the classic variety of web, there were webs in the shapes of fine canopies and intricate tents. They were elegant, grand even, as if a sprawling royal wedding party. The webs were densely packed and spread along the path as far as I could see. And between the tips of the taller blades of grass, single taut strands ran, connecting the whole mass, wiring it for communication and travel. These were not the webs of individual, isolated spiders I was walking past. It was an integrated metropolis.

As the sun dried the dew, it all disappeared to the eye. But the spiders were all still there, living their day.

The EuroVelo 6 runs from the Atlantic coast of France to Constanta, Romania on the Black Sea. Essentially up the Loire River then down the Danube. I played hopscotch with two French women on well-kitted bicycles. They were doing the whole length, over 3,500km. I imagined the mountainous terrain that must lie between here and there, but it didn't worry them. They weren't in a rush and were taking it day by day. Their venture reminded me of a cycle trip I had done the previous year. It was nice to meet kindred spirits off to new trails on their own. In that way we were similar, even though our current modes were different. What had compelled them to start? What had compelled me? Do any of us ever really know?

An acquaintance in the US, married to a woman from west of Ham, had asked if, when I finished, I'd be able to answer the question, "Why did you do this?"

Maybe.

But maybe not everyone has to have a question at the start or an answer at the end. I didn't know.

I wished the two good luck, and they did the same. I wondered if the captain and chief mate would be there in Constanta when the women arrived, home between contracts on the *Independent Pursuit.*

In truth, the three days walking up the Loire from Sully were not the most interesting or enjoyable. Too much of it was on asphalt bike path which was fully exposed to the surprisingly hot early April sun, and tough on the feet. Whenever I could I struck off on trails and wandered through forest and along field edges, crossing streams on fallen logs. A few of these trails ended up dead ends, but it was hard to go too far astray with the river always near.

On one dusty road I came upon a young woman in a white *utilitaire*. She was part of a research group surveying wildlife in the river valley.

"Oui, they are *ragondin*," she said when I described the beaver-like creatures I'd been seeing along the waterways since Belgium. "They are a problem everywhere."

I was out of water and thirsty. She shared her bottle with me, then drove off to meet colleagues for lunch. Take me with you! I thought, imagining the bonhomie around a table, good food and good conversation. Instead, I continued along the dusty road. How ironic, walking along the Loire and I couldn't find anywhere to fill water. Her name was Cami. Her water did more for me than she realized.

With a shift to the right bank in Gien, I escaped the bike path and followed a dirt trail in the trees all the way to Briare. It was by far the most pleasant stretch. People walking, biking, strolling, watching kids, picnicking. The Loire moving strongly, tea green and quiet except for roils along the grassy bank. I remember the small riverside park in Gien because I came upon a public drinking fountain – the first one I had seen in France!

Briare struck me as too chic to stop. I felt I'd stick out among the smartly attired visitors enjoying the afternoon in a crowded outdoor café. But the canal *over* the Loire? That was an impressive piece of engineering. Completed in the late 19th century, it replaced a perilous ferry point a little further upstream, in Châtillon-sur-Loire; boatmen, grappling goods across a sometimes-dangerous river, maneuvering in and out of locks on banks buffeted by current. This had been a major commercial crossing of the Loire, connecting southcentral France with canals linking to the Seine River basin and Paris. These rivers that were once great barriers or transportation routes themselves, are now barely noticed as we zoom over them on bridges, themselves underappreciated.

I did spend a very pleasant night in the old lockhouse in Châtillon-sur-Loire, at Mantelot. Its rooms had been converted into comfortable *chambres* for touring cyclists. Heavy beams, coarse floor planks, exposed stone walls and a solid bed – the best paid room so far. The moon was waxing gibbous. My last full moon was over the English Channel. This one would be over the Loire.

It was a night of frogs and owls.

And the next morning I ran into trees whose trunks had been sheathed in colorful knitting, lending a playful air to the forest. The lighthearted artistry reminded me I had seen postboxes and stanchions likewise adorned some days before. While those who had done this were not present, their positive energy very much was.

So maybe the days along the Loire weren't that bad after all. I got a closeup look at the nuclear power station in Belleville, venting vapor and surrounded by blossoming yellow colza. And there were more butter cows crowding along the fence in Rognan to see what I might have brought them.

Yet qualitatively there was a fundamental difference with the previous week where I had bounced across the agricultural lands, looking for a way and places to stay. There I did feel the traveler, the pilgrim, mostly because of how people interacted with me.

Are you hungry? asks Mme Chenu, having never seen me before in her life.

Along the Loire I was, before anything else, a tourist, the customer. My stay in Saint-Thibault near Sancerre exemplified the feeling; cheaply furnished room but expensive, "free" WIFI that came and went, dinner served as art not nourishment, and the "included" breakfast an extra-*petit-déjeuner* of micro bread that wouldn't satisfy a pigeon. It is in this sense, of feeling yourself merely a transaction for someone else, that loneliness can take hold. It's not a pleasant feeling.

I would leave the river valley after a night at La Charité-sur-Loire, and turn more westerly, towards Bourges. Ready in the zip pocket of my backpack's hip belt were the relevant pages of tomorrow's march. In an email, Klaas, from the Vézelay Route Working Group of the Nederlands Genootschap van Sint Jacob (a lead from Seamus in Compèigne), had sent me a link for the English version of the *Northern Variant via Bourges Guide* of the Vézelay Way.

The helpful, knowledgeable and charming *hôtesse d'accueil tourisme*, Marion, in the Office de Tourisme in La Charité-sur-Loire had directed me to the shop where the man expertly produced a two-sided colored booklet of the 70 pages. The Dutch know how to do directions, and it was a luxury to have them in English. But I didn't know how long I'd be able to take advantage of it, following the Voie de Vézelay. My next fixed destination was friends who lived in the countryside between Moissac and Agen, around 500km further south. Where to leave the Vézelay Way? Do I go all the way to Périgueux? Cut over from Bergerac?

I didn't need to worry yet. That decision was a week or two away. It would become clear in time.

Since I was joining the more traveled Voie de Vézelay, I expected I would run into other pilgrims. I looked forward to it, especially after feeling like a tourist along the Loire. The solidarity of other *pèlerins* would be nice. Since Rean & Jo and Rebecca, I'd only met one other; Emile, who'd come in late my first night out of Paris, in Vauhallan at the *abbaye*. He'd been kind enough to share information on *hébergement*, since I had no idea where to stay the following days. I think he put me on to the *presbytère* in Étampes, where I took the bucket bath. From Vauhallan he'd gone southwest to Chartres and Tours, and I'd gone southeast.

In La Charité-sur-Loire Marion had also given me the key for the *refuge des pèlerins*, which was essentially straight across from the Office de Tourisme. But for this last night along the Loire and first along the Voie de Vézelay, I was all by myself, again. Maybe I'd run into other *pèlerins* tomorrow, along the way, I thought somewhat hopefully. It was a clean, simple place. I left a half bottle of Pouilly-sur-Loire in the fridge for whoever came next. Okay, maybe a little less than half.

It had been an easy day to La Charité-sur-Loire, 20-25km, arriving by 1:30 p.m. After getting the printing done, I indulged my first haircut, which for some reason always feels restorative. The next morning I felt full of vigor stepping off on the Vézelay Way, direction Bourges. The Dutch guide's maps and directions matched the well-marked way. Lots of grassy roads, good shade, and rabbits and deer who preferred to keep nibbling rather than scamper away. And the blossoms of spring were upon me. From cascades of ornamental wisteria to carpets of tiny wildflowers – white, baby blue and sunburst yellow. There was suddenly color in the landscape, besides the industrial colza.

In addition to the rabbits and deer, there were pigeons, but these fellows were more skittish. They weren't of the scrappy urban, ground-pecking flocks. These were big regal individuals who'd burst from leafy limbs, the beat of their wings nearly always startling to me, lost as I was in the rhythm of my footfalls and ticking trekking pole. Usually in pairs, they'd wing and swoop and undulate, dashing through open air to another leafy refuge. Sometimes they'd leave a feather in their airy wake, rapidly spinning quill down, floating ever so softly toward the earth.

These birds had been with me all through rural France. With their puffed breast and upright posture, their vestment of feathers, they looked like flying popes.

Water. Again, it was at the forefront of my mind. And when thoughts of water start, they don't stop.

When my water bottle is low, or worse, empty, it's as if I'm dragging a heavy sled. Where will I find it next? How much further? A *ville*, a church, a shop, a person. In the mornings I fill myself like a camel. But as the kilometers pass, my eyes begin to search. In the countryside I wasn't inclined to drink from surface water because of all the agriculture – the cloying smell of sprayed poisons on the wind was not rare. Most of the little pockets of habitation were without the commercial establishments where I'd readily ask for a fill from the tap. Gien was the only public fountain I'd seen. I kept an eye out for spigots, though I never dared to enter a private yard. Sometimes the wall of the *mairie* would have one, back where they parked the cars. But church graveyards were the most reliable source. Aside from people.

I wasn't shy of asking. My only trouble was with the phrase itself, *de l'eau*. E-A-U. Three letters! *Avez-vous de l'eau ?* My pronunciation of this simple but essential word was so poor that I resorted to holding up my empty water bottle when I asked. (To the Spanish, I am eternally grateful for *agua*.) Every single stranger in France I asked for water obliged me without hesitation. Every one. It got so that I looked forward to the instant of spotting someone and saying to myself, ah, I will ask them. Such a basic request. I was always so relieved to get the water. I also think those who gave me water welcomed the honesty of the transaction, it being so elemental.

But it was actually sometimes quite difficult to find anyone to ask. I'd see houses, parked cars. I'd hear machinery, roads. But to see someone? For many hours for most of the days walking through France, it was inhabited landscape, yes, but empty of people.

I can walk hungry. But low on water I feel it. Brain and body slow; coordination and balance, thinking and focus, it all degrades surprisingly quickly. The sled tugs. But when I find water, or am given it, and slake my thirst, and I have 40 ounces of clean cool water on my hip, the sled falls away. There are no more obstacles, no more worry. I feel lighter, unburdened. I could go forever.

The woman at the *mairie* in Baugy where I paid the €6 fee and took the key said the *refuge des pèlerins* was empty and there were no reservations. Really, I thought, still, no fellow pilgrims? So I was horrified when I returned from using the WIFI at the *bibliothèque* to find someone had indeed arrived. Horrified because I had left the only sink in the shared bathroom full of my dirty clothes soaking in grey soapy water.

"No, no, don't worry," said the voice from the back where the bunkbeds were.

Out stepped Lucie, a vivacious woman from Paris who had driven to La Charité-sur-Loire at the crack of dawn and was walking the two days to Bourges. She would have arrived earlier but, "I lost my way many times," she laughed. "I am clumsy that way."

She was sunburned and blistered but wasn't bothered. Before I knew it, I was following her to the center of the *ville* in search of a *gastronomique* restaurant, the kind of restaurant that had an experienced kitchen and usually offered regional, seasonal fare.

"The food is always good in these places, and interesting. I search them out. It is the main joy in going to different regions."

But it was Wednesday, and the one place was closed. Disappointed but undiminished, Lucie, "Everyone calls me Lulu," led the way to the only other option, a takeout place of mediocre pizza. We bought a bottle of rosé – the only thing in the cooler – and drank standing outside, waiting. Lulu smoked another cigarette.

Lulu was a teacher in Paris, bursting with energy and confessed self-doubt. She was walking *le Chemin* like this, in small pieces when she had time. And not necessarily sequentially – she went wherever she was interested.

"The walking calms me. Otherwise, I'm nervous. Thinking too much about what I should be doing in life." She loved the feeling of being underwater while scuba diving too. Breath is central to both of these activities, isn't it? When you're relaxed, your breathing is relaxed, and the walk or dive can be almost meditative. But tense, with constricted breathing, it's a completely different experience. The breath can both reveal your state of mind and shape it.

I think there were three sets of bunkbeds in the small *refuge*. Though I had stayed in a few other *refuges* the preceding weeks, this was the first since the Gasthuys in Antwerp where there was anyone else. No, I'd had roommates in the traveler's hostel in Brussels, but that was the only exception, and none were walking the Camino.

I left Lulu under the stars outside, talking on her phone and having a smoke. I never heard her come inside.

The next day I had to scamper at times to keep up. Lulu strode with determination, blisters and peeling shoulders notwithstanding. We ate lunch in the shade on the grassy edge of a field then continued the march. The Bourges Cathedral – officially the Cathédrale Saint-Étienne de Bourges – dominated the landscape from a great distance. Truly dominated. It looked massive, out of scale to anything else in view. A giant black, featureless silhouette. If it so impressed me, I can only imagine the impact it had on travelers in the Middle Ages. I think Lulu told me it had been finished in the early 13th century.

"It's one of the great Gothic cathedrals. Very similar to Notre-Dame in Paris."

We arrived in good time and made our way through narrow streets of half-timbered houses. Called *colombage* in France, it's a medieval building technique where the rough structural timber is left exposed. The style reminded me more of Germany than France. At a café in the shadow of the cathedral, Lulu introduced me to *bière* Monaco, basically a shandy with a shot of grenadine. A little skeptical at first – how can I be seen drinking this pink fizzy thing? – but it was incredibly refreshing.

Then Lulu begged a piece of cardboard and a marker from the *garçonne*, wrote out La Charité-sur-Loire in big letters, and headed off to a likely intersection to hitchhike back to her car. And I went to get a bunk in the large but empty *auberge de jeunesse*, the city youth hostel. I wondered where and when Lulu would next set off. She said she didn't know herself.

My French must have improved somewhat because at dinner the next night I carried on a successful, if modest, conversation with the woman seated at the next table. It probably helped that we were the only two people in the dining room. That and the half bottle of wine I'd finished in the room before I came down. It was an organic Saint-Nicolas-de-Bourgueil I'd carried from Bourges. A random purchase at a *bio* market the night before that turned out so delicious, I felt it a crime to abandon it in the youth hostel. But never again. Even a half empty bottle was too much added weight. I felt it every step. And the nearly 40km of sloshing in a hot pack certainly wasn't lawful treatment of such tasty vintage.

And then there was the generous decanter of table red that came with the set dinner.

Julienne was from Douai, in northern France, near a famous Canadian World War I battlefield, « *Vous connaissez ?* »

No, I didn't know it, but wondered if my route had taken me near it. I later checked. Vimy Ridge is about 100km west of where I crossed the French frontier at Vieux Reng. The large site is still so riddled with munitions that visitor access is carefully restricted.

She was a retired teacher, and I think a professional children's storyteller. She had a soothing demeanor and exuded a kind of calm presence. The patience and insight developed through all her years of teaching I'm sure helped me have a conversation. Passing through a small village somewhere I'd come upon a woman whose bicycle chain had come off. *Je peux vous aider ?* I proudly offered, amazed I had the phrase ready. But after reseating the chain I hurried on, having used up all my French for the moment. But the circumstances in the restaurant allowed Julienne to draw me out, and I was grateful.

We were in the Pèlerinage Notre Dame du Sacré-Cœur, Issoudun. I had been expecting a regular *refuge des pèlerins*, but this place was more like a hotel. No sharing bunkrooms, bathrooms and kitchen. But it was modestly priced, €20 for a small, simple, clean room. Julienne was on her way to Vichy, for three weeks in a spa. I was pretty sure it was her who tapped the horn the next day as I headed along an empty road to Châteauroux.

If it seems like wine was a part of every day, well, as clichéd as it is to say in France, it mostly was. Part of it was its ubiquity. Part of it was my curiosity with the regional variations. And part of it was cost. A good bottle in France was at least half the price of a comparable bottle in the US. And actually, it wasn't that comparable. The American wines I was used to filled your mouth with a big, round, overwhelming taste. I admit I first found the French wines kind of thin. But I soon found the sharper taste more agreeable. It didn't drown out the food. What was it, more minerally? It would be pretentious to pretend I had even a smidgen of useful knowledge about wines. The only thing that really mattered was that I was largely enjoying my random selections, and even more so the recommendations of whoever was nearby. As stereotypical as it sounds, it seemed most of the people I encountered knew their home region's wines – they were proud. The wine was an accompaniment. It was meant to be taken with the food, the specific dish. And it was poured into small glasses, not the goldfish bowls I was used to sloshing around back home. All this slight refinement of imbibing didn't keep me from going through a half bottle some evenings, but somehow it didn't seem right to cap off a long day of walking through the French countryside with a mug of herb tea, though I confess I've since moved in that direction. Along the Camino I was lifting the glass of wine partially out of habit, partially to relax, but also in the spirit of a celebratory breaking of bread. It was a sense of community and solidarity, even if I was alone.

So, a couple of days after the wine-enhanced dinner conversation in Issoudun, I found myself using the indispensable Swiss army corkscrew to open a bottle of Quincy under a tree with Mona and her two children. Mona, Tania and Nil had driven from their home just outside of Paris to walk with me for a couple of days from Châteauroux, taking advantage of the school holiday around Easter.

What a delight. To stroll along with the three of them, they unencumbered by weighty packs, or by the uncertainties of bumbling through an alien landscape and culture. I was worried the kids would be bored, but they were enjoying themselves. None had walked the Camino, nor were they very familiar with it. As far out as looking for a bed by knocking on the doors of abbeys, convents and presbyteries seemed, it was M. Celo's assistance and M. & Mme Chenu's welcoming me into their home that impressed them most. Especially Mona.

"Impossible. That close to Paris? Maybe in the countryside. But this near to Paris. I am shocked."

I knew what she meant. People in cities can be guarded, and

Boissy-sous-Saint-Yon was close enough to be a bedroom community. It's a natural response to being surrounded by an unnatural number of constantly changing strangers. But that's just it. It's only a precautionary shell. Walking the Camino was reminding me that underneath, one-on-one, the vast majority of us are kindhearted and helpful. True, this is easy to forget living in our modern media vortex. But part of the reason we go through our days so over-armored against each other is that we allow a torrent of the most outrageous examples of human behavior to constantly pour through our eyeballs. This overconcentrated virtual  world of media and marketing distorts our perspective and drowns our better nature. Fortunately, not everyone buys in. I didn't get the impression M. & Mme Chenu allowed this to happen to themselves.

I'd passed two nights with Mona's family during my stop in Paris. During the day Mona and Jérôme, her husband, were at work, and the kids in school. I spent a pleasant time with Jérôme's mother, Nicole, who was visiting. She patched my trousers, already fraying, and showed me on the map where she lived, outside of Angers, a city toward Nantes southwest of Paris, on the edge of the lower Loire Valley.

Jérôme was born in Saumur, a town a little further up the Loire. Saumur is about 240kms downriver from Sully-sur-Loire, where I first joined the river. He was raised there by his grandparents the first four years of his life, because his single mother, still quite young, was posted to Paris as an official in Posts and Telecommunications.

"Of course Saumur has a château, but it is best known for its national riding academy, and Le Cadre Noir. I kept a strong link with my grandparents and spent all my summers and holidays with them until my mid-teens. My grandfather took me every year to the show of the Cadre Noir. It was incredible to see how the horses were very well trained." Le Cadre Noir is a world-renowned cadre of instructors who also put on classical riding displays. They are distinguished by their traditional black uniforms, hence the name. But in the end, it wasn't the horses that captured the young Jérôme. "My grandfather was also a fan of the Tour de France. We used to both watch it on TV in July. I think he inspired in me the passion for cycling!"

Jérôme has been a serious cyclist for a long time and has the sculpted legs to show for it. At 16, he and a friend did a month-long trip into the Massif Central. After this he was hooked. He joined a cycling club, and for 10 years participated in endurance events and competitions.

"I like riding in a pack, the peloton. I like the atmosphere, the times of suffering, the times of easiness. But when I look up, what keeps me going is the mountain."

Cycling is more popular in France than I'd realized. Walking, I'd think myself in the middle of nowhere, and a couple of cyclists would zip by. Or a whole peloton (French meaning small ball), shouting and calling, colored jerseys disappearing around the bend. It could have easily been Jérôme and his friends.

I asked him if he had a favorite part of France for riding.

"The mountains! But I have no favorite single region. We have so many places with beautiful landscapes and scenic roads. But for sure, I like to go back in Ardèche, Drôme, Cévennes, Alpes Maritimes, Alpes de Haute-Provence, Pyrénées and Corse."

In 2004 Jérôme rode solo from Paris to Beirut, almost 5,000kms in 35 days. Now he rides to work, rides most weekends, and still does longer trips in France. In their small, low-ceilinged basement hang a number of cycles. I asked which one he rode to Beirut.

"I left it in Mona's mother's house. So now, every time I go to Lebanon, it is there waiting for me to ride," he smiled happily.

In the basement there is a tiny slot of a closet which Jérôme uses as their wine cellar. It is full of wines from Anjou, his home region. I don't know if these wines are well-known outside Anjou, or Anjou-Saumur as the area is also known. But that's part of it. Jérôme knows them and knows them well. Why take wine from other areas when the Anjou-Saumur offers everything you could want? It's not necessarily that these wines are supposed to be the best, but they are part of his heritage, part of his innate *terroir*. That is what is important.

"We produce the red Anjou, but also Saumur Champigny, Crémant de Loire, and the sweet wine, Coteaux du Layon."

These may have been his favorites, but there are others which I can't recall. Jérôme is always eager to select something for whatever they are cooking, and it is always well-matched. The one time Mona brought home an alien wine of her selection – disaster. Even she admitted it was pretty awful. I thought it tasted like that kangaroo wine from Australia.

What Mona lacked as an oenophile, she made up with her cooking. Coming home with her from the office, we'd get off the Metro and make separate stops for vegetables, meat, cheese and, lastly, bread. Her butcher was one of the few who had horsemeat. My father had encouraged me to try it on one of my first visits, nostalgic for his days in the early 1960s flying C-130s out of Évreux. A very lean, dark red meat, it had been very popular in France then, only sold through specialty butchers (*boucherie chevaline*) I think. There is old signage for one near Mona & Jérôme's.

They indulged me on that visit, curious themselves since they had never tried *cheval*. The kids were not at all excited. Tania refused.

We didn't do horsemeat this time, but in the *fromagerie* Mona asked for a Maroilles, in honor of my passage through the town the second day in France. I remember this *fromager*. The very first time Mona took me there, after we'd picked up the *cheval*, she asked for a selection of cheeses for me to try, explaining I was a visitor.

The *fromager* said, « *Votre ami est Américain ? Vous pouvez prendre n'importe quel fromage, il va adorer.* » Basically saying I, as an American, would enjoy anything she gave me. He was right, of course

He'd be happy to know I've progressed a little since then. As I walked down France, I tried as many cheeses as I could and delighted in most. As with the wine, I've still no expertise, only enjoyment in the moment. The one thing I was learning though was that the cheeses I preferred didn't hold up too well in the top of the pack on a warm day. They'd ooze into a gooey lump, and if the breeze were from behind, would envelope me in an aroma stronger than my sweatiest of socks. Which I could not outrun.

The meals in their home weren't elaborate affairs, but they were always fresh. Both Jérôme and Mona work fulltime. The kids pitch in with preparation, especially the older Tania. Jérôme has an extensive collection of American Jazz and R&B albums, and maybe he'd play one of those. After dinner, if the kids were done with homework, we might get out a boardgame. I know there is a TV in their small house, but I don't think I've ever seen it on, and I can't say exactly where it is. I don't want to airbrush my friends' daily lives, and I risk generalizing, but I have the impression many French seem to live a less commodified version of life compared to most of us in the US.

Look, I was happy to patronize the big, brightly-lit, well-stocked Intermarchés and E.Leclercs, the grocery superstores I sometimes found on the edge of larger towns. Or head to the smaller SPAR grocers in town. Because a lot of times the alternative was nothing. As noted, many villages and small towns I was passing through, would pass through, had no grocery, no café, no *boulangerie*, forget a butcher or a *fromagerie*. There was nothing commercial. In the US, for better or worse, there's almost always a convenience store, as limited as they can be.

On more than one occasion during subsequent visits to France, a friend would point to an empty building and say, "There used to be a very good *gastronomique* there." To lose a restaurant of your regional fare, that's more than just a business closing. It's part of your heritage. I got the impression large swaths of the French countryside, as attractive and quaint as it was, was denuded of vitality. Later I'd read about the "empty diagonal" (*diagonale du vide*) a swath stretching from the northeast to southwest, characterized by its declining density of population. It turns out I'd spend a lot of time walking in it.

So not everyone in France is coming home from work buying fresh ingredients for dinner from different vendors. But many do, I think. It a practice kept alive because it is ingrained in French culture. It's not pretense. Sometimes, driving with the family, we'd pass a McDonald's — yes, there are more of them in France than you might imagine — and I'd ask Tania and Nil if they wanted to stop for a burger. "No! Never!" they'd shout genuinely repulsed by the prospect of corporate fast food. Contrast that with American children I'd been with who'd hold the car in a ransom of wailing, backseat pandemonium until they were sated with a mouthful of chicken nuggets.

Back to our picnic and the bottle of Quincy; (picnic, from the French, *pique-nique*.) Under the tree in a meadow was a spread of

Lebanese delights — including mujadara, kibbeh and fattoush — that would go perfectly with the dry white. I was happy to sprawl on the blanket with my shoes off, snacking and sipping. Nil climbed the tree. Tania had recently become too old for that.

The way from Châteauroux ambled through forest and along fields. The blossoms were becoming a riot now. There were wide meadows full of white fuzzy dandelion balls primed to sail with the wind. There were stands of flowers in the woods that looked like launching fireworks, with silvery-blue bursts sending out flaming orange sparks. There were blossoms of purple, pink, mauve, lavender, gold and burnt orange.

All the color, the sensation of life unbound, it was uplifting.

Mona and I had met 20 years earlier, in Yemen, where we both were working. As a little girl growing up in the Beqaa' Valley, Lebanon, she'd seen how the work of international aid agencies was so easily corrupted because its representatives would swoop in with money and technical assistance, then disappear. She figured she could do better, being someone familiar with ground realities. This is how she ended up in Yemen working for the United Nations. But eventually she came to feel that, in spite of the copious funding and expertise, these big organizations sometimes didn't do a very good job of reaching the individual, even with someone like her administering the program. Her mother had taught her and her six siblings to work for the good of others, which was the best way to do good for yourself. Mona turned from the prospect of a high salary and secure career. She met a handsome young man (Jérôme) who convinced her to continue her studies at the Sorbonne, instead of Harvard, and her life set roots in France. Now she runs a Paris-based organization that works to combat modern slavery and support its victims – not everyone's life is a carefree walk along the Camino. I can tell the work weighs on her, but I know she doesn't want to be doing anything else.

PARIS to CREUSE RIVER

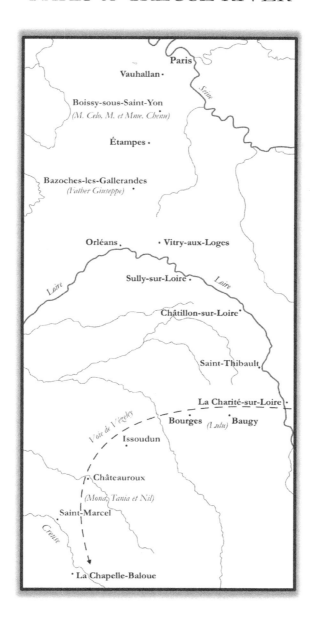

They Gave Me Water   **8**

Sumeet, at the family convenience store.

A public WC.
A butcher.
A man walking his dog.
A woman shaving her legs.
A man gardening.
A boy on a bicycle.
A marathon runner.
A man with four giant dogs, leaping, bounding, barking.

Bartenders, many bartenders.
The woman at the *boulangerie* chain.
Mairies, many *mairies*.

A church.

Graveyards,
       well-tended
             peaceful
                graveyards.

A farmer's wife sorting eggs.
A young man, just leaving.
The woman living in a camper.
A dusty mason, at the end of his day.

The woman, called by her son, who came out with her curious daughter and gave me a bottle of mineral water, explaining the farm's well water wasn't potable.

The beautiful young naturalist along the Loire.

The mother
of redheaded boys,
triplets
grinning on the farm swing set.

A woman with friendly spaniels in the garden,
"Water is the most important."

A man cutting his hedge,
"You are going far?"

In a forest, with 50s American music playing.

At the *salle polyvalente*, cooking on election day.

A man with a single, long curving yellow tooth and smile.

A shirtless, garrulous man with a running garden hose.

A girl tending her horses.

Fountains, so many *fuentes de agua*
one with a fleeing whale

A *señora* who offered, and I said, *"No, gracias, tengo,"* then 30
minutes later realized my error.

Another *señora* who brought a bottle of mineral water because
the garden *agua* was no good for drinking. She unlocked the gate
and asked, *"¿Necesitas algo más?"*

Earth

La Voie de Rocamadour to VIGNOBLE

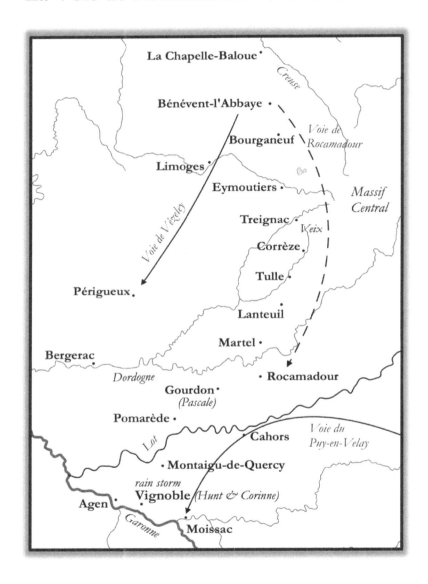

Poetry of the HILLs 9

It was only a brief interlude together, but I couldn't help but feeling a little emptiness in my heart when Mona, Tania and Nil got into the car to drive back to Paris Monday afternoon, *« Bisous ! »*.

I was alone again. Part of me was grateful to be alone again, for this singularity was an impelling component to this Camino: to walk over the earth, slow down and feel every footstep; to escape the routines that can ossify daily life, including the people; to clean the mind of its chatter, even the voices of others. I sought these solitary elements of the Camino even though, for instance, I had enjoyed sharing the day to Bourges with Lulu. Yet Mona and her children's presence reminded me of the essentialness of companionship, of relationship based on sharing, not expectation. I felt this absence.

I guessed it would take about two weeks to reach Hunt and Corinne, my friends who lived in the countryside between Moissac and Agen, though I still wasn't exactly sure how to get there. These days would turn into some of the most delightful walking on my traverse of France.

The walk with Mona from Châteauroux had taken us to the Creuse River region. I hadn't known we were heading toward the Creuse River. I was just following the Dutch guide of the Vézelay Way. Unbeknownst to me I was entering the Limousin, a hilly, upland area on the western side of the Massif Central. Later I learned the English word for chauffeured luxury vehicle, limousine, comes from the roofed but open-sided driver's compartment of the early models because this supposedly resembled the traditional hooded shepherd's cloak of the region. I could never have conceived such an origin.

The contrast to the days of flat agricultural lands was stark.

Like the Loire, the Creuse River rises in the Massif Central and we were now on its flank. We struck the Creuse at Argenton-sur-Creuse. It was beautiful terrain.

Rolling, lush, forested. Pastures of auburn cows, small vineyards of wooden *piquets*. A few narrow, steep paths, intimate enough I almost imagined myself isolated in some far-off mountains. And the church steeples, instead of spires, were blockish, capped by what sometimes resembled witches' hats.

It was such a refreshing change of terrain, the nearly 40kms the first day back on my own passed with pleasure. I reached La Chapelle-Baloue and stayed in the *chambre d'hôte* of an attentive Scottish woman and her French husband. They have their own chickens and fresh eggs and greens from the garden. She brings the

meal to you. And it was the first place I noticed it was truly dark outside. I could see the waning moon through the windowpanes. There had been high, lenticular clouds the day before, and it was supposed to drop near freezing the next few nights. A strong cold wind did begin to cut through the hilly landscape later, but the sky remained clear.

Studying the Michelin, Limoges, the urban center of Limousin, appeared as a big blob several days further south. I'm sure it is a nice city. I heard it is a nice city. But after coming upon this pleasant stretch in the Creuse region, I didn't fancy diving back into that kind of density of movement, noise and people. I puzzled over the map, trying to pick a way around Limoges, but it was looking convoluted. The Voie de Vézelay went right through the city.

"We take the bus."

A shadow must have crossed my face, sitting there in the tiny *refuge* in Bénévent-l'Abbaye the evening after La Chapelle-Baloue.

"It is difficult to follow the way in cities," she clarified. "The markers are hard to find. We always take a bus, from one side to the other."

My instinctive reaction was, you're not supposed to take the bus!

But there was no "supposed to" and who was I to adjudicate? In Spain I'd end up using a number of ferries. Was I "supposed to" paddle myself? The only real rule for the Camino I'd heard about was that to obtain a *compostela* (a certificate of completion), you had to walk the last 100km into Santiago. Administratively they had to draw the line somewhere, but really, how much did the paper *compostela* count against the experience itself?

It doesn't matter how far or how fast you walk, or what you carry or don't carry, or if you do it in one shot or in sections over many years. I'm sure pilgrims render a thousand judgements a day about these things, just as I had about the bus. But this judging only affects the judger, and risks turning his walk into just another competition, choked with rules, rituals and purity codes. All that matters is that you are on the Way. The Camino takes care of the rest, whatever "the rest" may be for each of us.

Though I kept expecting to encounter more pilgrims on the Voie de Vézelay, I'd only met Lulu, and now this pair. They were brother and sister from Germany, walking from Vézelay to Saint-Jean-Pied-de-Port.

Our two bunkbeds were in a room so small we couldn't sit opposite each other on the bottom without touching knees. The *refuge des pèlerins* A dos d'Ânes (On Donkeys) in Bénévent-l'Abbaye was run by a gentleman who had walked the Camino with his donkey, several times, I think. Besides walking and cycling, riding a horse or using a pack animal are also accepted modes of pilgrimage. Yves, the proprietor, stabled equines, in addition to his two bunkbeds, and the *refuge* faintly smelled of it – earthy.

"Rocamadour," said Yves, when I told him I was heading generally toward Agen but didn't feel like traversing Limoges. He ran a gnarly finger south along an old wall map, toward Cahors. I'd heard of Cahors and its wine. Rocamadour was new to me, but the name rolled easily off the tongue unlike so many French place names. I was having a tough time understanding Yves' French, but he was patient with me. I don't know if he said the way to Rocamadour was new, but he did say they had published a new guide to *La Voie de Rocamadour vers Compostelle* earlier in the year. Unfortunately, he didn't have any, and neither did the Office de

Tourisme around the corner when I checked. But I was interested.

Yves said the way was quiet, but it was well-marked, and the distances between places where you could find somewhere to stay were not that long, maybe 20-30km. There would be fewer *pèlerins*, and maybe no official *refuge des pèlerins*, but there'd always be a *gîte* or small *hôtel*. Probably about 200km. Probably take around a week.

Maybe he didn't say all this exactly, but it is what I found. Certainly he gave me the impression it would be a less travelled route through very good walking countryside, not that the Voie de Vézelay was over-traveled, with its three *pèlerins*. I'd had a number of near 40km days since leaving Paris. No other than myself had made me walk those distances, but I could feel they were wearing on me. Stages of 20-30km would be welcome. On those long-distance days all I had time for was rushing off to the SPAR before it closed, then eat-shower-sleep. What was the point of that? I needed to back off a little.

The next morning, I left behind the Voie de Vézelay and its impeccable Dutch guide, having been on it for just over a week. I'd slept well, despite the cramped quarters – only slight snoring from the brother.

It was bright and cold. I was excited as I dove into the forested trail, following the new waymarks. It was indeed tighter terrain: more forest and less timber tracts; streams, not canals; blue hills fading into the distance, not steeples on the horizon. More milk goats instead of beef cattle. Lunch was always along a deserted trail or lane, no one passing. For the first time I noticed what looked like "foreclosure" or "bank-owned" or "condemned" notices on properties. Houses empty, edging toward derelict. And the sign for Planchet, on the first day, was riddled with bullets – something I was used to seeing in the US, but not in Europe.

A deer poised in a tunnel of trees, staring intently as I walked toward her, then bounded into the wood. A weasel, reddish with a black nose, worked over the ground, moving, sniffing, pausing and looking. Something under the leaves? She leapt in a high arch, gracefully stalling at its apex, then down to pounce on – nothing. I crunched twigs and she flowed up a tree like furred quicksilver and was gone. I was more careful with the fox. He hunted the edge of a field, rested in the grass on his belly, eventually crossed the dirt road in front of me to continue out of view. And the blonde mare on a grassy knoll, slim-legged and finely muscled, the wind whipping her tail and mane; she looked like a waiting lover and never took her eyes off me. I was seeing more creatures than people along the Voie de Rocamadour. And of course, the flying Popes, bursting from their hiding places.

The sky was so clear these days it was like looking up from the bottom of a tropical sea. The ever-present white contrails of aircraft were actually the foaming wakes of surface vessels: the smaller ones jet skis and pleasure craft; the largest, put out by the four engine jumbos, container ships churning along global trade routes. Maybe the *Independent Pursuit*. And the waning crescent moon was actually an ethereal moon jelly, suspended between me and the maritime traffic above. I felt like a nomadic hermit crab, home on my back, scurrying along, feeding and looking for safe places to rest.

Thank you for this body. Thank you for this fitness. Thank you for this health. I know it is unearned and passing. But thank you.

Walking through one village a child started when he saw me and said something quickly to his mother. She laughed and told me he had asked if I was "from the jungle". The zinc oxide I wore on my nose and cheeks these bright days made me look like someone out of his storybooks.

The first place I stayed was the proudly named Hôtel Des Chevaliers in Bourganeuf, but it could have been the set for *Faulty Towers*, the old British comedy with John Cleese. Faded colors, peeling wallpaper, worn carpets, tepid shower, over-soft mattress, yapping lapdog behind the matron's door, and explosive plumbing. Merely sitting on the toilet could trigger a depth charge-like detonation in the pipes. It wasn't the first time I'd encountered the *ancien* plumbing of Europe – that first shock occurred in the deep quiet of late night Seneffe, Belgium – but it's nevertheless unsettling in the dark of an unfamiliar setting. To be fair, her WIFI connection was one of the best yet. And supposedly their *gastronomique* restaurant was a good one, but it was Wednesday, like the week before with Lulu in Baugy, and it was closed.

In Eymoutiers I lucked into another *presbytère*. A helpful elderly couple fetched me from the *mairie*. She spoke a little English and as we slowly walked, she pointed out some of the notable architecture along the way. They were proud of their town, and justifiably so, for it was very pretty. But if you looked a little more closely, there were closed businesses, broken windows and sagging roofs. She acknowledged this, with the heaviness of someone who remembers how it once was.

At the *presbytère*, real French priests! A pair of them, older gentleman, down-to-earth and easy going. They welcomed me wholeheartedly, even though the one spare room was taken for the night by a pair of *pèlerins*, Regis and Mary, a French couple who were doing an unhurried section of the Way. They'd be the only *pèlerins* I'd meet until Rocamadour.

While one of the priests prepared dinner, the other helped me set up a cozy place to sleep at the edge of the stage in the parish hall – bolsters, pillow and extra blankets because it was going to be another cold night. Then a hot shower and clothes wash. What else could I ask for?

Dinner!

Dinner was *pâté aux pommes de terre* and iron pot lentils, both Limousin specialties, I think priest said. The *pâté aux pommes de terre* had quickly become my favorite after I stumbled upon it at a *traiteur* in Châteauroux, where they offered ready dishes. It's basically sliced potatoes and crème fraîche baked in a pastry crust, a rich pie of goodness, perfect after a long day walking, especially when it was cold outside. It was only French around the table in the kitchen, and though I understood little, I felt completely included. We shared pears and cheese for dessert.

From my warm nook in the cold hall, I could see stars through the big windows.

The fourth day on the Voie de Rocamadour, as I climbed from Treignac toward Veix, I spontaneously started speaking poetry. Not memorized verse, but words which began to flow from a hidden place. These weren't lines I could try and remember – the words melted away after they were spoken. But I could feel their meaning, and their connection to the others in the flow as they formed inside me and rose into sound. I wasn't composing, just letting it happen, stepping out of the way. At first this seemed the most natural thing. Why wouldn't poetry be spontaneously issuing forth? Hadn't this happened before, in a dream?

Had anyone else been there, I'm sure it would have been gibberish. But to me it was marvelous. Even a little frightening, because it wasn't me doing this, or at least the *me* I understood. This went on for several minutes, and of course I began to wonder – this may have happened in a dream, but not while fully awake. What *is* this? As soon as *I* tried to become more directly involved, tried to analyze or control or influence or guide, the poetry scattered. Like startled birds, the words vanished, to resettle and reform somewhere safely out of my reach. Ah well.

I couldn't recapture the flow – its very nature made it uncontainable – but the lovely sensation stayed with me as I continued the 1-2,000ft climb up the Massif de Monédières.

Poetry is like kissing in public. Deep, passionate kissing I mean. It can be a little awkward for everyone involved, including the audience, though when the moment strikes, there is no stopping it. During my few days in Paris I had seen more passionate kissing under the beautiful blue skies than I have ever noticed anywhere. But maybe it's been around me always. Maybe it's me who has changed enough to finally see it. I'd felt joy for the couples, though I'd also felt sharply the absence of such intimacy. It is possible to hold these opposing emotions in balance, for the fullness of one lends hope to the hollowness of the other – in time the emptiness will fill. We hope. Walking to Veix there was no one to witness, no one to feel awkward about my deep passionate kiss. I experienced only delight. It was a moment of transcendental intimacy. I was sated.

Why had this happened? How did it happen? It was as if I had fallen into such a well-tuned groove I had opened channels normally blocked. Not just blocked, but unknown. There is no way to recreate the words that came. I know this. But the conditions, the physical/mental/emotional attitude, that is something I might be able to manage. But how? It's probably not willing myself to speak poetry. It's probably more like gardening. You can't make something grow. But you have to set the conditions and nurture it for there even to be a chance. You have to be open to the kissing.

How quickly the bliss evaporated. An hour later I was having a minor, curse-fill temper tantrum because I'd lost the way to Chaumeil. It's not like a wrong turn in a car that only costs you time, quickly made up with a little heavier foot on the accelerator. A couple of kilometers walking in the wrong direction can be an hour out of the way. There's no going much faster than the average 4kph. And more than that, your feet swell just a little bit more, the pack feels a little heavier, the sun dips a little lower, and maybe you're out of Mme Chenu's secret *gâteaux aux fruits* and the water bottle is low.

Nothing stays the same, however much we want it to. Everything changes, constantly changes, even my bliss. It's the most basic truth of existence and still I tense up, react negatively and become a victim of my own self-generated storm.

I tried to blame the map for getting lost, but of course I had misinterpreted the French instructions. I don't recall where I eventually found the guide to *La Voie de Rocamadour vers Compostelle*, but it was certainly more than adequate. Mistakes were wholly due to operator error.

More reasonable was to blame the wine, or more precisely my excess consumption of it. Sylvie and Rijk, the French/South African couple who'd lodged me the night before in Treignac, had popped open a number of very good bottles, the highlight being a couple of 1996 Cru Bourgeois from Château La Tour de By, Médoc AOC. Again, I'm an enjoyer, not a critic, but this wine seemed perfect for the table.

The hosts had invited two English couples and their friend for what was a delicious dinner and good time. I stayed up much later than normal and definitely imbibed more *vin* than usual, which led to the only morning along the entire Camino where I woke up feeling it – not again I vowed. But it was a convivial time and relaxing for me because it was all in English. I could freely contribute, instead of stammering a few rehearsed phrases, and I could understand what everyone else was talking about. Except for Rory, the friend. If I thought I'd had a hard time communicating with Yves, the proprietor/donkey driver in Bénévent-l'Abbaye, Rory was even tougher. Wherever he had grown up in England, the accent imparted was beyond my comprehension. When he spoke, I followed the lead of everyone else, laughing or nodding as appropriate. If he asked me something, I said "yes", which seemed to work. Maybe he didn't understand me either.

South Africans, Indians, Kiwis, Canadians, no problem. But the English, Australians, Scottish and Irish, it can be a challenge. Australia it's because they use words I've never heard before or in a context I have no idea what they mean:

"He spit the dummy."

"She's fair dinkum."

But the UK and Ireland, it's the rich accents themselves. I can't even decipher the words. Once, near Dublin, after I'd asked a teenager to repeat herself for the third time, she finally shot back, *"D'yi fockin' spek Anglish?"* I had to laugh.

Limousin is apparently one of the least densely populated regions of France, its population having slowly declined in the last century. In the area around Treignac I was surprised to learn there were many residents from England. I could see the region's appeal. Find a small pretty town like Treignac or Eymoutiers that still had services, or perhaps a place nearby in the bucolic countryside, just not too close to the foreclosures and gun-shot signs.

"We're here quite simply for the quality of life," said Ken at the table. "England's lost it. Too money grubbing and consumerist. The French, in spite of their problems, still know how to enjoy."

I finished the day with recovered good humor, reaching Corrèze via a pleasant off-trail way from Meyrignac. The dwellings along the way reminded me of homesteads in Appalachia. More dilapidated, families hanging out together with their dogs, enjoying a fine weekend afternoon amongst the sprawl of their lives. These rural farmsteads weren't the fortress farmhouses of the wider landscapes further north. Nor were the dogs as bear-like.

Fortunately...

On one long, quiet bend, five or six dogs come charging out of an open gate, barking excitedly and heading straight at me. I look to be the entertainment on this sleepy afternoon. Well, I've got the trekking pole, which might either keep them at bay or further  inflame them. Not sure which. I wait for someone to emerge to see what all the noise is about, but no one appears. No one is going to call them back. There is nothing to do but to wait for it. My calves begin to tingle. I remember the dog in Kathmandu who latched onto my left calf, and the cur in Delhi who went for the right. This gang is closing rapidly. With the first of the pack about 30 yards away, a hare bursts from the underbrush and takes off like a rocket. Hallelujah! Something more interesting. The barking rises an octave, and the lead dog veers off to give chase, now running as fast as he possibly can. The others thankfully follow, the last giving me a sidelong glance with a look of, "Next time you won't be so lucky." I thank the hare, pray for his evasive success, and hurry out of view.

It's election day in France (Sunday, April 23rd, 2017). Since crossing from Belgium, I'd come across displays of the portraits of the presidential candidates. They were all of equal size, plastered in a neat row, as if in designated spaces. I hadn't seen any yard signs or bumper stickers or flags or banners or billboards for individual candidates. The campaign seemed more of an administrative process, rather than the carnival I was accustomed to in the US. I think there were a dozen candidates, but I only recognized three:

> *Marine Le Pen*
> *and Mélenchon*
> *so many others*
> *plus young Macron*

Chrystelle, the owner of the wainscoted *hôtel* of creaking wood floors where I stayed in Corrèze the night before, said she was voting for Macron.

"I like Mélenchon better, but I think the country needs someone younger." A Macron presidency might be better for her business too. "We are trying to convert to a B&B. As an *hôtel* they tax you for everything. For music played here in the bar. For music played in the dining room. For this TV. For every TV in each room. That's why we took them out." I was the only guest.

I think it was on her bar TV that I glimpsed a popular weekend talk show. A couple of pundits (a word from India) sprinkled among the celebrities, and they were commenting gravely on the show's main topic, "Is the Third World War About to Begin?" They kept playing a video loop of the strongmen of North Korea, the US and Russia, their faces superimposed on the oiled physiques of naked bodybuilders, dancing around each other with ICBMs as erections.

Ah, the madness of the world. It was easy to forget along the Camino.

"If they won't let us convert to a B&B," Chrystelle continued as the missiles waggled, "we'll sell and move to the southwest and start something there."

The southwest. I wondered if Albert had finally been enticed into the van for the trip. There must be something appealing about that corner of France. It's where we all were headed.

I only ran into Macron and Mélenchon supporters along the way, at least that I knew of. I wasn't asking, but if the election came up, people volunteered who they were voting for. I didn't get the sense the French voter was as credulous as the Americans could be. Nor did their politicians come across as bombastic and fatuous. But really, how could I tell from my vantage point as a hermit crab at the bottom of the sea? I don't want to prejudge.

But racism? Here I felt there could be more commonality between the two countries. While the history may be different – colonial empire vs slave empire – racism in France might be as deep and pervasive, and as unreckoned with, as in the US.

Algerian rap music came through the wall of the room to wake me from a morning nap. How do they make these walls so thin, I wondered? Chrystelle had called ahead and reserved the last room at this 1-star for me. I had stepped out early for a breakfast sandwich but felt so tired after finishing it I opted to stretch out again rather than push off directly. The rap was catchy and the nap restorative. I was in Tulle, the former constituency of the current French president, Françoise Hollande. Apparently, he had been in town to cast his vote yesterday. I estimated only a few more days to Rocamadour from here.

Tulle was the largest town on the Voie de Rocamadour so far, large enough to have some grit to it, strange characters and itinerants hanging about. A wide road travels along either side of the channelized Corrèze River which cuts through the town center, adding noise and motion at the expense of tranquility and cohesion. But it's a relatively tight valley and there's no real alternative track.

Dropping in on Tulle yesterday had been a pleasant experience. The approach from Naves wasn't so nice – shadeless and exposed, it was an exception. But as I descended, before I could even see Tulle below, it began to communicate its presence like many hill towns do, if you're not sealed inside a motor vehicle. First the sound of the rushing river somewhere below, becoming audible at the invisible point where the sound waves were still in contact with the contour of the ridge. Then an engine, pulling up the steep road. An axe thunking into wood. Habitations clustered where they could find a grip. I smelled woodsmoke. I'd experienced these signatures approaching other mountain river settlements in other parts of the world. It's powerful how geography shapes us so similarly. The only thing missing here were the shouts of people communicating with each other and their animals over rough terrain.

Aubazine, between Tulle and Lanteuil, was so pleasant I had to stop for a mid-afternoon *café*. Entering the village I'd noticed a building having its roof extended, but what caught my attention was the quality of the new trusses. I'm used to seeing prefab trusses of lightweight pine held together by metal joint plates, mounted with narrow spacing. These trusses were made of large dimension lumber, and, because of the greater strength, were more widely spaced. They looked like they were built on site. And there were no joint plates – the connections were natural joinery. The ridge board was seated into the top of the king post, and the top chords were mortised into the post's sides. The joints were fixed by large wooden dowls. The webs were likewise mortised into the king post. The purlins were supported by wedges notched into the top chords. This didn't appear to be a special building, but the technique was striking. It was more like making or crafting, rather than merely assembling. Buildings are reflections of a culture's prevailing values, aren't they?

Walking through France I couldn't help but be struck by the existence of so many traditional buildings, some in need of serious repair, but many in quite good condition. True, there were some ill-conceived "upgrades", but by and large the integrity of the original building, at least externally, remained intact. Visually this was extraordinarily pleasant. One of my favorite features I saw on houses all through France, new or old, were the window shutters. Heavy, functioning shutters that did everything from secure the house, protect glass, block light, keep out heat, keep in warmth and maintain cool. We'd long ceded this functionality in the US.

While other forms of noxious pollution are obvious, visual pollution is insidious – look around, how much of your built landscape is an eyesore? In contrast these traditional buildings and structures, made with local materials, contributed to the cohesion of the environs, whether countryside or town. These were not sights to avoid or ignore. They were to take in. It was enriching. I got the sense that the French were serious about their *patrimoine*.

Apparently it is extremely difficult to build anything on designated agricultural land in France, which must account for the limit on endlessly sprawling suburbs like you find in the US. And many structures, and even entire villages, are listed as protected, or "of interest", and thus subject to special rules. A friend of mine told me about the *Compagnons du Devoir et du Tour de France*. At first I thought she was talking about the bicycle race. She wasn't. The *Compagnons du Devoir* is a national program of apprenticeship in traditional skills, many of them related to building. The apprentices and journeymen work under masters and live in group houses, moving around the country to learn the particularities of different regions, hence the *tour de France*. The process can take a decade before the individual is ready to settle and begin to practice independently and teach apprentices. This commitment to quality, traditional workmanship must also influence regular artisans. I felt that's what I was seeing in those solid trusses in Aubazine.

The last couple of days to Rocamadour turned into a bit of a blur because for much of it I was head down in drenching rain, the first real rain since entering France. My backpack cover was working, but my old North Face jacket was leaking:

It's soaking me through
It's soaking the ground
It's harder now
The rain coming down!

This verse is far from the spontaneous poetry that flowed on the way to Veix. But I'd taken to composing simple, repetitive marching ditties, and I'd sing them or hum or whistle for long stretches, sometimes until I'd worn out my voice or realized I'd better conserve my breath for the walking. It was creative and fun, sparked by the simplest things, like coming upon the line-up of the presidential hopefuls' smiling faces in a sleepy *ville*. It was certainly better than obsessing over directions or worrying how far I needed to go, or where I'd find water.

Somewhere after Lanteuil the earth turned red. Long gone were the gnarly flints from around Paris. *"Raato maato chiplo baato,"* a Nepalese expression that warns about slippery red trails, popped to mind. But it didn't have the cadence for a marching ditty, and this red earth wasn't very slick anyway, just wet. Collonges-la-Rouge was built of the red stone. It was beautiful, as if the ground had animated itself into a human village. Though the village looked like it had been heavily adapted for a regular flow of tourists, with the sodden weather I was the only one. I stopped for *un chocolat chaud* and to wring out my socks, the latter a futile gesture but the hot chocolate restoring.

The rain kept coming. Farther on I ducked into the entrance of a 12th century church, in Saillac, to escape the deluge and finish a day-old baguette and a terrine of *porc*, both quite good. The stonework displayed an impressive variety of beasts consuming humans. The red earth disappeared without me realizing it.

Somewhere there are groves and groves of *noix* in my memory, the walnut trees slick and grey like the sky. Probably after Collonges-la-Rouges. I stop in Les Quatre-Routes-du-Lot to get out of the rain again and to get my bearings. And for a *café*. With great certainty I'm told Mme Valade, who runs the *Tabac* down the road, will have the Michelin ZOOM Map 161, the next map I'll need. She doesn't.

Later on this wet afternoon I lose my way in the forest after Ripane. But it is a minor detour. I've been a little uncertain all day, so it doesn't seem like much. Eventually I arrive in Martel, a pretty, medieval town of pale stone, a stark contrast to the ruddy red of Collonges-la-Rouge only a few hours north but feeling much further away. Maybe it was in this valley of Martel, approaching the Dordogne River, where I walked through the *noix* groves. I don't know. Martel means hammer, and there are hammers on the town's seal. Maybe they use them for the walnuts. I remembered the bin of walnut shells in the engine room of the *Independent Pursuit*, for cleaning the turbines. Where is that ship and her crew now?

In the town center an old woman quite sensibly doesn't come out in the rain, but gives me the key to her guest house on the other side of the overgrown garden.

The ground after Martel was comprised of broken, light grey stones in thin layers. There were old walls in the forests, fallen into ground, covered in cushions of moss. Whose hands had toiled on them, what had their lives been like? Sheep grazed in the wood, their bells clinking. The languid cuckoo clock birds of the timber tracts north of the Loire were back. And the flying Popes too, fat and grey like the clouds. I was across the Dordogne and heading for Rocamadour, which I knew must be getting close because of the exposed cliffs in the landscape. I rarely saw people. There were a couple of Polish cave divers near Montvalent, but that was about it.

To Rocamadour
Then to Cahors
And if I can
I'll do a bit more

Then to Moissac
There's no turning back
Heading to Spain
To see Saint Jack!

I apologize for subjecting the reader to these ditties of mine and promise only a few more.

There'd been some charming if touristy *villes* the last few days – Aubazine, Collonges-le-Rouge, Martel – and in fact Collonges might have been too much except the rain had virtually shut down the place. But Rocamadour had completely succumbed.

It was a beautiful setting, a village built into the cliffside of a forested canyon, unlike anything I expected to come across in France. In spite of the threatening weather, motor coaches were disgorging their loads and pumping out diesel fumes near the welcome center on top.

There's a qualitative difference between a place you visit where your interactions barely perturb the people going about their normal lives, and a place where the way of life has become dominated by these interactions. The evolution is probably a subtle process at first, but once it happens, the results are stark. The place becomes a faux representation of itself. A movie set. Such intense tourism ends up smothering the original, however imperfect it might have been. You're sold a make-believe version of the world, which ironically becomes its own reality.

I'd soon pass through Prague on another trip, a place I'd heard so much about. What I saw when I arrived: Throngs of visitors massed under their country's flag, guides shouting in their native tongues; fiberglass knockoffs of 1920s convertible roadsters bouncing down streets, passengers more interested in their smartphones; hundreds of currency exchange shops, notorious for scamming unsuspecting visitors; gift shops stocked with Russian nest dolls and imitation Iberian ham, pink and sweaty; signage for massage parlors, skydiving, river trips, whatever your thrill. And numerous McDonald's and Starbucks. Granted, I was only in the central area. Would Times Square feel any different? But still, this was Prague of gorgeous buildings and great history. Maybe it was my expectations that were the problem. But I can't help but wonder, why do some places maintain their integrity, like Paris, and some lose it like Prague and Rocamadour?

I wound down the tight and charming streets of Rocamadour and stopped in a place to have the worst rubberized crepe in France. Or the best, depending on how you look at it.

Rocamadour lies along a variant of the Voie du Puy-en-Velay, from Figeac, and it was here that I participated in the type of pilgrim's dinner that characterized these regularly ways. People pitching in in the shared kitchen with whatever they had to produce a simple meal. All were invited. I contributed a bottle of wine to the table. Around it were more pilgrims than I had met since Antwerp.

We were staying at Lou Cantou de Nostro Damo, a *refuge des pèlerins* on the edge of Rocamadour run by sisters. Tiny rooms, but private, clean and functional. There was a pair of strapping Frenchmen. An elderly South African couple catching the train to Bergerac. Two women leading a blind man. A few others, and I met my first Americans, two younger women in great spirits, going as far as Moissac.

You must be American. I can tell from your smile. This was said to me in Paris, and the guy didn't mean it as a conversation starter. It's the most antagonistic thing ever said to me in France, but I wasn't on the Camino. I was at a reception. He was right. We Americans tend to smile a lot. But what do *you* do when you feel joy? I wanted to ask, because it really was joy I was feeling that evening. But yeah, standing around with a big dopey grin, baring your teeth, could be misinterpreted. I guess the opposite is true too. Some Americans probably think the French unnecessarily dour because they don't smile as wantonly. Then again, more times than not on the Camino I remember coming upon locals in an isolated setting, they not sure what to make of me, nor I of them, but then a smile would relieve our uncertainty and lead to warm nods and greetings.

I loved Meg and Judy's familiar smiles.

For over a dozen people in limited space, sharing kitchen and toilets, everyone tried to be mindful of each other. Who knew how someone else's day had been? More than that, what other burdens might they be carrying besides their backpacks? It was all new to me, so I was a little more circumspect, making sure I didn't commit any grand faux pas. Really though, it was obvious. Respect other people's space, clean up after yourself, don't take forever in the loo, and minimize the noise. Of this group, especially those who came to the table, everyone was open and easy to engage. And with the luxury of a private cubby, snoring was pleasantly muffled.

Sister Cecilia offered blessings in the morning, out front of the glowing warm stone of the *refuge*. Despite my ditty, I wasn't heading south *on to Cahors, and then to Moissac*, but more west along the GR 64 to Gourdon. It was Sisters Cecilia's suggestion. I'd found the Michelin 161 at the welcome center, thanks to Rocamadour being a tourism hotspot, and angling off to Gourdon did look a better way to get to Hunt & Corinne's than Cahors. She said it was less traveled, which was appealing, plus one of my best friends was named Gordon, which was somehow reassuring. I hugged Meg and Judy, who were headed to Cahors, then we went our separate ways.

I followed the winding ravines of the l'Alzou/l'Ouysse River drainage out of Rocamadour. I thought I might be in for more rain, but eventually the sun broke through. I paused on the bridge over the A20, watching the cars and lorries whoosh along. Their speed felt so alien to the walking pace. A different world. I didn't linger.

In the woods I begin to notice small, hand-painted signs for a place called the Brockbar. They are so persistent I begin following them rather than the trail markers. Eventually I come to a string of old bicycles, dozens and dozens of them fixed along the fence line of a dirt road. Of course I must follow them. They lead deeper into the woods. I can see an isolated house. Should I go closer?

I do, a little carefully. Am I trespassing? But there are all those little signs. Maybe they are obsolete, from some past event? There is all kind of scrap and junk and art outside. But the house seems dark. Deserted? Closer. Now I can hear something. Music? American rock music, from the 1950s. Really? It should be alright to go closer. I call out. No response. Just the music. Where is the main door? I make my way around the back. Now I am committed. More interesting objects, old cars, a VW van. If someone comes out and finds me here, they'll think I'm stealing something. I call out again.

A dog. A bull terrier. Watching me silently. Of course there is a dog. But silent. That's unnerving. He's not going to be distracted by a jackrabbit. Why had I followed the line of bicycles? It was a spell, they enchanted me, pulled me here. Maybe witches live here. I'll be cooked and used for potions.

I take a tentative step back. He doesn't like that. He growls. We spin slowly, until he has me pinned against the VW van. Then he starts barking. Well, at least now he probably isn't going to jump me.

Finally, a door opens.

The very friendly woman let me eat lunch on her deck and made me a cup of coffee. The man, surrounded by antiques, collectibles, curiosities and cast-offs stayed inside, spinning records and bopping his head to the rhythm.

Fortunately, my raddled body wasn't good for potions.

From a distance Gourdon appeared to perch on a cone. Indeed, when I reached it, I found the center a hillock of tight lanes 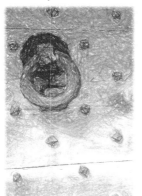 topped by a fortified church. I'd encounter this again as I walked, old settlements that grew along terrain features, saving the flat land for agriculture and providing a defensive advantage. They have a completely different feel than places built by bulldozer.

In this pleasant town I found Pascale and her 150-year-old house, which was in the process of getting a new slate roof. Under that renewed roof Pascale put me in a bedroom of all white; white walls, white linens, white curtains, set off by the browns of the wooden floor and furnishing. It was the complement to my first night in France, in Aulnoye-Aymeries, the room of black walls, curtains and bedspread.

In this bed of white I slept with such tranquility, such undefended peacefulness, that the poetry of Veix rose in me again. And even though I was sleeping, I knew not to make the mistake I had made while walking. I let the words rise freely, unguided, uncomprehended, and felt them fully. Music too. Not the music of the day's lone house in the woods, nor of any song or melody I'd ever heard, but music as if it were always there, rising inside us, like the poetry, rising through my chest, through the crown of my head, a connection that is always alive, or always possible. A kind of unitive cosmic symphony.

I can't conjure such dreaming on demand. It's only in setting the conditions, tending the garden. And what blossoms are instances of eternity. That is what I know, even if only barely.

"I lived on Réunion for 25 years," she told me that evening as we ate. "My daughter and my two grandchildren live in Los Angeles. I'm studying English for them," she laughed. She was using her phone, speaking French into it and then playing back a toneless English that was a very rough translation. She frequently cut it off midway, waving her hand and saying, « Non, non, non, » then trying again with different phrasing. It was better than we could do directly with each other, and we were having fun. She was a practicing dentist, taught, wrote, painted and enjoyed cooking, as evinced by the delicious duck stew she served after we shared an aperitif. Her breakfast was equally nourishing and tasty – not yesterday's baguette dipped in weak coffee! It recalled the hearty plates of Jean & Jeanne in Braine-le-Château and the host in Seneffe, Belgium. I wouldn't be served another breakfast like it in France. And Spain would be worse!

I didn't get the sense these things Pascale did were mere pastimes. I think they were pursuits which allowed her to express herself and connect with others. I could feel a kindness and openness and patience in Pascale, even if we couldn't speak to each other. She was a wounded soul, as I think we all are in our different ways. But she had opened to that wounding, rather than hiding it. Isn't that one of the messages from the Cross, to accept our vulnerability and grow with it instead of denying it?

She'd lost her son, her only other child besides her daughter. His death might have prompted a separation from her husband and move back to continental France. We didn't go too deep on the subject with the digital translation.

"I wanted to walk the *Compostelle*, in his memory. But I fell. I broke my leg, and it is impossible. So, I thought, I will open my house to *pèlerins*. If I cannot go on *le Chemin*, I can bring it to me. And in this way, I can honor my son's memory. Constantly, not just with one walk." She said this not with sadness, but with gratitude. In retrospect I think it was her gentleness and wise contentment that somehow reached into me as I slept and opened the flow of poetry and music. That glimpse of the eternal symphony. The poetry of the hills.

Fifty Days Passed **10**

Plane-filled blue skies stayed with me the next days as I stitched together a route of small country roads heading for Hunt & Corinne's. I had left the intimate trails of the Voie de Rocamadour behind, but this was still good walking country, the Lot, so called for the major river I'd soon cross. No other pilgrims. Nights touched freezing and mornings were cold, with frost on the ground, but the sun soon warmed the air pleasantly. More than one local told me the freezing was unseasonable and that it had severely damaged the local vineyards. And the curled black leaves I noticed on trees? Stone fruit orchards too.

The moleskin was working. The miles walked in soaked shoes to Rocamadour had softened the skin on my feet, creating hotspots, the warning sign of a coming blister. Each morning I cut shapes out of the small sheet of drugstore moleskin and pressed them in place, the adhesive backing sticking to the surrounding good skin, the felt-like cushion creating space for the tender area to breathe and minimize friction. The stuff is unchanged since my first hikes in the Appalachians of the mid-1970s. Cheap, simple and highly effective, it was one of the most valuable things I'd brought along. And thanks to it, I never did get a blister.

The small roads, indicated white on the Michelin, were generally very quiet. I'd go for miles without a vehicle, then three in a row would whoosh by. Near Montcléra I came upon the first cattle I'd seen with a real set of horns. Theirs were broad, like the upturned handlebars on a beach cruiser. They had shaggy coats of deep ochre and horse tails. Impressive beasts.

It was a quilted landscape, shaped by winding streams and rivers, chief among them the Lot, which rose in the Massif Central. After I crossed it at Puy-l'Évêque, I followed the D44 as it wound and climbed through a bright green forest of scrubby oaks with twisted, black and silver trunks. It was wadi-like geology, with the same deep flat layers of whitish, sometimes chalky broken rock I'd seen crossing the Dordogne and approaching Rocamadour. The twisted oaks and aromatics reminded me of places in California. On top, the road curved along a large vineyard.

Tiny flowers, most white, some yellow, filled pastures. Along the roads, banks of red Remembrance Day poppies bloomed. Donkeys had become more frequent and didn't mind getting nose to nose across a fence. In tiny, sleepy Saux, a fellow with bad teeth, an Englishman not a donkey, popped out of his dwelling to offer me the key to the church belltower, if I fancied. I did. Then accepted a cup of tea. He and his partner were preparing Thai food to take to a community lunch at the *salle polyvalente* the next day, a Sunday. The *salle polyvalente*, or multi-purpose hall, seemed a well-utilized facility in the communities I walked through. I'd regularly see them in use. There may no longer be commercial establishments in these *villes*, but there was still community life. The Englishman and his partner put me on to a place to stay in Montaigu-de-Quercy, from where I thought I could reach Hunt & Corinne's.

The clear blue surface of the sea overhead was about to be thoroughly roiled.

Besides some nominal familiarity with Paris, the area around Hunt & Corinne's place was the only part of France that I could claim to know somewhat. Thus, I had clearly visualized strolling along the narrow lane from Perville, where Corinne drove every morning for bread, turning left at the water tank that looks like a giant golf tee, then turning right at the letterbox labeled Vignoble, and marching triumphantly along the gravel farm road to where they were tucked in among field and wood.

Lying in the grass in Montjoi eating lunch, I suspected my arrival would not be as envisioned.

The sky to the south was beginning to darken. Not a slight greying of a possible shower, but the bruising purple-black of a growing stormfront. I knew I needed to get up and get moving, but I was pretty fagged out. The last two days had been 30-plus kilometers each, and this one would be too. I still had 10 or so kilometers to go – two hours for sure.

With sanctuary so close, all the miles from Paris – no, it's better to say all the steps, because that's what they'd been, one footstep after the other – I was starting to think about the resting, rather than the get-up-and-going, the everyday movement that keeps the underlying fatigue at bay.

Je suis fatigué. Just shy of a month since the Paris break. I looked at my bare feet, still catching the sun. I looked at the sky. The towering black and purple wall was higher. Now it looked like it reached into outer space.

The gale ran me over soon out of Montjoi. It was just what I needed. The shaking thunder and bolts of lightning, the cold wind and lashing rain. I was quickly soaked through, the North Face breathing its last and clinging to me like wet newspaper. But I was invigorated. Head tilted down against the stinging rain I marched, actually marched. Swinging my walking stick and waving my other arm I belted out every marching ditty I'd ever learned or composed, sometimes raising my face to the storm and howling along with it.

For two hours.

Along fields, among the trees, through Perville, past the golf tee, down the lane and finally into a room with a glowing woodstove.

Fifty Days Passed

A big stormfront
A wall of black
The thunder roared
The lightning cracked

A few cold drops
Then some more
With a cold wind
It began to pour

Fifty days
Already passed
I was done
All out of gas

The Devil came
In a white car
He said *Pilgrim*
It's very far

Don't tempt me!
I'm on the track
For Hunt and Corinne
And old Saint Jack

The thunder clapped
The heavens cleared
The storm was gone
The sun appeared

And here I am
With my friends
Drinking tea
At Hunt and Corinne's

"Bravo!" Yes, I actually did perform that for them, marching in place in their kitchen. I was hoarse, but happy.

It was Corinne who first introduced me to the Camino. During a visit a few years before the three of us were driving a shaded avenue near Moissac, when Corinne matter-of-factly said, "Ah, there's a pilgrim."

I looked and saw a man in a broad hat adjusting the load on a donkey under the pollarded trees, soft green with spring growth. I didn't understand what she meant. Pilgrim? This man looked like a period actor for some type of tourist setup. Or maybe a bionomic farmer. Or maybe he was from a group similar to the Amish. Did they have Amish in France? All those made more sense to me at the time than the idea of a pilgrim.

I knew devotees in Hinduism went on pilgrimages. And Muslims made the pilgrimage to Mecca. But *pilgrim* was kind of an archaic term, at least to me. It's the word we use for the first of the English who established themselves on the North American continent. And that usage itself was an inaccurate, elementary school, Halloween costume concept. Better to call them settlers or traders or adventures or speculators or colonizers or invaders or emigrants, rather than something that primarily connotated pious religious seeking. Anyway.

When Corinne said the word pilgrim, I couldn't get the image of the brown coconut we kids, using construction paper, dressed as a turkey for the centerpiece of the Thanksgiving table in Miami.

"What do you mean, the Camino?"

"The way to Santiago, in Spain. Thousands walk it every year."

"It goes through here? How long is it, where does it start?"

The overall concept of the Camino was harder for me to grasp than her usage of the word pilgrim. And I had never heard of Santiago. Why walk there? I was trying to make this Camino thing fit into the long-distance hiking trail category, like the Appalachian Trail, or Pacific Crest Trail. Something that had a start and a finish, a fixed distance, a particular way. Corinne couldn't give me the answers I wanted because I was asking the wrong questions. At the same time, I couldn't comprehend alternative explanations because I couldn't conceive them. It's fascinating to me to see how the mind can completely close itself off to the possibility of something even though it's very real. We continued with whatever we were doing that day and the pilgrim/Camino notion receded to obscurity.

You may wonder how I had not heard of the Camino de

Santiago in the early 21st century. Honestly, I didn't know anything about it. But the seed had been planted by Corinne and the man with the donkey. Could it have been Yves, of A dos d'Ânes in Bénévent-l'Abbaye? Over the next couple of years I met a handful of people, mostly Europeans, who had walked "the Camino". They all spoke about it with such enthusiasm, from such a sincere place in their hearts, I began to feel the tug of the Camino myself even though I still didn't really know what it was. Still I asked them, how long is it? Where do you start?

Six months before I boarded the ship to Antwerp, I met an Italian woman in Manali, India. Same story: she glowed when she recalled it, but didn't have much to say that I could absorb. I took off on a solo cycle trip through the Himalaya shortly after this. At a particularly challenging juncture, I remembered the joy in her eyes and realized this "Camino" was in my near future. My thirst for movement remained deep and unslaked, but in that instant I never wanted to get on goddamn bicycle again. Ironically there were many moments along the way in France and Spain when I wondered why I hadn't instead walked those broken roads in the Himalaya and saved the cycling for all the fine pavement I was pounding along here!

A more accurate cartographic description of the Camino de Santiago is not a trail, but a watershed. Rivulets flow into streams which flow into creeks which flow into rivers and finally everything ends up in Santiago. There's no one way, but it's all moving in the same general direction. In that way the Camino is like the Hindu and Muslim pilgrimages. You start wherever you are and get there however you can.

I remember houses in upper Egypt where those who had made the Hajj depicted their journey on their exterior walls. Usually there were images of buses, boats and airplanes. If I had a house to go back to, I could, so far, paint a ship and a pair of shoes.

Let's see what else I might add? Ah, a car. There had been that lift in Écouen to get across the highway. Oh, and a *utilitaire*. My last night in Belgium, after the old men chuckled off my question about a place to sleep, a tradesman had loaded me into his *utilitaire* for the last 100 yards to the Giselle's *gîte* when he realized I couldn't understand his directions. So my mural was already with substance.

Hunt & Corinne had converted a modest farmhouse into their comfortable abode. Built in the 1840s, it had been left unoccupied for about 40 years before they acquired it: one outside water tap, a single electric light, a fireplace for cooking and heating, and no road.

"The woman who lived here as a girl is now 100 years old. Madame Linon. She still lives nearby," Corinne said. "She walked to school in Perville and in winter shared the bed with her sister because it was so cold. The attic, our bedroom, was inhabited by your friend the owl who came and went through the open little windows."

Perville is about 5km. The owls remain nearby too.

"We did what is best described as a total renovation, hopefully in keeping with tradition. New windows, shutters, floors, doors, bathrooms, water, electricity, heating, plumbing, septic tank, etcetera, as well as the road. We incorporated what is now the dining room, which was the *atelier*, or workshop, and the guest bathroom upstairs, which was storage, accessible from the threshing area behind the house. The *pigeonnier* was a heap of rubble and we rebuilt it with the stone using old roof tiles and old beams."

They'd certainly done a tasteful job, incorporating basic conveniences while maintaining the essence of the structure and setting.

The *pigeonnier*, a pigeon house, stood next to the main house. It looked like a squared stone silo. Hunt, a retired diplomat, had made it into his office. He was forever writing some obscure history book, the current project focused on mid-19th century Californios, the descendants of Spanish and Mexican settlers. He emphasizes these are not deep works of original scholarship.

"I'm merely plugging gaps, highlighting subjects for a general readership that might not want to wade through the troughs of academia. I pull together information that's already out there and simplify it. From real experts. They know much more than a former Marine with a liberal arts major ever could."

He is dogged, and I admire the way he cranks them out.

"I write because writing is the *only* thing in life I do better than average. But I rarely sell many. Hoping for that school contract. Really I just want to be immortalized by having my name in the British Library," he laughs.

I think he had 15 books in there to date. I'm hoping he does one on the Viking raids up the Seine River. Vikings in Paris? They'll make a movie out of it.

It was an idyllic setting; the small house of yellow limestone and graceful *pigeonnier*, surrounded by deep rolling fields of plowed brown earth, young green wheat and greyish colza finally gone to seed. I realized I'd watched the rapeseed pass through its full cycle over the weeks since Belgium; from those first tough and smelly, deep green stalks, to the vibrant yellow blossoms, and now the oil rich seeds ready for harvest.

There wasn't another structure in view.

"You don't want to be here in winter," said Corinne. "We're fine with it, but it can be quite dreary. Everything is mud."

The weather was perfect for the three days I spent with them. Cold enough at night for the wood burner, sunny enough for lunch at the table set outside by the linden tree.

"It buzzes with bees all spring. People still use the leaves to make tea here."

We made a foray to Agen for socks and maps – it felt very odd to ride that distance in a car – but otherwise stayed in our hidden vale. I was more than content to fill the hours soaking my feet in Epsom salts or watching hoopoes terrorize whomever was living in the soil beneath the linden tree. I'd only ever seen hoopoes working the dusty earth in South Asia. How did they end up in France? Followed the great tits?

Hunt did the cooking and most of the talking, and Corinne mostly did everything else. Corinne, from the Netherlands, had worked for her diplomatic service too, in an administrative capacity.

When I told her the heartiest pilgrims I'd met so far were all Dutch, she said, "Well, I'm not surprised."

Corinne was in her late 60s, Hunt his late 70s, and we'd met thirty years before in Kathmandu, Nepal, when we were all a little more conventionally employed. But some of our essential characteristics persisted: Corinne sharp, focused and somewhat reserved. Hunt chatty, flirtatious and somewhat scattered. Me still a little impulsive, and more than a little judgmental.

It was beautiful sleeping in that tranquil house. A crisp firm bed with cozy quilt. Window cracked for fresh air and night sounds. Owls in the predawn. Then down the creakiest stairs in all of France to boil water for tea. The next sound after the kettle would be Hunt's wakeup sighs, a series of long primal moans that astonishingly neither of them noticed.

Hunt was full-on patter when he came downstairs, usually pointless questions about where he should live if he moved – he wouldn't. Or he'd obsess over improbable scenarios about their 1991 Volvo station wagon breaking down – it wouldn't.

One interesting vignette I didn't know came up when we were talking about life aboard the *Independent Pursuit*. In 1956, with his father and brother he'd traveled by ocean liner between New York and Naples. "I bought one glass of Mumm's Cordon Rouge champagne for a 16-year-old girl I met for a few minutes. Alas, end of story right there – nothing more to report!"

Normally his commentary was more circular:

"If by some wildly capricious act of God my darling Corinne departs this earth before I, or leaves me for another man, where shall I go? New Mexico? Are there noble people in New Mexico?"

By the second morning I remembered an answer wasn't actually required for Hunt's questions. He asked them for the asking, not any resolution. I could continue with my tea until diverted by Corinne and our run to the *boulangerie* in Perville.

"Corinne," Hunt asked as soon as she entered the kitchen, "shall we have duck for lunch?"

Of course we'd have duck for lunch. It was Hunt's go-to meat. In a country that force-fed millions of the birds to engorge their livers for foie gras, there was of a surfeit of *viande de canard*. You could buy duck confit almost anywhere. There were tins of it in gas stations.

"I'll prepare some duck legs, and beans. Very typical in Gascony. We're on the boundary here. There is a bottle of Cahors. A red with lots of tannin. It goes well with this heavy and oily fare. What do you know about Oregon?"

My twin nephews were graduating from high school the first week of June and I wanted to be there. I couldn't believe how expensive a one-way ticket was.

"Buy a roundtrip. It will be less expensive," Corinne said quite sensibly.

"I don't want a roundtrip." It's always bugged me that most legacy carriers, especially the American ones, create such a disincentive for one-way tickets. It bespeaks an unimaginative concept of travel as merely out and back.

Plus, a roundtrip would be wasteful because I wasn't coming back. Resting in Vignoble, I'd decided I could reach Santiago in time and fly back from there. I'd calculated all I needed to do was walk 40km a day for the next 30 days.

Now, if the reader has been paying attention, I've only done a few days over 40km. And just the last three 30-plus kilometer days were tiring. So, 30 days of 40 kilometers – what was I thinking?

It's as if we're composed of different, competing entities. My heart immediately knew this was wrong-headed. My body was incredulous. But the little, self-absorbed corner of my mind was certain. Thirty days, 40km a pop? Bah! Easy breezy.

Corinne merely shook her head. Living with Hunt for so long she knew it was pointless to try and change the mind with reason. Reality would ultimately step in and assert itself at the right moment. She went back to reading.

I finally did follow her advice about the ticket. The roundtrip, arriving one day before one nephew's graduation, and returning a week later, the day after the other's, was less than half the cost of the one-way ticket. But I wouldn't need the return. I knew.

Hunt's daughter had sent Corinne a brand-new North Face jacket from California which turned out to be too big. Corinne kindly gifted it to me. So, with a smart blue jacket, new wool socks, recharged by companionship and full of duck, I set out for Santiago, only a month and 1,200km away.

VIGNOBLE to SPAIN

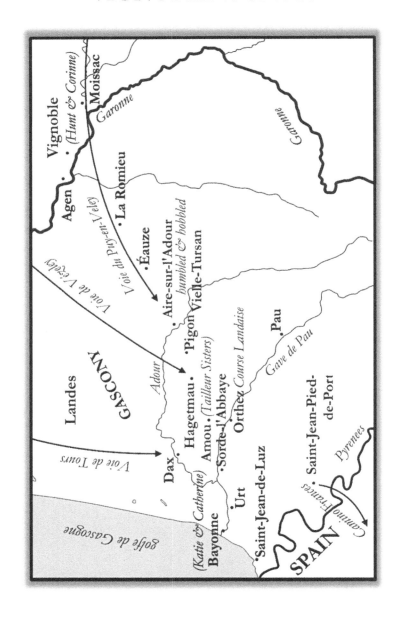

Shadow of the Pyrenees **11**

After a full day and 40 kilometers I joined the Voie du Puy-en-Velay in La Romieu. Two hours after leaving Hunt & Corinne's I'd crossed the Garonne, one of the largest rivers yet. Loire, Dordogne, Lot, Garonne, these were names I'd heard, but now, to walk along and cross them, I could put them in some sort of context. I was struck by how riverine this part of France was. This was due to the Massif Central, with its highlands south and east tipping the flow of rain and snowmelt north and west. But this was changing on crossing the Garonne.

Some rivers from the Massif Central do flow into the Garonne's right bank, including the Lot, but the Garonne's primary source is the Pyrenees, the mountain chain further south which forms the frontier with Spain. It would be these snowy mountains that held sway over the land from now on, not the Massif Central. Broadly defined I would be crossing Gascony (Gascogne) as I made my way southwest, until I reached the Pays Basque, near the coast. Unbeknownst to me the English had exercised control over Gascony for approximately 300 years in the late Middle Ages. I wondered if this explained something I learned later about southwestern France that took me completely by surprise: the popularity of rugby in the region.

I shared the *refuge des pèlerins* in La Romieu with four others, all women. The youngest, a solo walker, sat on the edge of her bunk, needle and thread in her hand. It looked like she was sewing a large flap of skin back onto the bottom of her foot. I recoiled slightly at the sight. Jesus. Actually, what she might have been doing was draining an enormous blister that covered her heel; using a needle to pull knotted thread through the blistered skin, leave it overnight, letting the fluid drain out along it. I would see this done numerous times on the way to Santiago. Thanks to the moleskin I wouldn't have to try the technique, and I'm not sure if I would have had the stomach for it. The young woman said she wasn't going any further.

The oldest of the *pèlerins* nodded approvingly when she noted the terrine I brought back from the *épicerie* across the street. "You made the right selection. Always get the *entier*. They don't mix in the bad pieces." All credit to Mona in Paris who had explained these things to me at her local grocer.

The church bell in La Romieu marked the hours all night. It was the only place in France where I noticed this. It is possible I dreamt of the bells' clang, but I don't think so. Usually, I found the first bells of the day were at 7:00 a.m., or maybe 6:00 or 8:00. Bazoches-les-Gallerandes with Father Giuseppe was the only place I heard them at 5:00, and I assume this reflected the central role agriculture played in daily life there. Why all night in La Romieu? I found it soothing. It reminded me of the chowkidars in India tapping their lathis and blowing their whistles through the night. A reassurance that, "All is well."

The woman who approved of my terrine accompanied the bells, snoring most of the night. Snorting really, but not too loudly. But who was I to complain? I also snorted, especially falling asleep on my back. Heavy sighing too. The three younger women were absolutely silent, invisible presences in the dark. It was an early lesson about who to sleep far from if you had a choice.

In hindsight, it was an extravagance on my part to even note the light night sounds of this woman and the German fellow back in the tight room of Bénévent-l'Abbaye. These few *refuges* in France were as peaceful as an empty church compared with what was to come in Spain.

But if there was one slightly more legitimate preoccupation I had with these pilgrim accommodations, it was the tendency of people to keep any windows closed. Instead of a fresh injection of cool night air, we recirculated each other's warm, humid breath.

Perhaps I was the odd one with this preference – I sleep as close to the outdoors as I can. Nevertheless, despite the contrast with the dream-like tranquility of Hunt & Corinne's, La Romieu was a cozy, very satisfactory first night back on the Way.

Only 1,160km to go.

The Voie du Puy-en-Velay was clearly a well-traveled Way. For the first time I saw signs in the countryside, nailed to trees or posts along the path, indicating places to stay or have a meal. And local residents, especially on the more isolated stretches, might set out a thermos of tea or coffee, maybe some  snacks, and a donation box for those so inclined. This was different from everywhere I'd trod so far. Reassuring and generous on one hand, but maybe a little too overdone on the other. With places so clearly indicated, it took away that sense of uncertainty that kept you keen. The trail was so well marked I didn't have to pay much attention to where I was going.

Knowing I needed to average 40km a day I pushed to finish 25km before I stopped for lunch. I was truly marching along, maintaining a brisk pace, at times firmly striking my heels into the tarmac as if I were on the parade ground, the shock of the impact perversely a relief to my aching feet. This was probably inflicting repetitive stress injuries that would nag me for life. I closed my eyes too, to see how long I could hold a line. Not very.

I was back to the marching ditties, having fun trying to remember the ones I'd conjured the previous weeks and trying out new ones. The few ditties I recalled from the days of being a Marine officer candidate in Quantico, Virginia were so laced with profanity, not to mention sex and violence, I couldn't imagine uttering them on the *Compostelle*. In fact, the energy of these ditties was so utterly different, they wouldn't come out of my throat. The words withered. But the underlying tempo was perfect, and I built on the scaffolding.

There were netted plum orchards – Agen is famous for its prunes – more colza seed, and stone walls covered in purplish roses. Caudecoste's center was comprised of half-timbered houses, *colombage*, like Bourges, their walls leaning and rolling with the centuries. The vineyards around Condom were leafing out. Most marvelous of all, tall banks of poplar trees released their seed on the wind, storms of cottony puffs swirling across road and fields, blowing like snow. It reminded me of scuba diving one night in the Red Sea, when I found myself in the middle of a coral spawning, also as dense as a snowstorm. Both phenomena unexpected. Both so wonderous.

The prettiest girl
I ever saw
Was driving a truck
Along the Loire

Lovely smile
Long brown hair
Freckled nose
And very fair

The day was hot
A clinging shirt
And on her hips
A tight little skirt

She said, *Pilgrim*
I'll give you a drink
But anything else
Don't even think!

Lo right-a-left
Left right left
A lo right-a-left
Love to double-time!

This was as risqué as the ditties got. Spring was in the air.

The last seven kilometers into Éauze was a lovely, shaded path. Far ahead I could see two figures ambling along, and I closed ground on them steadily. I was grateful for the wide, flat path, and to have them pulling me along because I was feeling the day's 40km. Sometimes they stopped, maybe looked at something, had a sip of water, clarified a point of discussion, then they'd resume, two silhouettes in the tunnel of trees,  walking side by side. Now that's walking I thought, walking and enjoyment.

A sound caught the attention of my right ear. Even though I was focused on the two figures in the distance, I couldn't miss this. It was smooth and continuous, very unlike all the other little discrete sounds that came from the trees and brush on either side of the way. Snake, I thought, big snake. But that seemed preposterous. How could a snake make such a distinct sound? Sure enough, in a gap in the foliage the muscled flank of a *vipère* slid by, looking like a freight train plunging into a tunnel. She was moving fast and steadily, but calmly.

Holy cow, how big is this snake?

At least as fat as my forearm. Brown. That's as much as I saw. This wasn't one of the little fellows living in the mâche beds along the River Juine. The last thing I needed was for her to turn across my path. I pushed on quickly, leaving her unperturbed.

I caught up with Marc and Jacques just as the way reached Éauze. Or rather, Marc and Jacques, when they noticed me during one of their regular pauses, stopped and waited for me. They suggested I tag along, since I had no idea where to stay, and soon they introduced me to Laurence, the proprietor of the most pleasant little *gîte*, the Lou Parpalhou in the center of town.

There was something about Laurence's smile I remember to this day. Maybe it was the way it turned up at the corners of her mouth, or maybe it was the way her brown eyes animated it. But she seemed to genuinely enjoy running this *gîte* which she and her husband had started a few years before. She served and sat with the three of us for an aperitif in the kitchen, and said she'd run laundry if any of us required it. I never turned down an offer.

The old center of Éauze had a circular aspect to it, like Gourdon, but it wasn't a hillock topped by a fortified church. The boulevard ringing the center follows the trace of the medieval fortifications, I think. Long before that, the location was the site of an important Roman town. Now Éauze sits in the region which produces France's famous brandy, Armagnac. There were still quite a few well-preserved half-timber structures, and the small lanes were filled with shops, *épiceries* and restaurants. I had explored a little after a shower but felt so knackered it was enough to just pick up a few things at the SPAR for a simple feed back at Lou Parpalhou.

Much to my regret, I realized much later I had zoomed through the whole Armagnac region without tasting the famous spirit. Worse, I didn't even think about it then.

Marc and Jacques had rested, cleaned up, and were going out to find a *gastronomique*. It sounded very civilized. They asked if I'd like to join. Yes, I would, but I didn't have it in me. Is this how it'll be the rest of the Camino, marching and sleeping, marching and sleeping, for the next 28 days?

Jacques, the shorter of the two, emerged from the bathroom. He was shaved, perfumed and dressed smartly, ready for a night out.

« Voilà ! »

Marc smiled and said, "He is like that," and we all laughed. I barely woke when they returned.

"What color would you like?" Laurence asked. On the *gîte's* cachet was a butterfly. *Parpalhou*, I believe, means butterfly in the Gascon language.

"Pink," I said, and she colored the wings with a marker.

"Laurence, I noticed you sat with me this morning the whole time I was having breakfast. You know, keeping me company." It seemed an odd thing to ask about. While having breakfast I even hinted she might have other things to attend to, but she said she was fine.

"When I was on the Camino," she said, "sometimes I found myself alone at breakfast, or would notice others alone. And that's when I would feel homesick, for Patrice and my daughter. To start the day alone, I think it's always good to have someone, to share this with. That's why I sat with you. So you know even though you are by yourself, you are not alone."

Wise beyond your years, I thought, and gave her a big hug.

The first glimpse of the Pyrenees: black and grey specters, low on the southern horizon. It was a cloudy, windy morning. I stopped in Nogaro for *un chocolat chaud*, imagining the cold of the alpine peaks. I knew nothing of these mountains.

But I wouldn't be crossing them, as many pilgrims did from Saint-Jean-Pied-de-Port, where the main routes in France converge at the "foot" of the range. There the Camino Frances commences, traversing the mountains then passing through the main cities of Pamplona, Logroño, Burgos, León and Lugo on the way to Santiago, this the most popular route. I would walk along Spain's north coast instead, on the Camino del Norte.

Part of this choice was wanting to avoid the more heavily trafficked Camino Frances and what I suspected would be fairly hot weather in the interior by the time I got there. But also, I wanted to be near the sea. I grew up near the ocean. It was a part of me. And when I'm away from it for any length of time, I start to feel its absence. I was looking forward to its presence again.

The brisk morning of hot chocolate and distant snow peaks turned into a never-ending afternoon blaze. I kept motoring on. This relentless approach to walking wasn't conducive to moments like climbing the massif to Veix, when the poetry began to flow spontaneously. Or to the continuation of that flow in dreams, like during the night of words and music in Gourdon at Pascale's. I knew this but kept going.

I had experienced several instances like those in Veix and

Gourdon while on the Himalayan cycle trip, where something inside of me opened up and connected to energies I didn't comprehend. But I had let those moments fade to faint shadow, barely retrievable.

Why? Why had I not immediately connected them to Veix? Why had I likewise let Veix and Gourdon dissolve into the background?

Perhaps I'm too conventional. I never had much exposure to ecstatic traditions and have no reference points for this kind of encounter. Maybe I cynically assume such things are just aberrations. Maybe I'm worried about being considered strange or weird for having them.

Maybe I'm afraid.

Afraid that this little self I'm so comfortable with will be overwhelmed and dissolve into this greater mystery. Maybe I'm afraid to admit that this is one of the things I most desire. When I regard this troublesome fear, I can't help but recall the last lines of Mary Oliver's poem, *The World I Live In*:

Only if there are angels in your head will
you ever, possibly see one.

It was definitely different climate this far south in France, and not just because it was early May. I was seeing air conditioners on buildings for the first time, and pines that looked like they came  from California. Though the Pyrenees announced the proximity of Spain, seeing Hispanic names on signboards truly made it feel near. France had seemed to go on and on, so much so that at times over the past weeks I couldn't believe a country in Europe was so big. But here I was, close enough to feel Spain seep into France.

Laurence had booked a room for me at the cheapest place in Aire-sur-l'Adour, another one of these worn out, formerly grand 1920s *hôtels*. Its saloon was briefly packed for an end of day drink, then emptied out and shut. It didn't seem like there was anybody else staying there.

I'd leave the Voie du Puy-en-Velay here and turn more directly west, with the ultimate goal of crossing into Spain on the coast. I didn't have an exact route in mind, but Hagetmau looked like a good destination for tomorrow. According to the Michelin it was only 34km along country roads. That was a relief after doing 40-plus kilometers each of the last three days.

I massaged the top of my left foot and ankle. I'd felt a funny sensation at times during the day. Not pain, but little sparks. Strange, I'd never experienced such a thing before.

You're running a bit hard, I said to myself.

Well, you've got to stay on pace.

Yeah, but I feel like all I'm doing now is rushing to find the *supermarché*, eat, sleep, shit and pay.

Let's not whine. You were the one claiming you'd probably do 50km a day.

True, maybe in my early 20s, but not my early 50s!

You can do this. Just keep at it. Stay steady.

You're right, and now that we're heading more west than south, we'll make more progress with the earth spinning past underneath our steps!

There turned out to be a Canadian couple, also *pèlerins*, staying somewhere in this rambling establishment. He was still walking, but she had started using the bus.

"Tendinitis," she said, showing an angry looking ankle. "I need to stay off it until it's better, then I can start walking again."

The bus, I thought, that's got to be a downer, pull you out of the rhythm of the Camino. Could it really be that bad? I heard myself think, the judgement creeping in like it had with the brother and sister back in Bénévent-l'Abbaye who were going to bus across Limoges. Don't be a jerk. It was admirable how this couple had adapted to make the situation work for both of them and not just give up. I told her about the strange pricks I had felt on the top of my ankle today.

"You came all the way from Éauze? That's quite far. Don't overdo it. That's exactly how mine started. It's very painful. And once you have it, there's nothing you can do about it. You should be careful."

I nodded, appreciative of her intention, but it wasn't advice meant for me. I'd be fine.

The next morning:
A grown man acting like a boy, believing the world was made for him, that he would always get his way, that rules and limits and routine were for others, that he, of everyone, was somehow beyond it all.

On a drizzly morning a few kilometers outside of Aire-sur-l'Adour, along the quiet D335, someone whacked my left shin with a club. That someone was the Camino de Santiago.

I wouldn't listen to the misgivings of my heart. I wouldn't listen to the doubts in my head. I wouldn't listen to the signals from my body. I wouldn't listen to the advice of a fellow *pèlerin*. So, the Camino stepped in, grabbed me by the ears and said, *stop this*. Stop the hurry. Stop trying to get somewhere rather than be somewhere. Stop ignoring your inner voice. Listen to what you heard in Veix.

I limped off the road and found a wet stump to sit on. I rocked in pain. It wasn't a twist. It was like fire. Go back to Aire-sur-l'Adour? I thought of the Canadian woman. She had been exactly right. Bang, tendinitis for the first time in my life, completely self-inflicted. And it hurt like Hell, really hurt. I felt I owed her an apology.

The collapsible trekking pole I'd swung so jauntily to keep rhythm with my ditties was now a cane, supporting my weight as I hobbled along the shoulder of the narrow road. The grass was wet and uneven, but it was excruciating to tread on the asphalt. It was too far to go back to Aire-sur-l'Adour, so I continued, hoping to find somewhere to stop soon.

I limped, pain and frustration pulling tears from my eyes. I would have been a pathetic figure to see. But there were no cars that morning along the D335. I only recall fields of corn. Silent fields of corn. Yes, M. Chenu had said I'd find corn further south. Here it is. And the Pyrenees, long off over the rolling countryside, a jagged horizon.

Jean B.
Lucien
Augustin
Jean M.
Jean B.
Jean B.E.
Pierre J.
Jules P.
1914-1918

Most of the carnage would have been in the northern half of France. This only dawned on me after I realized I hadn't passed any war cemeteries or battlefield memorials on my route south of Paris. There was the simple stone monument a week ago just outside of Montaigu-de-Quercy; two young men executed by the Gestapo, on the edge of a field. The terror was everywhere, even if not the major military actions.

But in every town and village I crossed throughout the country there were monuments. Monuments with the names of the local men, many sharing last names, killed in the World Wars. Sometimes the battle was noted, sometimes the ages. Probably few if any of the bodies made it home – they were in the cemeteries I'd passed or churned into the earth where they fell.

These places may not have a *boulangerie*, or any other commercial establishment, but they all had a monument to the men lost. A well-maintained monument.

These are not monuments to something far away, but of something here. Our savageries are kept close, made present and

147

personal. Descendants, if the lines hadn't been snuffed out, are still there to read the names of their family. To remember. I wonder if this presence is why Europeans as a whole, or I should say the French, seem more cautious about the idea of war than we Americans. We have our Civil War memorials, and the names on the Vietnam Memorial, but we don't have the same intimacy of communal death and homeplace.

I must stop at one of these monuments, I said to myself every day walking down France, and write down the names, write down the names as acknowledgement. But I was moving, always moving. Next time, I'd say, next time.

It took being wounded, being confronted with my own weakness, to take the time. To witness.

To the men of Vielle-Tursan and your weeping mothers, fathers, sisters and brothers, wives and children; I see you, I acknowledge you.

Forget getting to Hagetmau. I needed to get off my feet as soon as possible.

I'd inched my way five or six kilometers to Saint-Loubouer, I think it was, but found nothing. There were a few *chambre d'hôte* emblems on housefronts and gates, but no one answered. How far was the next village? I kept moving, short lopsided steps. The next place had to have something. The road felt long and empty. Vineyard and corn. I didn't know how much further I could go. Leaving Ville-Tursan, after resting at the monument, another *chambre d'hôte* emblem. My hopes lifted when I saw a woman, lugging a crate to a truck. All I could do was point to the sign. She shook her head. They didn't take guests anymore. She indicated there might be a place a little further on. Turn left, I think she said. If that didn't work, it was only more empty road.

I come to the first turn and take it, following the road downhill.

Yes, another sign at a lane. This must be it. Halfway down the gravel drive, as if to affirm it, a warm breeze picks up and pulls the seed loose from a lone tree. The air is filled with a swirl of silken tufts, flowing toward the farmhouse, leading the way. I follow them to the farm of Philippe Labrouche, a man with hands just like Michel Chenu. By 2:00 p.m. I was showered and stretched out on bed. I slept all afternoon.

They normally don't provide meals, but Philippe and his elderly mother shared their simple dinner with me, since I had nothing and there was nowhere to go. A glass of the local Tursan too, a somewhat sweet white. But I was soon back to the room, which was in a separate building. Lying in bed I noticed the exposed timber was fixed with big, hand-hewn pegs. A lowing cow, cooing doves, and birds settling down. The purplish scallop with its string of beads hanging from my pack – oh for the company of my meditation companions now. But even with the nap I was soon asleep again, before the night fully arrived.

The sailing silken seeds, swirling along the breeze, landing where it pleases. They need fertile and protected ground to develop into the giants that they carry within. Most perish. We too, the billions of us, are seeds, seeds of God, scattered on this Earth. And likewise require fertile and protected soil from which we can grow to full consciousness, grow toward God, grow into God. But there are so many perils. How many among us even begin to bloom, before we are cut down? How many of us know we must tend our own garden? Most of us perish without a trace. No wonder God must sow so many, here, and in other soils too.

The next thing I knew Venus was as bright as I'd ever seen her, and the Pyrenees were shrouded in cloud. Vineyards fell away from the farmhouse. There were even a few palms and banana plants. I clasped Philippe's hand and thick round fingers, so grateful for his shelter.

It's Sunday, and the French vote again today, the second round in the presidential runoff. And I walk again too, to maybe Hagetmau, only 15km away. Hobble really.

There are cherry trees along the narrow country road, ripe and full. I stop, not 30 minutes out from Philippe's, because now I have time. Now I'm not trying to reach anywhere. I reach, pluck, eat, spitting pits, the flesh thick and juicy. My fingertips redden, as I imagine so do my lips. But there is no one to tell me in this quiet piece of countryside.

On the edge of Aubagnan, the first village I come to, I find a *boulangerie*, open, doing brisk business. This is another thing it took me a while to figure out in France. On Sundays, businesses were open in the morning, till lunch, after which they were closed for the day. Perhaps another finger in the eye of the church?

« *Bonjour !* » says the busy *boulanger* from the back as I enter. A young man, he is white with flour.

« *Bonjour ! Une baguette au tradition, s'il vous plaît. Et qu'est-ce que c'est ? Un gâteau basque? J'aurai la cerise, bien sûr.* »

My words didn't exactly flow that smoothly, but we understood each other: A scrumptious looking little torte caught my attention, I pointed and asked what it was, and nodded when given the choice for cherry. I'd never heard of a *gâteau* Basque, but it looked too good to pass up. Small, it was heavy, which I considered a good sign.

At the next village, Serres-Gaston, I fill water at the *salle polyvalente*, where they are cooking a huge meal for the community. A little beyond town, on a knoll along a dirt road among fields, I find a giant, solitary oak tree. It provides shade, bird song and a fine view of the clear and snowy Pyrenees. My left leg throbs. The *gâteau* Basque is wonderful. No wonder it's becoming harder to find Odile's *gâteau-aux-fruits* in the shops. Who would buy them when you have these!?

Resting there I think, why do we do this so often to ourselves, race along to some destination self-defined as critical, oblivious of everything passing by around us, unconcerned about consequences, only focused on our objective? I knew better. I know better. I also know it is a continuous struggle. It's so easy to slip back into this default sense of urgency, this idea that if I only get one more thing done, walk one more kilometer, then everything will be just right. The key, I guess, is continually nurturing the intuition that will recognize this delusion and allow you to stop yourself. And to hope you have someone to step in, like the Camino, when you fail.

When I told Corinne of my predicament, she didn't say I told you so, as I might have. She expressed sympathy, asked if I needed anything, and said quite simply, "Now you can slow down and enjoy yourself."

And I did.

Sitting under the big oak I felt relief. Now I didn't have to walk 40km a day. I could walk as much or as little as I wanted. Stop and eat all the cherries I could. Thanks to Corinne, I had a roundtrip ticket in hand. When the date arrived, I'd jump a bus wherever I was, catch the flight, then come back and pick up where I left off. I'd had the milage equation backwards. In your twenties you can aim for 50km, but in your fifties, aiming in the twenty-kilometer range was plenty. And for the foreseeable future, 10-15km would be just fine with me.

I regarded the lenses of my reading glasses and the screen on my Nokia. Both had long been scratched fuzzy from the incessant movement in my thigh pocket. We were all wearing down.

Man my foot and shin were throbbing.

The blue sky, fine and clear, was full of streaking airplanes, leaving their wakes across the surface of the sea. I, hermit crab, sat on the bottom, satisfied to watch them race urgently on. *Thank you for this body. Thank you for this fitness. Thank you for this health. I know it is unearned and passing. But thank you.*

I remember Hagetmau because they charged €5.50 for the *refuge des pèlerins*. Why the 50 cents?

I sat in front of the *refuge*, watching the swallows devour insects in the late afternoon sky. At a particular angle, when they'd flare their wings, white spots would appear on their undersides, shimmering as if electrified. I'd only seen this for certain once before, in the Himalaya. I remember being surprised and doubtful at the time – swallows don't have spots! – but at that moment I was thinking, this is familiar somehow. Maybe I have seen this before, maybe when I was less prone to determine what I see, maybe deep in my youth, maybe in a dream. So this time in Hagetmau, when the swallows shared this little secret with me again, I only nodded, as if I'd expected it. I bet in Veix the swallows always shimmer.

Next time you're lying on your back watching the sky at dusk, try to see the spots. They are there, I promise.

There was also a handsome black and white magpie up to something. Every 10 minutes or so he'd fly past, lower than the swallows, first one direction, then back. Then again. What could he be doing?

And in the open end of the sign pole that extended over the road, a finch had found a fine nesting spot. You see a lot waiting for the world's slowest washing machine to finish. Oh why didn't I select *Express*? It's the same word in French!

I hadn't realized it, but I was back on the Voie Vézelay in Hagetmau. The Way was approaching Saint-Jean-Pied-de-Port, less than a week I think. Next stop, Orthez.

A fellow *pèlerin* turned me out of the small room where I had set myself up.

"I'm not with them," she explained, referring to the three men with whom she had just arrived.

Neither am I, I wanted to say, and point out that dorms weren't segregated on the Camino, as far as I could tell. And I promise I neither snore nor bite. But she didn't look in the mood for banter. She looked like she needed understanding and space. So, I joined the three lads next door in the lime green room. One Dutchman and two Belgians, two of whom seemed to prefer to roam around shirtless, airing their bellies. I see why she wanted space.

For the first time I mashed in a set of silicone earplugs a friend, Leigh, had given me in the US. She wears them because of her husband, likewise of noble belly. A paunch, I knew, was an indicator of snoring, and these fellows looked serious, so in they went as a precaution. But it wasn't as bad as I expected. The night ended up being a mild symphony whistles, sighs, snorts and rumbles. I don't recall, but I think I only ended up using the earplugs once more, in Santiago on the very last night. Still, having them was reassuring, and I thanked Leigh for the peace of mind.

It was a warm, companiable room, but I was happy to slip outside before dawn with a bowl of tea and enjoy the subtle sounds of night we miss in our pilgrim huddles. And of course, the shooting stars.

Do You Like Rabbit? **12**

Now that's a cemetery to spend eternity in, I thought, coming into Brassempouy along the D21. Situated on a peaceful slope with an unobstructed view of the Pyrenees, well-tended. There was a bouquet of on one of the graves that looked like it had just been put there. There wasn't much to Brassempouy, but it was the site of a couple of famous Paleolithic caves. I thought I'd take a look in the museum, but everything was closed for some reason.

On the other side of the *ville* I greeted a woman loading the trunk of her car. She was slim, wearing a straw sunhat; Isabelle Tailleur. She was collecting a few things from her aunt's house, who had recently passed away. It was she who had left the fresh flowers on the grave.

Isabelle lived with her sister and mother in Amou, only another 7km along. It's where I hoped to reach for a short, restful day.

"Ah, you are walking the *Compostelle*? I have a sister who walked." Maybe two actually, but not the one she was living with, I didn't think. Our communication was slow, but we were making it work.

"But the Office de Tourisme is closed today," she interrupted, finally understanding what I was trying to explain. « Le jour de la Victoire. »

"Victory Day?"

"Oui, then end of World War II, between Germany and France. Today is May 8th."

"But there is a hotel, or *gîte*?" I asked hopefully, wondering how I'd fare without the helpful, knowledgeable and charming *hôtesse d'accueil tourisme* to guide me.

She said there was.

Good, something will work out I thought. Amou is not far, and I'll be arriving early enough in the afternoon to look around.

Despite the throb in my left foot, I was beginning to enjoy this easier rhythm.

« *Aimes-tu le lapin ?* »

I don't know how I recognized the word for rabbit. Maybe the presidential campaign. Even if I hadn't liked rabbit – I didn't think she had in mind a pet – I would have said yes. For I surmised this generous woman was about to invite me to lunch. I would eat whatever was served.

« *Oui, j'adore.* »

"My sister is cooking rabbit for us. Would you like to join?"

"Well, yes, you are very kind, but I don't want to intrude on your sister's lunch."

"It is my rabbit."

If Isabelle might at first give the impression of being frail, and even anxious, her forceful spirit soon came through. Soon after the rabbit had been dispatched, she was on the phone with another sister. Though my comprehension was far from perfect, her side of the conversation went something like this:

He is walking the Compostelle, and you have walked the Compostelle, you need to come talk to him.

You can give him advice on directions from here.

I know you have plans, but you can make time.

I'm not telling you what to do.

Now, you should come now.

It's not out of the way from Dax.

Then you can take him with you.

And that's how I ended up 15km south in Orthez, sitting in a 100-year-old bullring. Not exactly 100 years old. I think it was built in the 1920s. And not exactly a bullring. This was the *course landaise*, a traditional form of bullfighting in the region, especially in the department of Landes. But it's wrong to refer to it as a type of bullfighting. They don't use bulls and there is no fighting. I had never heard of anything like it.

If bullfighting is a classical performance, a mortal struggle, albeit lopsided, the *course landaise* is more like jazz or ballet, but with broken bones. I have never seen anything like it.

Geneviève seemed the opposite of her sister Isabelle. Full and self-confident, more gregarious and social. On the way through town, just before we reached the arena, she pointed out the medieval bridge over the Gave de Pau. She told me the bridge had been used to toss the condemned to death in the river below. Since capital punishment is about demonstrating power, the pretty *pont* would have been the perfect place to maximize the viewing opportunity of your subjects. I remembered the time I had almost been run over by a coal train on a high trestle in Virginia. At the last moment I was fortunate enough to slip through the ties and onto a support pylon. The memory still gives me chills. I could kind of relate to the horror medieval Orthez's condemned might have felt just before the plunge.

We relaxed in our seats in the simple arena, Geneviève waving and speaking to those she knew, which was quite a few. An *harmonie musicale* of trumpets, saxophones and clarinets played. Various towns and villages supply these wind orchestras, which are specialized in playing Spanish music. "They are an essential part of the event," Geneviève said.

Between general announcements, a man read the names over the public address system of those who had made a small donation on entrance, a *prime*. The event organizers send invitations, so technically if you receive one you don't have to pay the entrance fee. But custom is to give a *prime* in the like amount. I think the men in the ring can dedicate part of their performance to a patron, and receive some of the donation in return, but I'm not exactly sure. It seemed just about everyone there had given something. It was an intimate, social atmosphere.

When a man is hit with some force and knocked down for the

first time I look at Geneviève.

« *Non, non,* » she pats my knee, "it is normal."

I glance around and no one else seems overly concerned. I thought the hit was an exception, but I guess not. The downed man wears a blue *boléro*, a short-waisted jacket, with silver brocades. His thick black hair is swept back, his lantern jaw clean shaven but with permanent shadow. His colleagues help him up, support him, and talk with him until he regains his bearings. He acknowledges the crowd, and we cheer him in return. The other men then assist him from the arena. He must be done, I think. But after a brief interlude he returns, stands without support and waves to us. We cheer even louder. The blood from his nose shows brightly on his crisp white shirt. He turns to wait another charge.

In the *course landaise* they use cows, *coursières*, because these females are smaller and lighter than bulls, faster, more agile, and  have more stamina. The man in the ring with the animal, I want to call him a matador because I don't know what else to call him. But he's not a matador because they don't kill the animals. The word matador comes from the Spanish verb *matar*, to kill. Geneviève tells me the proper term is *torero*.

The *torero* stands alone in the center of the dirt ring. There are no horses, but a long rope is attached to the *coursière* at the base of the horns for safety and control. I'd never seen cows so aggressive. They were like wild animals, a different species. The *coursière* bangs and gores the wood of the gate. She snorts and stamps the earth madly, full of energy and eager to get at the man and his cape. She's finally let free of the stockade and bursts into a full sprint. The goal is for the *torero* to dodge the charging *coursière* at the last instant, as elegantly and as closely as possible. Sometimes it is perfect and graceful, the *coursière* past, and now looking about for the object of her fury. And we cheer. Sometimes the *torero* is grazed and staggered, and we collectively wince. And sometimes he's knocked to the ground, the rope goes taught as the tenders try to pull the inflamed animal off the downed *torero*, whom she is intent on finishing with her horns. When he gets up, we cheer even more.

All the *toreros* go down eventually, one by one. The stocky one with the crewcut. The tall one in the black *boléro* with pink piping and animal talismans – the impact when he is felled is so solid we feel the thud where we sit, and this time all of us gasp. And Loïc Lapoudge, the reigning champion, in his gold and blue *boléro*, who was facing the champion *coursière* with her wild long horns. He was the only one who could stand with his back to the animal and safely spin away at the last instant. Almost every time.

Eventually the champion *coursière* gets him. Her name is Ibiza. Lapoudge goes down hard on his face. But he doesn't bunch himself into a protective ball like the others. He slowly rolls onto his back and props himself up on one elbow, smiling like a sated lover. Ibiza, *the golden horn*, trots toward him, the ropes slack.

"She will not attack on the ground," Geneviève explains. "She is the only one like that."

Ibiza, breathing heavily, stands over the Lapoudge, her horns sweeping high at different angles. The trumpets, saxophones and clarinets play. The *torero* finally gets up for another round.

They all did. They all, however slowly, got back up to face a final charge.

At intermission Geneviève introduced me to the champion from a few years earlier. He was slight of stature, had a short, wide scar under his left eye, possessed the looks of a fashion model and the taught body of a ballet dancer. I had never met a man more beautiful. But his beauty didn't come from only his looks. It came from his poise and bearing and presence, his sense of confidence and humility, the deep reservoir of calm that one would need to stand and face a charging beast with only your wits and skill to rely on and faith in the men supporting you. I felt a jester in his presence.

The *course landaise* is a team event. The men in the ring are a team. They are scored individually and as a whole. There are arenas throughout the region where the teams perform, and I realized I had seen one in Hagetmau – it was near where we paid for the *refuge*. The teams are not in the arenas together but are evaluated at events by judges over a long season, stretching from March to November. This event was part of the Landes-Béarn *Challenge*. But it isn't just the men who are judged. The animals too.

"She was the champion last season," Geneviève had explained to me, indicating the *coursière* with the wildly sweeping horns. *Corne d'or*. The golden horn. "Ibiza. And he, Loïc Lapoudge, he was the champion too," she'd said of the *torero* standing up and dusting himself off again.

The roll call of names and *prime* amounts continues. Geneviève nods when she hears her name. The *harmonie musicale* keeps playing. This is indeed a special event she has brought me to, with both reigning champions present.

The first time Fabien was announced in the ring I didn't know what to expect. A young man, he looked 17, dressed in white slacks and long sleeve shirt. Tall and lithe.

The crowd buzzes a little bit. Fabien walks to the middle of the ring and stands, feet together, hands at his waist, facing the stockade door. Behind him another young man crouches. The stockade cracks open, and the head of a *coursière* appears, jostling the heavy door and raring to break out. She gnashes and bangs against the planks, stomps the earth. Behind Fabien the young man starts waving a cloth at ground level. The *coursière* spots it and becomes even more animated. I have no idea what is about to happen.

The door swings open and the *coursière* charges, dirt exploding from her hoofbeats. Fabien doesn't move, except maybe his fingers. His partner behind him gives one last wave of the cloth then backpedals as fast as he can. On the animal comes, head lowered, gathering mortal momentum. At the last possible instant Fabien springs straight into the air, flips forward and rolls, and lands on his feet with his arms outstretched, the *coursière* having flown beneath him, goring the air.

It was too much. I'm sure my mouth was open in amazement. Fabien Napias was apparently a champion too, which I didn't doubt. He performed more acrobatic feats flying over the animals, sometimes with his legs tied together. Geneviève later explained that *torero* was a general term. The man who dodges the animal is an *écarteur*. The one who leaps, like Fabien, is a *sauteur*, from the French verbs to brush aside and to jump over, respectively.

At the end everyone, except the animals, came out for a bow. Fabien in his white shirt, the woman who conducted the *harmonie musicale*, the men who handled the ropes, and the *écarteurs*. When these *écarteurs* stood together to present themselves at the outset, they were immaculate, as if dressed for a formal ball in colorful outfits and pressed shirts, their *boléros* regal.

Now they are dusty, scuffed and bruised. One or two are limping, one or two are holding their ribs. And one is missing, the one with the bright red blood on his white shirt. But he'd be back, Geneviève is sure.

I wondered how they could keep it up, the season really just getting underway. The tall *écarteur*, in the black and pink *boléro*, the one whose impact we felt in our seats? He had started out as a *sauteur*, like Fabien. Geneviève said he once spent a year recovering from an injury.

And here he is.

The 30km sounded a little ambitious with the tendinitis, but Geneviève told me there was a nice *refuge des pèlerins* in Sorde-l'Abbaye, near Peyrehorade. I aimed for it, fully cognizant I may need to stop short. But Cécile, the sister who cooked the rabbit, had put me on to Flector, an anti-inflammatory cream that was already helping. She was a nurse who for now was caring for their mother at home, who suffered from Alzheimer's. Meeting these three sisters and their mother had buoyed me, made me forget about the pain in my lower leg. I was in good spirits for this final bit to Spain. I couldn't believe France was about to end. Until I'd seen the Pyrenees, I wasn't convinced it would. But what a change of outlook compared to four mornings ago when I sat immobilized a few kilometers out of Aire-sur-l'Adour, feeling sorry for myself.

Just before I set off, Isabelle took me to Comblat, her great grandfather's house. She was restoring it from a dilapidated state. "It was a dream of my father, but he couldn't do it. So I will."

The structure dated from the 1850s of similar age to Hunt & Corinne's place, but of completely different style and material. It was a small square building, its walls comprised of neatly mortared layers of river stone. It had a low-angled, hipped roof of red tile,  and a broad, arched door and a few small windows. It sat isolated among flat fields and an edge of trees. "My great grandfather Valentin bought it and the land in 1921. They grew corn and raised cows." Its exterior looked solid, and the broad door made me think the ground floor might have been for animals, the upper for the people. But it had been left empty since the 1930s, even longer than Hunt & Corinne's. Unfortunately, Valentin's son Raymond died at 38. His widow Louise and their young sons left Comblat for the village, Amou.

The small building glowed beautifully in the morning light. "There's still much to be done. The whole interior. I raise money where I can. But Comblat is my dream now. My sisters call it my obsession."

Flagging slightly in the late afternoon, the terrain fortunately flattened out as I entered the floodplain of the Gave de Pau. I passed another communal laundry, a *lavoir*, the second one of the day, and I'd pass another one tomorrow. I hadn't noticed any before and wondered if it was something about this region that they were preserved here. The cement and stone of the wide wash basins had been restored, the heavy timber trusses looked solid, and the tile roofs were in good shape. These would have been centers of activity when laundry had to be done by hand. Water still flowed through them.

It took me a while, but I finally realized I was walking through vast orchards of kiwifruit. They looked like vineyards on steroids – fat *piquets*, thick vines reaching twice as high, broad round leaves, heavy netting, and big fuzzy fruit. I remember first seeing kiwifruit in the 1970s. It was an exotic item you'd be served in first class on a Pan Am flight, and not know how to eat it. I thought they all came from New Zealand.

"Non, France produces quite a lot," said Claire proudly, a freckle-nosed young woman in overalls. She gave me a tall glass of cold kiwi-apple juice. I sat inside her shed and drank it as customers came and went. It was the needed boost to Sorde-l'Abbaye.

Bernard, the chatty caretaker of the *refuge*, drove me to a *supermarché* in Peyrehorade to get a bottle of red. At his suggestion, it might have been a Madeiran. Whatever it was I shared it with him and the only other *pèlerins*, a couple, who shared their dinner with me. Bernard was very curious about my route and had gone through my *credencial* in detail as we sat round the table, nodding and making approving sounds. He was delighted to find the Tailleur name where I'd written it into the latest space. He asked of Geneviève.

It was a pleasant *refuge* in a repurposed old house with a wide arched door like Isabelle's grandfather's barn. It puzzled me there was such a nice little *refuge* here, but it turned out it serviced pilgrims coming down the Voie de Tours and a way that hugged the coast. I was crossing the flow, again. First the *voie* from Vézelay, then Le Puy, Vézelay again and now Tours and the coastal route, about which I hadn't been familiar. The couple was heading to Orthez, then on to Saint-Jean-Pied-de-Port,  as most did coming through here. But she had a terribly sprained ankle, very swollen. Her spirits were down. She was going to continue but wasn't sure how far she'd get. They retired early to a small room in the rear, and I had the main bunkroom to myself.

Part of what helped the 30km from Amou go by was my idea of finding a boat. Peyrehorade sits along the Gave de Pau which joins the Adour to flow through the middle of Bayonne and into the Bay of Biscay. Oh to lounge on the deck of a barge, resting against my unweighted pack, swollen feet bare in the sun! I was feeling much more understanding of the bus riders.

But the signs weren't good. Bernard didn't know of anything, and I saw no docks or marinas, not even channel markers on the wide river. And in the morning it started pouring rain. Not like the gale that welcomed me to Hunt & Corinne's, but more like the steady, two-day deluge heading into Rocamadour. A couple of days of that again would be a bit of a downer, especially with my game leg.

I was stalling in Peyrehorade's vibrant, if soaked, Wednesday market, contemplating next steps. If I'd only known when I passed through Aire-sur-l'Adour that the Adour flowed to Bayonne. But I was so much further north and east I hadn't imagined it. Like the Garonne, the Adour rises in the Pyrenees. But instead of flowing northwest to Bordeaux, the Adour is bent back to the west and south in a broad, fan-like sweep, joining the Gave de Pau a little down from where I was. Its shape perfectly illustrated the tilt of the land in this corner of Gascony. But I wasn't musing over geography. I was imaging having found a boat in Aire-sur-l'Adour and sailing from there. But I had been in a rush. What else had I missed, besides the Armagnac? Ironically it was the very rush that had ultimately slowed me down. I may have missed the Armagnac, but I'd found the cherries, the *gâteau* Basque, the Tailleur sisters and the *course landaise*.

I stopped in front of a *saucisson* vendor. Why not, I thought, and bought a salami labeled *Âne*. I'd heard about donkey sausage, and here it was. I did feel a little awkward as I tucked it into the top of my pack, remembering the curious fellows who'd greeted me at fence lines along the way. And what would Yves, the man who'd done the Camino with his donkey, think?

The rain didn't look like it was going to let up, but I figured I might as well get underway and see what happened. I let the idea of a boat float away to join other fanciful notions. A beautiful darkhaired girl was selling umbrellas. She was so pretty she knew she didn't have to give me the discount I suggested. I would have paid whatever she asked. The rain stopped before I crossed the bridge over the empty Gave.

It was flat easy walking, a 20km hop to Urt along the river. No barges and no boats, except for a few fishermen rowing their nets. Too bad Claire used trucks instead of floating her kiwifruit down the river.

Urt. What an abrupt looking name, and it didn't look at all French to me. It should be an easy one to pronounce, in contrast to Peyrehorade. Only three letters. But was the "t" supposed to be silent? I still made a mash of French place names. I didn't fool myself. Three letters didn't necessarily make it easier, witness my struggle with the word for water, *eau*. Friends live near Pau, through which the Gave de Pau flows. My pronunciation of that city's name still brings looks of sympathetic puzzlement to French faces.

It didn't dawn on me I was entering the Pays Basque, even having gorged the *gâteau* Basque a few days earlier. I flipped over a postcard in a small shop in Urt, trying to figure out what was this interesting symbol I had started noticing. Kind of a Celtic cross, or swastika, or pinwheel, maroon on a white background. The *lauburu*, it said, the symbol of Basque Country. So, I was here.

It was a refreshingly simple insignia, even elegant in comparison with so many others, crowded as they are with shields and swords and lions and horses and castles. It reminded me of neighboring Béarn's two red cows, which are likewise pleasantly unencumbered.

When I think Basque I think of Spain, not France. That's probably because during the late 1970s and 80s I'd read about the violence of the Basque separatist movement in Spain. I've been told that France didn't experience the same extent of unrest because its modern political system didn't try to suppress Basque language and culture, like the Franco regime in Spain did. The Pays Basque is also geographically more accessible than the traditional Basque lands in Spain, and thus more integrated. Or diluted. The Basque population in France is a fraction of what it is in Spain.

Urt. It was a sun drenched, sleepy *ville* the afternoon I spent there, spilling along a bluff overlooking a bend in the Adour. The *église* looked more like an adobe Spanish mission church, something out of Hunt's New Mexico. And as much as I tried, I couldn't find a cheap alternative to the only *hôtel* in town.

And neither could I find a bicycle to rent.

Since there were no boats plying the wide Adour, my next idea was to ride the bike path which looked like it ran all the way to Bayonne, squeezed between the right bank of the river and the D74. It was less than 20km, but riding would be much better than limping along the exposed asphalt. But limp it was the next morning, full sun blazing.

The Basque houses were appealing. They were stout, heavily plastered, but with the large stones on the corners and around the doors and windows left exposed. Windows were small, the roofs low-pitched, and no balconies or verandas. They looked solid and cozy. In front of one I came across a splash of gaillardia, bright orange and yellow, my favorite flower. I was surprised to find them

here, knowing them as natives along the sandy coasts of South Carolina. When reading about them later, I learned they had been named after a French botanist, perhaps explaining this presence so far from home.

Unfortunately, the colorful gaillardia and elegant *lauburu*, symbol of the ancient Basque people, were soon obscured by the roadside jetsam of Starbucks, McDonald's and KFC. Bags, cartons, wrappers, cups and straws were everywhere. The fine breezy weather carried the sounds of traffic, airplanes, sirens and construction. I finished the *saucisson âne* for lunch. It tasted greasy and full of guilt. And I was thirsty. But there were no graveyards in the floodplain where I could take water.

Two months after I'd entered the English Channel, there it was again, the sea. On a rocky promontory overlooking the *golfe de Gascogne*, we celebrated with shaved *jambon de Bayonne* and a gorgeous bottle of Châteauneuf-du-Pape – no more donkey sausage for this pilgrim.

My dear friend Katie and her oldest daughter Catherine had trained from Paris, where they'd  been living the last couple of years with three younger sisters and a neutered cat – a veritable girl posse. We were walking together along the coast, my last couple of days in France. A welcome benefit of my enforced slowdown was I could easily adjust my timing to accommodate their days off from work and school, and not be worried I wasn't "making progress". When Mona and her two had joined, they had walked a half day at a time. Part of that was having to shuttle their car, and the younger age of her children, but part of it too was that I was maintaining a fairly cruising pace at that point, even if it wasn't the self-destructive 40km X 30 days fantasy.

Standing on the promontory I took in the expanse of the *golfe de Gascogne*, the Bay of Biscay, the watery horizon, the Atlantic. The sea's pull was more than being something I grew up near. The special place the sea occupies in many of our lives is more than being a thing of beauty and recreation and restoration, or even livelihood. The ocean is where we come from. It's where all the life we know comes from. It's the reason Earth is alive. It is what sustains us all, even if we live our whole lives without seeing it. If the oceans slowly rose to engulf the planet, we'd find a way to adapt and carry on. But if the oceans drained away, leaving Earth a bare exposed rock, I imagine that would be the end of us too.

Someone once asked me what was sacred in my life. I had no ready answer, but after some thought I said, if I had to choose a place, it would be the ocean. Why? Because it represents both life and oblivion: the yawning oblivion I felt while crossing the North Atlantic on the *Independent Pursuit* when I imagined plunging over the stern into the black water; and the primordial sense of the unfathomable moment of life's creation.

In our current incarnation we like to settle down and live near the coasts. Something is pulling us there. It is, I think, this connection with creation, a sense of the wild nature we intuit in the oceans. A wild nature we have nearly extirpated from the land. It's a bit of a self-deception though, isn't it? For the sea is just as denuded as the land. Only we can't see this profound damage. Instead, we imagine that the depths beneath its surface are still burgeoning with God's original abundance. Nevertheless, something remains of the original. Something critical to our sense of being.

What is sacred in your life? It's kind of an awkward, corny question, but it is worth trying to answer. You may find it's not as you think it is.

Katie, Catherine and I hiked along the coast at an easy pace. Admittedly a lot of it was heavily built, this being a crowded corner of France. Perhaps Albert was somewhere nearby? But the concentration of population didn't bother me. This was a celebratory juncture, reaching the sea and Spain, and I was glad to share it with these two, whether walking past empty seasonal apartment blocks, or along windswept bluffs. And Katie is a take-charge person, so I happily shifted into follow mode. This was more of a relief than I expected, but after two months of calculating each step, it was nice to let someone else lead the way. I only had to intervene once, when a shirtless, flirtatious man holding a running hosepipe in his garden would have chatted with this pretty stranger for the rest of the afternoon. I'd only asked to fill my water bottle.

Katie's French was excellent, and, a talented cook too, she knew her cuisine. She found a *gastronomique* restaurant for an inexpensive dinner in Saint-Jean-de-Luz that might have been my best plate in France – seabass and roasted artichokes. Simple, local and delicious. And for the first time I tried *vinho verde*, a young fresh wine from Portugal.

My only culinary contribution those three days was a mandatory stop for affogato when I sensed Catherine was flagging. When the glass of gelato swimming in espresso and topped by a pile of whipped cream arrived, her smile returned. She forgot about what her friends back in the 7th arrondissement might be doing.

It was actually a stressful period for Katie, so I appreciated her taking the time, with all she had going on at work and home, to traverse the length of France.

"I didn't think I could manage it," she told me, "but the opportunity to escape the pressures of Paris, spend a few days simply walking and experiencing nature, with nothing to *do* except put one foot in front of the other, and have time with you and Catherine, it pushed me to make it happen."

Her work was high-pressure, she had a critical French exam in a couple of weeks, they were moving this summer, and Catherine was making tough decisions about starting college. "She's had a difficult year." Katie hoped this little piece of pilgrimage might create for Catherine a space for self-reflection. When I spoke to Katie later, she said the experience, as brief as it was, had definitely touched her daughter – and her too. The power of the Camino.

A short ride on a crowded little ferry from Hendaye marina to Hondarribia and we were in Spain in time for lunch. We sat in the sunny central plaza under battlements pocked by cannon shot. Flowers filled window boxes and the table was crowded with the delights Katie had ordered, among them grilled *pulpo* (octopus) and squid, *pimientos de padrón* (sautéed green peppers), and a sangria so soft and mellow I soon ordered a second.

But lunch eventually finished, and they left to catch the TGV back to Paris from Hendaye. I had expected to stay right there near the plaza, sipping sangria all afternoon, but the young man at the Oficina de Turismo had been unable to find me accommodation in busy, weekend Hondarribia. He was helpful but not as resourceful, and certainly not as charming. I would end up using these tourist offices very little compared to France. I walked a melancholy hour to the rugged headland of Higuer. I was sad to see them go, mother and daughter. Our time was brief, but having Katie and Catherine along made it an experience shared, of moments passed together, even if perceived differently. Though I do value my solitude, solitude stagnates if not refreshed regularly by the company of others.

I don't want to gloss over what I felt leaving France behind, even if it had been as simple as a short ferry ride. I left France with a heavy heart. Being with Katie and Catherine masked that feeling somewhat, but the sensation rolled over me unrelieved as I walked past marina, *la playa* and the port. I don't mean that suddenly I somehow belonged, or that I understood French culture or the issues shaping French society. Or that I could magically speak the language and offer insight and informed commentary. Far from it – I still had trouble saying the word for water!

But I did feel like I had a better appreciation of France, that I had at least gotten beyond the American caricature of the place (Freedom Fries!) and the dominance of Paris in our imaginings. France had daunted me. Still daunts me. But from Seamus & Claire in Compiègne, to M. Celo and M. et Mme Chenu in Boissy-sous-Saint-Yon, to Isabelle and her sisters and mother in Amou, to every man, woman and child who met me with a *« Bonjour ! »*, or who gave me water, France had extended its hand. It had generously helped me along, a solitary *pèlerin* not exactly sure where he was going.

I'll never forget that.

I'd also had other handholds along the way. My friends in Paris. Hunt & Corinne's tranquil abode. And the companionship of Mona and Katie and their children. These familiar presences reassured and steadied me, more than they know.

But now it was time for Spain. I had never set foot in Spain. And unlike France, I knew not a soul there.

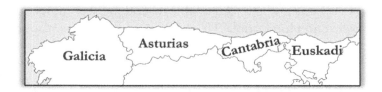

Txotx! **13**

"*Txotx!*" the burly man called and turned the key. A thin stream of *sidra* jetted from the enormous barrel. We were lined up and ready, each one in turn dipping our wide glass in the arching liquid for a finger's-worth, making way for the glass behind, trying to keep the *sidra* stream from reaching the floor in the transition. Then the four of us would regroup, down it, and compare it to the last round from a different barrel, keeping an eye on the big guy with the key to see if he was going to open another. The cellar was long, cavernous, dim, damp and cold, with a nose crinkling citrusy, sour smell. Giant wooden barrels lined either side, and a drain ran down the middle of the cement floor.

"For centuries the Basque fleets whaled and fished cod off what is now Canada. They could go farther and stay longer because of the *sagardo*, the *sidra*. Unlike water or rum or wine, the *sidra* had vitamin C, from the apples. The crews didn't suffer scurvy. It was our secret weapon, even if the reason wasn't precisely known." Joxe smiled.

We were back at our table in the dining section of the cider house, or *sidería*, or more appropriately in Euskara (Basque language), the *sagardotegia*. Waitstaff circulated plonking down platters of different courses of the set menu, the first of which, if I remember correctly, was chorizo. Through a glass partition we could see the main course, slabs of beefsteak slow grilling over open flame. In between a heaping omelette of salted codfish would appear. And more cod with sautéed green *pimientos*. And for dessert; Idiazabel sheep's milk cheese, quince jelly and walnuts, if you could fit them in.

Though it was toward the end of the Basque *sagardoa* season, the tables were filling up. At one, three young men, dressed unremarkably, arranged themselves in the aura of a stunning young woman.

"The tradition started as a way for the farmers to attract buyers to sample their *sidra*," Joxe explained, while his oldest son and son's friend tried to keep their eyes on the food. Me too.

She was tall, made taller by heels, with long, shining blonde hair. Her skin was flawless and tanned, and it seemed to encompass the horizon.

"They'd eat a little, sample different barrels, eat a little more."

What appeared to be one piece of cream chiffon was fashioned into a tiny skirt with swaths that metaphorically cloaked her breasts and tied behind her neck. She was like the ancient Earth, naked with ocean, only a few pieces of land visible on the mysterious surface. The three guys orbited like moons. How could they even have an appetite?

"It was a long way to come out to these orchards, so the food was an incentive." The four of us had driven to Astigarraga, an area famous for its *sagardotegiak*, inland from San Sebastián.

She could be walking the carpet at the Oscars, cameras flashing.

"She's got to be Russian. Or Ukrainian."

"I think she's American."

"No."

"Yes, I heard her accent."

I had no idea apples played such a central role in Basque agriculture, even culture and history, especially in Gipuzkoa, the name of this small Basque province where I'd stepped into Spain.

When they got up for a round in the cellar, we followed. For the *sidra*, of course.

I say "Spain", but Spain is a looser national entity than I realized, notably so compared to France. While France has its strong regional distinctions, it is politically and administratively oriented toward Paris. Madrid's authority and influence, by contrast, can be quite limited. Spain is organized by autonomous communities, some of which exhibit robust local identities, like the Basque Autonomous Community. This independence and encouragement of local culture stands opposite the highly centralizing Franco dictatorship which gripped the country until the mid-1970s. A sharp counterreaction to it even, rebounding back to a more nuanced and natural arrangement. So yes, while practically speaking I was in Spain, and Spanish culture, i.e., Castilian culture and influence, interpenetrates all parts of the country to varying degrees, I was first of all in Basque Country. Or, as it is referred to by most of the locals, Euskadi.

Sidra apples are generally more acidic than eating apples, and there is an endless variety that produces a range of ciders. I was certainly delighted when Joxe proposed we head out to a *sidería* in the countryside for my second evening in Donostia-San Sebastián, though I hadn't been that keen on the cider aspect of it. My experience was limited to English cider, which for me is too sweet. An evening of that would mean a big headache in the morning. But this was different altogether; tart, sour and citrusy, the Basque *sagardoa* was refreshing. It isn't carbonated, but develops a fleeting effervescence from the long pour, which is always short – we never filled the glasses, not even to halfway. A few sips between courses refreshed the palate. The

sagardoa wasn't that strong, at around 5%, and you don't drink that much of it in the end.

So, it wasn't exactly true that I knew no one in Spain. Joxe (pronounced Hosha) and Elisa had hosted another one of my nephews on a student exchange, and unhesitatingly welcomed me to their beautiful town when my brother encouraged me to reach out. I had been unsure about suddenly imposing myself on them with such a tenuous connection but shouldn't have been. The first evening we walked from their flat into the old town where we moved from tavern to tavern sharing *pintxos*, which are similar to tapas, and *txakoli*, a dry, sparkly and slightly bitter regional white wine. It went perfectly with the *pintxos*, many of which were seafood-based. In Euskara the *tx* is pronounced like the "ch" in church, so the call at the *sagardotegia* sounded like "choch!". *Pintxo* sounds like "pincho".

Though in mid-May it was still a month before tourist season really took off, places were jammed with patrons, including many locals, spilling into the narrow streets. But Joxe & Elisa knew where to find the best *pintxos*, and how to get served through a scrum three deep at the counter.

Donostia-San Sebastián is an old settlement, but the present cosmopolitan town was built out over the last two centuries. The Basque call it Donostia. Spaniards and foreigners call it San Sebastián. It can certainly feel touristy, and it is expensive, but it has character – it hasn't turned into a Disney façade like Rocamadour and Prague. It must have something to do with the resilient Basque culture.

I asked Joxe about his family's background, and Elisa's. He said it was nothing special.

"We are ordinary people. Our grandparents came from the farm. Families used to have many children, more than 10, and all the properties were inherited by the first son in order not to divide them. Basque Country's farms have small lands because of our orography. So, the other brothers usually became priests or monks, worked for others, migrated or went to the cities to find any job. And sisters became nuns, got married with other farmers or with men that migrated and came looking for a wife for their destination. Some of them went to the city. That's the case of all of our grandparents. They came to San Sebastián. They were simple workers and their wives. In three generations we have been able to reach a university level. So, it's not very entertaining but it's the philosophy of a hard-working country of things well done."

That family history may sound humble, or *nothing special*, but I could tell both Joxe and Elisa are very proud to be a part of it, as I imagine are their two sons. What more could you ask than to be a part of *things well done*?

I stayed across the bridge in Gros, a vibrant urban area with a great surf beach right out front, Zurriola. Looking at the beach with the beautiful water, the intimate topography of surrounding hills, the small bars and coffeeshops, the fresh food and animated people from all over world I thought, "Why leave?" But as vibrant as it was, and as welcoming as Joxe & Elisa's family, I pushed on after two nights. Any longer and I couldn't trust myself not to give in.

While heading out of town along the sweeping Kontxa beach promenade toward Zarautz, the day's destination, I ran into the Canadian couple from Aire-sure-l'Adour – she who had foretold my impending tendinitis. They were coming in the opposite direction. Her tendinitis had healed, and she was walking again, but they were running out of days to reach Santiago, so they were catching the train to Bilbao.

My left ankle and shin had improved too, only a general throb, but ever since crossing into Spain four days before, my right ankle and shin had gotten worse. It was a little frustrating the right becoming afflicted even though I had significantly eased the pace since Aire-sur-l'Adour, ten days before, but I was grateful both sides hadn't seized up at the same time. And, with the roundtrip ticket to the States in hand, I had all the time in the world and wouldn't have to worry about making up distance via bus or train. I knew I couldn't merely blame the 40km days after Hunt & Corinne's for this acute pain. I had been consistently overdoing it all through France and the effect was cumulative. Had I been smart about sustaining myself for the long term, I should have kept the daily average below 30km, preferably 20-25km. I need to accept that I wake most mornings stiff as old bamboo, not as the supple young palm I sometimes imagine myself to be.

Despite the two rest days in Donostia, despite the less than 25km to Zarautz after the two days of rest, my right shin and ankle were now truly on fire. It didn't make sense. It shouldn't be this bad. It should be getting better, not worse! *Aren't I being careful?* I whined to myself.

Too much *sidra*, too much *txakoli*, too many *pintxos*? Too much longing for Zurriola beach in Gros?

No, it was just a little reminder from the Camino, making sure I'd imbibed the lesson of Aire-sur-l'Adour, to *Be Here Now*, as Ram Dass always said. To accept the situation as it is, rather than what I want it to be. To let go the struggle of unceasingly trying to reach ahead and drop back into the spaciousness of fuller presence.

Slow down.

Quit trying to get somewhere that isn't there.

But *Be Here Now* is not merely being attuned to what's around you, where you are, and what you're doing. It is the capacity of moment-to-moment observational awareness of processes unfolding below the level of superficial consciousness, including your thoughts and reactions. Especially your thoughts and reactions. It is to see *as it is*. This is work, not passivity.

I know, it sounds a little fluffy. But declutching from our normal obsessive patterns allows us to perceive things differently – we don't realize what a chokehold we maintain on life and how blindly we blunder on. The capacity to observe, internally, not just externally, brings greater awareness, finer discernment. It allows our life to breathe. Easing up opens vistas to places like Veix and its road of poetry. Granted, fleeting moments, but if I had the skill to extend those moments little by little? Maybe even to connect some of them, into something greater? Then what?

It was a grey morning leaving Donostia along the sweeping Kontxa beach and raining lightly by the time I arrived in Zarautz. And it was coming heavy the next morning and expected to continue all day. Good. I was relieved and quite happy to ask the receptionist at the Txiki Polit for a second night. I watched two Dutch ladies zip their slickers and push off. They were doing a two-week section from Irun to Santander and weren't at all fazed by the weather, chatting amiably with each other as they entered the deluge. I went back to the room to stretch out.

Ana and Miriam had put me on to the Txiki Polit, a busy place on top of a boisterous restaurant in an empty wet plaza. It wasn't actually that busy and boisterous, but you could tell it would be in the summer season. I think it was the only place I stayed that used key cards, to give you a sense of it. Maybe the *hôtel* in Urt? But it wasn't fancy, just functional.

I had met Ana and Miriam my first full day walking after leaving France, the morning after Katie and Catherine caught the TGV back to Paris. I'd had one of the bunkrooms at the Camping Faro de Higuer to myself, woke up at a leisurely time that first morning, but eager to set off. I headed to the campground canteen up by the entrance at 8:00 a.m. with backpack, ready to go.

They would only open at 10:00 a.m. For breakfast.

Welcome to Spain.

Now this has left me flatfooted I thought. Nowhere to get anything to eat until 10:00 a.m., really? There were no other options on this isolated headland.

I took inventory: two nectarines, which will be as delicious as they were yesterday, and some day-old bread which will only be worse than it was yesterday.

Chugging across the river from France to Spain was like throwing a switch. The coffee got way better, and the bread got way worse. The *fromage* turned bland, excepting the Basque Idiazabel and some in Asturias. But the *nectarinas* were truly exquisite; tart, sweet, succulent with cool firm skin and never a mealy one in the bunch. And the fruit vendors didn't *tut-tut* when I fingered the produce, like in France. Water was freely available at public fountains, if sometimes over-chlorinated. Early morning and siesta were dead zones, but places were open later in the evening, so I didn't have to rush to the *mercado* (usually an Eroski) like I did to the *supermarché*. And the language – while I only had a smattering of Spanish, at least, unlike my struggle with French, I could distinguish spoken words and read signs, and basically pronounce them. *Agua* vs *eau*. And the people, to grossly generalize, while in France I sometimes sensed a propriety, in my first weeks in Spain I was struck by an earthy vivaciousness, almost a heat, as if in crossing the river I was transitioning from reserve to exuberance. And yet, I immediately found myself missing the ready salutation of the French, the *bonjour* and *bonsoir* for all. I was all prepared with my *buenos días*, but to my great disappointment it seemed most Spaniards were content to pass a stranger in silence.

Two nectarines and some bread wasn't much, but it was only about 20km to Pasai Donibane, just short of Donostia, where I hoped to get a bed at the Hospital de Peregrinos. Leaving the shuttered canteen behind, I stepped onto the GR 121 in perfect walking weather; clear and fresh. The coastal terrain in France I'd traversed with Katie and Catherine had been low and gentle. But across the frontier the earth jacked up. The grey outline of these mountains had been on the horizon since before Bayonne. Now I was upon them.

And being a Sunday, so were a few locals. Most *peregrinos* walking the Camino del Norte, I learned, start off in Irun, the Spanish city across from Hendaye, on the backside of this massif. I wouldn't run into any of them until converging in Pasai Donibane. I was the sole *peregrino*, with my big backpack and aching feet, on this Grande Randonnée, or Gran Recorrido as they are called in Spain. The path climbed and wound and dipped down toward the rocky cliffs and frothy sea. Much of the way was open and grassy, with wide vistas. It was windswept coast. In my memory I carry a spectrum of blues and greens, browns and greys. And a tactility of the crunch of earth and scuff of rock. Sometimes I could hear the sea, but always the breeze and my footsteps.

A couple of times through this reverie my subconscious would register another sound. I'd turn just in time to step out of the way of a zooming mountain bike.

At some point I began to hopscotch a group of four women. I'd be resting and they'd pass. They'd be resting and I'd pass. We'd acknowledge each other but hadn't spoken. They seemed to be enjoying the day thoroughly.

I eventually came upon them in the afternoon, relaxing around a picnic blanket. I looked at the remnants of their lunch before I looked at them. Crumbs. My *nectarinas* and bread were long finished. I guess my gaze was obvious, because one of them (María, I learned later) offered me chocolate. Normally I'd politely decline and wait for the person to insist before I accepted. This time I didn't hesitate, afraid a second offer might not come. I grunted and nearly trod the picnic spread trying to reach her outstretched hand. The chocolate squares went right into my mouth.

This little boost of energy gave me the momentum to detour off the GR 121 for the final stretch into Pasai Donibane. The trail swung high along a crest that reached the narrow mouth of the small Pasaia Bay. The way was so steep and narrow at places, I felt flutterings in the soles of my feet and pit of my belly, like the wingbeats of tiny, panicked birds. Was this really so smart? I wondered, negotiating the knife edge of the ridge in my backpack.

No, not really. It was typical impulsiveness and self-testing.

But it is really beautiful, I thought, looking down on the foliage clinging to the weathered cliff face. And I encountered no one on this spur.

Down along the flat edge of Pasaia Bay there they were, the four women enjoying a glass of beer in the sun. They waved me over. This is how I connected with Ana and Miriam.

Four evenings later in rainy Zarautz the three of us met for, what else? *txakoli* and *pintxos*. Wednesdays are *pintxo pote* night at the cluster of bars in the center of town, where a *pintxo* comes with your drink. While Zarautz can't compare with Old Town Donostia's vibe for *pintxos*, we had such an enjoyable couple of hours we decided to do it again the next night. So it wasn't purely the rain and my feet that kept me in town an extra day.

One of the first things I noticed about Zarautz was its beach. Nice and wide and long and packed in the season with visitors, Ana and Miriam said. "The population doubles in the summer. We only go at low tide."

Zarautz is small, maybe a tenth of the size of Donostia. It counts on the seasonal tourism.

But Zarautz doesn't get so crowded that they feel they need to escape. "Our favorite season is summer. The weather, the temperatures are better. The days are longer and we can do more activities outside. Like walking and cycling, go to the mountains, to the beach. Rollers."

"Rollers?"

"Skates," said Miriam. "I don't go, but Ana does."

"With my niece."

"I thought you might have been talking about the waves."

They laughed.

"I prefer land sport," said Ana.

"Yes, also me," Miriam agreed, "but we are mainly known for our surfing. Some years ago the World Surfing Championships were celebrated here. This beach in September has big waves."

Even in May, especially with the grey weather, the water seemed cold and full of energy. I could see why they preferred the dry land.

"And we are also known because a famous chef that has a beautiful restaurant in front of the beach, as a castle. Did you see it? Karlos Arguiñano. He makes TV programs, writes books."

The place hadn't registered when I walked to the beach – I was more focused on the waves. But now that Miriam mentioned it, I had heard about a special restaurant in Zarautz. Had Joxe & Elise told me?

"Every year there are more schools, more surfers. My oldest daughter tried it."

"Okay, you live in a famous surf town, along the Camino, and you love doing things outdoors. Surfing isn't your thing. But you haven't walked the Camino?" I teased.

No, no, they protested. "We are planning to walk. But for now, we can only do it in stages, on weekends. Because of work, and family. It may take a few years, but we will get to Santiago!"

The Camino is not at the forefront of people's minds in Zarautz, as it might be in smaller places, especially along the Camino Frances, the main way in Spain. Miriam and Ana admitted they didn't really notice or pay attention to pilgrims passing through. I was the first one they'd actually bumped into and connected with.

"But we are making a list of reasons," said Ana, explaining how they were motivating themselves for what seemed like a logistically challenging endeavor, doing the whole Norte in such short stages, packed into the occasional open weekend. She ticked off the list so far; "Know new people and traditions, practice English, know new places, be on contact with nature, doing exercise...When we finish the Camino, we'll tell you!" They ended up doing their first *etapa*, Irun-Donostia, the next month, on June 11th.

Ana and Miriam, somewhere in their 30s, have been friends since they were six years old.

"Six!?"

"Yes Jerry, our relationship is longer than many marriages," Miriam joked.

They first met in elementary school – their gang included María who handed me the chocolate – and started their outdoor adventures bicycling together. As they got older, they began walking in the surrounding hills, spending time at the beach. "When we finish the Camino walking, maybe we'll repeat it cycling!"

Miriam takes the train to Donostia, where she works in a natural products shop. Ana works quality control in a machine tools factory. "In Elgoibar. It's a village with lots of industries dedicated to manufacturing machine tools." That was another thing Euskadi was known for, besides its unique culture – its successful manufacturing base.

Despite it being off-season and rainy, I found Zarautz quite animated. People were out. I heard more Euskara than I had in Donostia, which I attribute to Donostia having more of an international population that would, if anything, speak Spanish. I say Euskara, but it's not that I recognized it. It's that it was the one wholly unintelligible tongue, so I assumed it was the local language. And I heard it not just among the older generations, but younger ones too. I knew it had been suppressed for decades – fearful centralizing governments do this – so it was encouraging to see/to hear.

"In Zarautz," Miriam told me, "and in general in the small villages and towns, people speak in Basque. In fact, in the schools all the lessons are in Basque, apart from one Spanish subject. Only in the big cities is possible to learn in Spanish all the subjects."

But this is different from not too long ago, right?

"Yes, very different. When we were young, we studied in Spanish. But my sister is four years younger than me, and she did school in Basque."

Exploring the wet streets, I came upon a procession of stilt walkers in large-headed costumes. They'd halt and commence dancing and spinning, the crowd drawing close. Further on people gathered along barricades of a blocked-off street. Intermittently a bewildered calf would come skittering along the narrow lane. Children and adolescents would run in front, yelling and squealing when the calf picked up speed, kind of Pamplona's running of the bulls with training wheels.

"The festival of the Santa Marina neighborhood," Miriam explained later. "They do it every year, around 21st of May. This kind of festival happens in every town and with different games in different dates of the year. Stilt walkers are very known here. Giants go dancing through the streets accompanied by music and the smaller ones go chasing the children hitting with water balloons. Some faces of the stilt walkers and giants are famous here. Karlos Arguiñano is one of them."

The chef?

"Yes. At night famous musicians have concerts and the people dance in groups and take drinks. During the day there are some games for children. The festival lasts about one week."

And the running calves?

"The little cows, *vaquillas* in Spanish. It's very funny to see and sometimes some runners jump over them."

The extra day and the hospitable spirit of Ana and Miriam boosted me. My feet were feeling better, and the weather had cleared. It was time to dip more deeply into the Camino del Norte.

Out of the six nights I'd been in Spain, I'd spent only one in an *albergue de peregrinos*, the night in Pasai Donibane before Donostia. It was the fullest pilgrim hostel I'd been in, though to be honest I didn't have that much of a sampling to go on. I did a rough count flipping through my *credencial*. Out of the approximately eight weeks I spent traversing Belgium and France I'd spent just over a dozen nights in official pilgrim hostels. I knew this would change along the Camino del Norte, despite my 1:6 ratio this first week. And though the Hospital de Peregrinos had been packed, the night had been fine. At least for those of us in the upper room.

This first pilgrim *albergue* back before Donostia was small, and I don't think it had a shared kitchen. It was clean, but the showers in the basement left a lot to be desired. There were basically two sleeping rooms, an upper with three bunkbeds, and a lower with more. I lucked out, getting the last free top bunk in the upper room with a beautiful large skylight right above me that we kept open to let in the fresh air. Hallelujah! We were a young Spanish fellow and four women: two Swiss, one German, and an American from Washington state.

"I just finished the Camino Frances," the American told me. "It felt so good walking you know, all the crazy thoughts, my problems, they went away. I thought I had worked everything out. But when I got to Santiago, they all came back. I don't know what to do. I've got another week before I fly home. So I came here. To walk more. To figure this out. It's the only thing that makes me feel okay right now."

I was a little taken aback by her frankness – we'd only just said hello. But I respected her candor. There was a lesson in what she was saying, in what she was experiencing – the walking merely functioning as a distraction rather than as an aid to honest reflection. It is probably a very common phenomenon: motion as solution. I know I've done it, still do it. But even if common it doesn't mean it's easy to discern and escape. Why do we like to keep ourselves so busy, always moving? Why are we uncomfortable with things like silence and boredom, being alone, stillness, even freedom? Reflection and contemplation is actually quite demanding. She was brave to recognize this and give it another try.

This ready openness among pilgrims was something I'd see and experience frequently along the Norte. It was almost a guilelessness, certainly more candid engagement than in everyday life. The normal calculations of maintaining status and reputation were diminished, if not absent. We were away from home. We were all a little uncertain. We all shared the soreness and fatigue. We all had sweaty shirts and smelly socks. Our clothes were overworn and our hair unkempt. We woke up together with bad breath and a need to get to the loo. No one really cared what you did in "real life". We cared more about what had brought you here. Because maybe what brought you here would help me figure out what brought me here. Maybe give me some fresh perspectives to consider. Or maybe I had some perspective that would help you. I came to recognize this directness among pilgrims – at first awkward for me after so much time alone – as one of the finest attributes of walking the Camino with others.

Back to that first *albergue* before Donostia:

Peregrinos normally enter Pasai Donibane from the other direction, so there was no signage to the *albergue* coming from the mouth of the bay like I was doing after leaving Ana and Miriam's group. I had to ask around a few times before someone put me onto the stairs that climbed the hillside behind the village.

When I finally find the *albergue*, the first three *peregrinos* I meet  are three enormous men from one of the Baltic states. Not just fat, but obese. Every element of them engorged; earlobes like little croissants, necks of bulging tires, bellies sliding like earth before a bulldozer, calves like Ibérico hams, fingers like pickles. They are sitting outside taking shots of some kind of clear liquor. I couldn't imagine the strength, stress and strain it would take to move those bodies, and their backpacks, especially over this terrain. I wouldn't have it in me.

Fortunately, they were in the lower bunkroom, a windowless crypt. I didn't go too near the stairs for fear of being drawn down. One of them snored the whole night. Not a light snore, but like a tractor. With a rusty muffler. And he started early. Having had his share of whatever they were imbibing, he was in his bunk before dark. So his roommates knew what they were in for when they walked down those darkened stairs to find their bunk. His reverberations were muted by the time they reached us upstairs. I counted my blessings for my quiet bunkmates and the stars through the cracked skylight.

The next morning the three giants had impressively set off early, but I soon found them red-faced, drenched in sweat, and looking a bit shellshocked. They had just started up the steep headland on the other side of Pasaia Bay and had stopped to drink water. I felt fortunate it was merely my feet which were challenging me.

It was only 5km to the *pensión* in Gros, Donostia that day. I walked a spell with two other young Spanish men and a very chatty young German woman. Young, meaning in their twenties. Most everyone seemed to be just starting out, having left Irun the previous days. New *peregrinos* have a different energy, a kind of eagerness mixed with uncertainty, maybe expectation and joy too. I think I had been this way those initial days out of Antwerp. I wondered what energy I gave out now? I found it refreshing to be around the carefree openness of these new walkers. I enjoyed the encounters and exchanges.

Two days later it was the same positive energy but a different cast, leaving Donostia for Zarautz. There were the two older Dutch ladies on their way to Santander. Another American woman, from New York City, toes killing her on the downhills. A young Swiss guy singing along who had started out from home in St. Gallen, from where my paternal grandmother's family hailed. And a French girl in sandals, carrying very little, not even a rain jacket for the coming deluge, looking a little bewildered by the circumstances but not at all intimidated. She was a waif if I'd ever seen one.

Most of the *peregrinos* I'd encounter in Spain were from Europe, but I'd also meet people from South America, Mexico, India and East Asia.

I don't know why I feel compelled to mention everyone's nationality. I guess it was the easiest shorthand in the moment among strangers, a convenient identification; "You haven't met an older Dutch couple, have you?" I'm sure we all carried our stereotypes about what someone from a particular country must be like. As inaccurate as this could be, it at least provided a point of departure that could be adjusted if one was willing.

But of more importance than nationality was the fact of being a pilgrim. That's where the connection was strongest. Granted, there was the whole spectrum of motivations for being on the Camino: from my bunkmate's struggle with her personal issues, to Rean's more traditional piety, to a woman somewhere who barely slowed to tell me she was doing it for speed, to the young Mexican girl I met in Santiago. She had walked as prayer, that her ailing father receive a donor kidney in time.

Whatever our individual compulsion, we were sharing a common experience. This sharing fostered a ready openness that was powerfully attractive.

Still, I felt ambivalent. The Camino in Spain seemed like it could be cut off from the life around it, too self-contained. Walking over-marked trails, spending nights racked tight in *albergues*, up and out in the morning, constantly moving, consulting your map, reading your guidebook, face in your smartphone, other pilgrims always in sight, the country and culture around you a blur. I hadn't experienced this exactly those first days in Gipuzkoa, but I sensed it could be near.

In Belgium and France, I felt like an individual wandering the landscapes, not just another pilgrim hoofing along a proscribed route. Joxe & Elisa and Ana and Miriam had spoiled me my first week in Spain, showing me glimpses of the world I was walking through. Still, during those first few days in Euskadi I'd seen more pilgrims than in all my time in Belgium and France.

I'd known that I would start thinking this way – this is *my* pilgrimage, *my* special trip, who are all of you!? Belgium and France had been solitary. Spain already felt crowded.

The coast road leaving Zarautz ran toward Getaria, a small fishing village nestled at the base of the sloping mainland. I wouldn't have noted it except for Joxe.

"Do you know the first man to sail around the world?"

Magellan? I ventured.

"Elcano, Juan Sebastián Elcano."

"I confess I don't recognize the name."

"He was a navigator. After Magellan was killed in Cebu, Elcano eventually took command and completed the journey. The first man to sail around the world. A Basque. From Getaria."

That's right, I remembered, Magellan was bogged by low tide and speared in Mactan, by Lapulapu's warriors, during a misguided attempt at forced Christian conversion. But that's as much as I knew, and only because I'd passed through that part of the world some years earlier.

Abashed by my ignorance of such an historic undertaking, I later looked it up. (Joxe recommended the book by Laurence Bergreen.) What an epic. Five ships sailed and only one completed the expedition (1519-1522). Magellan wanted to find a route to the Spice Islands from the east, i.e., by sailing west across the Ocean Sea, as the Atlantic was then known, and through a rumored strait at the bottom of the landmass south of Brazil, if it were possible. The Portuguese controlled access to the lucrative trade from the west, via the southern tip of Africa. The king wouldn't support an effort that might open trade from the east, so Magellan renounced his Portuguese nationality and successfully petitioned the King of Spain. The voyage, requiring risk and daring, fortitude and endurance, courage and instinct, and knowledge and great skill, also involved mutiny, execution, murder, betrayal, desertion, malnutrition and slow, painful death by scurvy. Elcano, not innocent of certain events, limped home on the surviving ship, the *Victoria*, a compliment of only 18 men at the end. He risked capture by the Portuguese in attempting the circumnavigation. After finding a route to the Spice Islands from the east and filling their holds with cloves, the ships were supposed to return to Spain the way they had come, not via the Indian Ocean and Africa.

Cloves.

The whole expedition had been sponsored and financed by the prospect of the immense wealth that cloves would bring in the European market. Elcano perished from scurvy four years later, somewhere in the middle of the Pacific Ocean, on a similar, profit-driven journey. He was just shy of 40.

I recalled passing a replica of a Basque ship under construction. It looked nearly complete. Was it his ship, the *Victoria*?

"No, the *San Juan*, a whaling ship that sunk in Red Bay, Newfoundland, later in the 16th century," Joxe told me. It went down with a cargo of 1,000 barrels of whale oil, discovered with the wreck in 1978. The Basque had maintained seasonal camps and tryworks along the coast of Newfoundland that processed the oil for Europe. But, unlike the later English and French, they weren't colonizers. So this history is buried under the stories of the later, more permanent settlers. There is a belief that the Basque were in that part of North America long before Columbus made his voyage.

As impressive as the ship was, and I can still see the replica clearly in my mind, I couldn't remember where it was that I had passed it. Zarautz? But Ana and Miriam didn't know of such a project nearby.

"You saw it at the Albaola," Joxe said, "in Pasai San Pedro."

Pasaia? Before I even got to Donostia?

Pasaia had been a major whaling port for several centuries. It's from where the Basque oceanic fleets set sail. I had spent the night there and had no inkling. But now I recall the Albaola. A facility sitting by itself at the edge of the Pasaia Bay, just before I would have turned up the headland where I found the three Baltic giants resting. It specializes in building historical Basque boats and ships with traditional methods.

The replica of the *San Juan* is based on details collected over years of excavation and research at the wreck site, which now has a World Heritage designation.

It looked tiny.

The size of a school bus. Okay, a travel coach, maybe a little bigger. I had to look up basic vessel particulars for comparison. The *San Juan* was about 90ft long, 250 tons. Elcano's *Victoria* significantly smaller, about 60ft long, 85 tons. Sixty feet. My pickup truck is 20ft long. The *Independent Pursuit*, the container ship on which I'd crossed the Atlantic, is gigantic in comparison. Well over 600ft and 26,000 tons. With about a third of the crew of the *Victoria*. It's impossible for me to comprehend what it must have been like on those vessels.

The tiny ship, the tiny village of Getaria. When the crews cast off on those voyages, they were on their own. What an alien concept in our world of multi-layered connectivity. How many of these sailors never came back, like Elcano? What would it have been like as family, waiting, not knowing? At what point do you move on? Or could you?

"The Portuguese and Spanish favored Basque navigators. They were the best in the world at that time." Joxe.

According to background reading María guided me to, the Basque, in the 16th and 17th centuries, had mastered their abundant oak and iron ore and built the finest oceangoing vessels in all of Europe.

The hills overlooking Getaria were covered with the vines of their famous *txakoli*. It was excellent walking terrain along narrow, coarse country lanes. But after passing through Zumaia, a town set down by a river, I was surprised to see *peregrinos* strung out along the bucolic track in front of me. Or not that surprised. It was happening. Ones and pairs, until they disappeared around some green hill.

Is it going to be like this all the way to Santiago?

Like a gift from heaven there soon, at noon, was a junction, with the Camino pointed left, and the GR 121 pointed right along a smaller, rougher looking track. Right it was. I was surprised to find the GR 121 again but delighted. I saw no one else for the next three hours, until I reached Deba, the day's destination.

But what I did see as the GR 121 climbed up and down where land met sea were some fascinating geologic formations; the Zumaia flysch. A flysch is a sedimentary deposit of alternating strata (I had to look it up). Along this stretch of coast, 60 million years of geologic history has been rolled on its side by tectonic energies and exposed by the erosive force of the sea. Earth's layers are nearly vertical, sweeping up out of the sand and breakers. Like a book on the shelf, ready for its pages to be read. While I couldn't really understand the words, the picture was enough.

The *albergue* in Deba occupies the upper floor of the train station, a stout little stone building standing by itself beside tracks which followed the river. A dozen kilometers upriver was Elgoibar and its machine tool factories, where Ana worked. To get in the *albergue* you had to register and take a number from the Oficina de Turismo. Turismo Bulegoa in Euskara. It didn't reopen until 4:00 p.m., so several of us lolled in the shade and sunshine on the curb, quiet and tired. When I finally got in and paid the €5, the woman handed me a receipt with the number 38. Thirty-eight, I thought, that's a big number for a little place.

The *albergue* was like a mill, a clean efficient mill with a couple of volunteers processing *peregrinos*. It looked like it could hold 60 of us and it was filling up. No shared kitchen either, I don't think; less mess to deal with I guess, and it encourages *peregrinos* to patronize the local economy. The bathroom was large and well-lit, as busy as a high school locker room. If I felt the *albergue* in Pasai Donibane had been full, this was of another magnitude. We *peregrinos* were everywhere; some arranging their stuff, some relaxed, some exasperated they couldn't sleep in peace, some on a great social outing, some in a daze.

Number 38 was a bottom bunk, and across from me a girl with a runny red nose was reading a book.

"Sorry," she laughed, rolling over onto her stomach, sniffing. "It's from walking in the rain. I was completely wet. For me it's very easy to get a cold and have runny nose. Unfortunately I know it well. But it's okay," she smiled. "I have my bed, my book, I don't need more."

Tereza, 25 years old, from the Czech birthplace of Budweiser Budvar. Her laugh filled her bunk space like an aura.

She had started walking, solo, four days earlier.

"Now that sounds more interesting," she said when I responded Antwerp, "everyone else I ask starts in Irun, like me." She put down her book.

It was the first time I considered that the two months I'd already been underway might seem a little unusual, or be "interesting" to a fellow pilgrim. Every day the miles were new, so it wasn't like I knew anything more about the route than anybody else. Granted, it wasn't how you passed the miles, but how the miles, in their accumulation, passed through you. Maybe that's what made it interesting. This accumulation.

"I can't imagine walking so much kilometers. But I want to. For me 900 kilometers for the Camino in Spain seems unthinkable. Maybe too much. I only did 70 kilometers to here. My longest hike before this, before the Camino is in the Slovakai mountains, called Nízké Tatry, 100 kilometers. But I want to know if I can walk so many kilometers in one journey."

Tereza worked at an outdoor store in České Budějovice and as a kayak guide in the Šumava National Park, near where she had grown up. Her mother had homeschooled her and her sister, and their father worked in the various protected areas in the region. On many weekends the family hiked and camped.

"My childhood was about being in nature. My dad said that I ask for my first small backpack when I was four. I'm not sure if it is true, but if it is, it tells a lot," she laughed.

Tereza knew a few other people who had walked the Camino, but it was really seeing the 2010 film *The Way*, which inspired her to try for herself. "Do you know it?" I'd heard of it, but I hadn't seen it. "I know, it isn't original. A lot of people set off on the Camino after watching this film. I wrote it down on my bucket list, but it was for me so unthinkable to realize this dream. But everything comes at the right time, and this was the same. I wanted to quit my job and I thought about my possibilities. What can I do with my time now? I had a look on my bucket list, and I chose the Camino. I don't know why."

She'd almost started the Camino Frances. "Only one week before my flight I changed my plans. I read a book about the Camino del Norte, and the writer said that the choice of this Camino was the best decision that he made. I thought about it for a while, then I decided for the Camino del Norte too. There were more reasons. There's less people than the Camino Frances, and the coast. I love view of the sea."

I told her I felt the same, how wonderful it is to finally reach the sea and walk along it.

"I am excited. I'm not sure if it is exactly just about the Camino. Maybe it is simply about walking, about freedom during walking the Camino. This is amazing for me. The Camino is the line which I can follow. And I am proud of myself, because I am not afraid to start one of my big dream."

When she asked me about my motivation, what brought me to this point, I realized I didn't have such a coherent answer as she did. I told her a little about my cycling trip in the Himalaya, how its difficulty made me swear my next venture would be on foot, and I told her how I'd ended up in Antwerp because of the container ship. But really, why had I come? Was I really just using the walking as distraction, "motion as solution", like the American woman I'd met in the Pasai Donibane *albergue*? "I really don't exactly why I'm here Tereza. It's like there is a force inside, you know, that pushed me here, that encouraged me to come."

"Yes, I know. And you have to listen to that force."

We were quiet for a moment. People arranged their things, passed in and out.

"What was it like before here, in France, it is very different, yes?"

I told her the most obvious difference was the generally solitary nature of my time in France. This, with so many other pilgrims around, felt more intense.

"Yeah," she said, dropping her voice and looking around, "some people here..." she raised her eyebrows and I laughed.

I asked her if she had seen the flysch today.

"The what?"

I told her about following the GR 121 markers.

"No, I followed the normal way, like everyone else."

I left Tereza in her bunk and went to find something to eat. Tereza may have just *"followed the normal way"* today, but in our short conversation she struck me as quite spirited and self-confident, not someone who'll merely follow the *normal way* in her life. I was happy to be sharing the Norte with someone like her.

The hum of activity in Plaza Foruen attracted me and I found a likely *cafetería*. Alas, the kitchen didn't even open until 8:00 p.m., a bit late for a *peregrino*, at least on my early-to-bed rhythm. A dinner of *pintxos*. This was another stark difference from France, how late dinner got going.

The plaza, in full shadow, was in full swing. Kids of all ages running, shouting. Young people in groups. Parents having a *cerveza*. Elderly women meeting for coffee. The sounds echoed off the building façades in the great cacophony of human settlement. I hadn't happened upon anything as animated in France.

It was too much. Not the activity in the plaza. That I loved, sitting there taking it all in, even if as only an observer. It was pure exuberance for the life we'd been given.

I meant the crush of *peregrinos*. I wasn't ready for it. Not that I had any special claim; I deserved nothing more than any of the others. But I hadn't realized how the previous two months had conditioned me, had shaped me for solitude. I love close contact with others, the intimacy of it, but waiting in line at the train station *albergue*, clutching number 38, no, I needed a little more time and space to reorient.

Giant headed clowns burst from a dark passageway and raced into the plaza, scattering screaming kids, the littlest ones clinging in terror to the legs of their laughing parents. "Does this go on every night?" I said out loud, amazed. Deba must be getting ready for a festival, like Santa Marina in Zarautz. Or maybe, I thought a bit enviously, they always shared such a good time here.

I had found an English guidebook to the Camino del Norte at a small *librería* in Donostia's old town. It was a well-done guide, in fact almost too well-done. The outline of everything you'd need as a walker, all you had to do was make a few choices, fill in the blanks.

193

It showed the Camino heading inland from Deba to Guernica and Bilbao.

No. I wouldn't go that way. Part of it was Bilbao didn't appeal to me. My brother had been robbed of everything he possessed when he visited, and he was the only person I knew who'd been there. Certainly it was unfair for me to judge the city solely by this. What crime had I faced along the Way? There had been that overwrought warning of gypsies and the banlieues nearing Paris. And the caution of walking through the *forêt*. True, I would meet a young *peregrino* nearing Santiago who'd had his new iPhone filched in a large *albergue* – he left it out overnight charging. But that was it, from Antwerp to Santiago, and in fact that incident occurred along the Camino Frances.

When I was first walking into San Sebastián an elderly woman had gestured to me to help her cross a busy street. Why me, an obvious stranger? For an instant I thought it must be a setup, a pickpocketing scam or something. But I regained my senses and offered her my arm. Being overly guarded almost kept me from that simple yet immense pleasure of helping. No, even if Bilbao did have a bit of a reputation, I wasn't giving it a miss because I was worried about it. I just didn't want to follow everybody else.

Put the guidebook away. Stay on the coast, I told myself.

True, it didn't look like a natural line of travel. None of the coastline of Euskadi was a natural line of lateral travel. The connectivity ran inland, along the short rivers, basically north-south not east-west. I could see on the Michelin 144 that the few motorways that ran roughly parallel to the coast from Irun, these all bent further inland at Deba, like the Camino.

Poking around I learned there was another Gran Recorrido, the GR 123. Maybe not as popular as the GR 121, but still, it was something. I'd follow it, as best I could, along the ragged, bulging coastline, see where it took me, head west and finish Basque Country keeping the sea in view and aim to rejoin the Camino del Norte where it came back to the coast in Portugalete. I could tell from the Michelin this would take longer than staying on the Camino proper, but that didn't concern me. It looked *interesting*, as Tereza might say, and with no guidebook, somehow fresher.

It would end up taking five days to reach Portugalete, and I wouldn't encounter another *peregrino* the whole time.

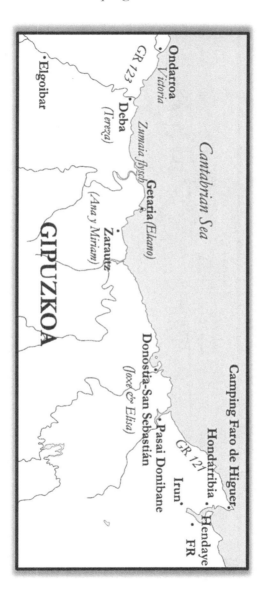

EUSKADI

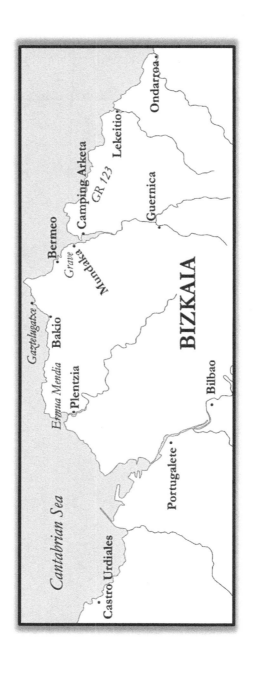

Eskerrik Asko **14**

One serious challenge in Spain is that they plonk a bottle of wine on your table with the *menu del día*, normally the most affordable plate on offer. *Blanco* or *tinto*, you choose. In the 1960s this bargain meal was initiated by law, known as the *turist menu*, as an incentive for tourists to patronize restaurants. Now it's up to the establishment, but most seem to still offer the deal. In France I heard it was still mandatory to offer a moderately priced *plat du jour* at lunch, though I never ran into a full bottle of wine being included. They are generous in Spain. You can take a sip or drink the whole bottle by yourself. It's part of the *menu*. But this generosity can derail any ambitious walking intention for the afternoon.

That first day out of Deba off-Camino I wasn't going any further than Lekeitio, so it wasn't an issue. I'd finished the 30km before 3:00 p.m., in time to catch the long Spanish lunch hour, the *tabernas* ringing the harbor full of people. I could drink the whole bottle.

The GR 123 had been well-posted. I'd made a sharp right turn uphill exiting Deba, while my fellow *peregrinos* streamed inland. I'd worried someone would call me back, telling me I was going the wrong way, and I'd have to explain, but no one did. The way dipped down from hills and cliffs to small towns gathered tightly at river mouths along the way – Mutriku, Ondarroa. I paused at an overlook to view the wave energy plant at Mutriku, apparently the world's first breakwater power station. It looked just like that, a breakwater, rather than a steaming powerplant, which is part of the point. But the ocean appeared sleepily calm. I wondered how it was performing on a day like this.

And then tiny Ondarroa, which I thought nothing of as I walked down into and up out of except to admire its setting. This village had given the world the *Victoria*. Elcano's ship, the first to circumnavigate the globe, had been built here. But unlike Elcano, the *Victoria* had sailed on for nearly another 50 years, ultimately disappearing on a voyage across the Atlantic in the late 16th century. I learned this much later.

Somewhere in the hills between Mutriku and Ondarroa I left the province of Gipuzkoa and entered Vizcaya, or Bizkaia, another province of Euskadi. Bizkaia is more industrial than Gipuzkoa, probably because of Bilbao, but there was no obvious difference where I was – around me was mostly green pasture and pine forest. In Mendexa, approaching Lekeitio, I was accosted by geese fortunately restrained by fencing. They were as menacing as the farm dogs of northern France, and I gave them a wide berth. It wouldn't be the last time.

The *tabernas* around the marina in Lekeitio began to empty out, as did my bottle of *blanco*. The streets, sun drenched, went quiet. It was siesta, and I was having a hard time finding a place to stay. There was a 2-star, smug and expensive (€88!), and unnaturally hushed. More to my liking was the salmon colored 1-star. The patrons of the *taberna* on the ground floor had forgone siesta and were boisterously forging on, like passengers making the best of the last moments of their sinking ship. I was hoping for a room upstairs to join the fun, but they were full. I made my way to the only other option, an *albergue turístico*, kind of like a YMCA, toward the far edge of town.

I waited two hours for someone to return from siesta, then underwent the world's slowest check-in process. The WIFI didn't work only for me (my little MacBook wasn't *that* old), and the washing machine door wouldn't open to give me back my clothes. The only other people staying there were a chaperoned group of special needs kids making all kinds of racket having a blast – it was the kind of building that sent sound bounding along every corridor. Everyone was very nice, and I settled right in.

For dinner I stumbled into the Pizzeria Santi, at dark, for the best pizza of the whole Camino. It might have been the only pizza, I can't remember, but nevertheless it was excellent. No, there had been those sad slices with the vivacious Lulu, back in Baugy, and perhaps others forgotten. But I love good pizza (my father makes the tastiest I've ever had), and the meal was a perfect way to celebrate my first day as a solitary *peregrino* again. I felt relief and back in balance. I don't mean that with any sense of superiority. But, having encountered the main Camino current of *peregrinos*, I recognized it is a powerful flow. I hadn't been prepared to handle all its energy.

Heading back to the hostel the streets had filled with people, spilling out of *tabernas*, bars and small restos. Laughing, drinking, talking animatedly. True, it was Saturday night, but I couldn't help but wonder again, does this happen every night?

There was no one else in my small bunkroom, so I could hang my laundry over the other bunks. The EXIT sign above the door was so bright I had to cover it with a shirt. The group of kids were settling down. I slept well, knowing there were good people nearby.

The blossoms and blooms that had erupted as I walked through spring in France continued in Basque Country, though a little more attenuated in the rugged coastal terrain. I stopped to watch a hummingbird feed on tiny pink and purple flowers. The buzz of his wings and blur of motion had caught my attention.

Wait, there are no hummingbirds in the Old World. What is it then? Just a big beetle? Was I seeing things?

A hummingbird moth! I had never encountered one. And here one was, flitting along the edge of the trail. When he stopped to dip his long proboscis down a flower's tube, I could make out his antennae. Fascinating, a perfect example of convergent evolution.

The Basque terrain was the most demanding I'd traverse. Zooming along highways belies its difficult geography. Hilly, mountainous, cut by short narrow rivers that disgorge into seas that are treacherous in winter. No wonder the language had survived the arrival of Indo-European tongues, and its culture millennia of regional war and conflict. The area was a natural redoubt where a people could carry on relatively unmolested. It was a demanding land not naturally coveted by those looking for lucrative conquests.

Traveling laterally, east to west, was near constant ascent, descent, ascent, descent. The GR 123, having been well-marked the first day, began to fade. I strayed from it regularly.

I stopped in Ispaster to try and get my bearings, a small settlement in an interior valley. For a scratch of a place, the *taberna* served an excellent espresso, and the whole town had open WIFI. It looked like I could follow country lanes to Akorda, an even tinier place high on a massif overlooking what appeared to be the widest river mouth on the Basque coast. I wondered if I could find my way across the river to Mundaka, or would I have to walk upstream until I found a bridge? That could be as far as Guernica, I realized, where 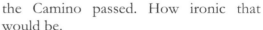 the Camino passed. How ironic that would be.

I filled my water at the fountain under the pollarded trees of the plaza. No, there's got to be a way, a skiff or something. What a luxury to have these fountains everywhere, I thought again. In Lekeitio I'd come across a small cast iron handpump, forged in 1888, displaying a crewed longboat, harpoon at the ready. In the centuries before the advent of the oceanic whaling expeditions, I believe almost all the coastal Basque towns (and many in coming Cantabria and Asturias) hunted whales locally, spotting them from lookouts on shore. This carried on until the Bay of Biscay had been virtually emptied of the creatures.

Further along in another small town I see a woman carry a surfboard into a building.

"Let me ask my girlfriend, I'm not from here."

I'd asked the guy standing by the car waiting for the woman about the GR 123.

"But I'm not sure how much longer I'll be her boyfriend. I think she is bored of me." He looks as if their recent road trip might have been a little tough on him.

When she comes back downstairs, he translates her directions, which are straightforward.

"You'll find it on the road, just short of Ibarranguelua."

She shoots him another burst.

"She says you should check out San Pedro de Atxarre Baseliza. An old church on top of the mountain."

More instructions.

"You'll see signs for it on the trail. After Akorda."

She disappears inside.

"I don't surf. She loves to surf. She's crazy for it."

She returns with a bag of snacks for me, almonds. I ask about surfing in the area.

She becomes animated and the words spill out too fast for translation. It doesn't matter. I can feel the passion of what she is saying. She is lean, her hair long and straight. She might have a broken tooth. Her ropey arms move with her speech. The only word I catch is brutal.

"It's her favorite English word. Maybe her only one. She uses it to mean really good, or cool.

She is the real thing, hyper-focused. I want to talk to her more, tap into her energy, but the moment is not right.

"She thinks I'm boring, but I'm crazy about her. I think she only keeps me for the car."

I'm guessing she was Basque, and he Castilian.

The remote peak chapel of San Pedro de Atxarre Baseliza was indeed impressive. Not the structure, per se, though building it would have been a task, but the view; the broad, sandy river mouth emptying to blue Cantabrian Sea, and green mountains all around.

Far below on the opposite side of the river mouth Mundaka clung to the hillside. It is home to a world class surf break. I could imagine the woman down there when it was going off, fighting for position with guys from around the world, not conceding an inch.

I wish I had gotten her name. But I didn't want his name, only hers, so I didn't ask. Not to go back and find her one day, but just to give me a little traction on her spirit when I remember her.

Online in Ispaster I'd seen a campground on this side of the river, at the base of the mountain. It'd be a long afternoon otherwise, searching around for other accommodation, but she had confirmed it was there when I'd asked her boyfriend. Now, far below, I could see it scrunched in a tight green draw.

When you don't have a marked trail you have to lift your eyes from what is just in front of you to what is all around you. How does this land lie? How do air and water flow along it, how do people and animals move over it?

John 15:5; *a branch cut from the vine bears nothing*. The Guru Granth Sahib; *the branches of a tree are drying up, that is cut off from its roots*.

I don't know why these sacred passages came to me at this particular time, in the dense forest below the chapel. From two very different traditions. Christian and Sikh, saying basically the same thing; cut off, disconnected from world and spirit, we as separated individuals are nothing but scrap for the fire.

Another example of convergent evolution, or better, convergent wisdom.

Halfway down the side of the forested mountain an unmarked trail broke right, and I followed. Like a hollowing wave face, this is where the energy was flowing, and sure enough, it took me to a bluff right at the back of the campground. Sometimes it's better when you're not blinkered by a map, guide or smartphone.

"You can use my son's tent. Wait."

I thought they'd have a dorm or little cabins to rent, but they didn't. When she realized I'd have to keep walking, maybe another hour or more, to find accommodation just because I didn't have my own tent, she was quick to find a solution.

"It's small but it works. I'll only charge you for the place. There is no one in back, so you can stay wherever you like."

Miran. How one person can make such a difference. Giving

me a tent to let me stay instead of turning me away. Calling to arrange a boat across the river. Looking up information on the GR 123, coming up with ideas for places to stay the next couple of nights, describing the clifftop walk for the final stretch into Portugalete. She was proud of her region and happy to do anything she could for a stranger.

I asked her about all the trailers. They looked semi-permanent, with awnings and informal structures attached, even a little fencing. And most seemed unoccupied, not as if they'd just drove in for the weekend.

At this she shook her head and sighed, "Yes, some caravans have been here since the 80s. Not camping anymore. But once in, you can't get them to leave. It's hard for the owners to make any money." I would notice this about these "Campings". Sections of them looked more like crowded trailer parks.

The bar outside the entrance didn't start serving proper meals until 8:30 p.m., so it was another dinner of *pintxos*. Lying in the small dome tent I could hear the forest settle down to sleep and the owls wake. The tent had no fly. Light flecks of rain ticked the nylon, and I wondered if I'd have to decamp to the awning of an unoccupied caravan, but the weather passed. At 8:00 a.m. a woman motored me across the river in her skiff. The break at Mundaka, without the winter storm swell of the North Atlantic, was deceptively quiet. I started up the mountain on the other side.

From Mundaka the trail climbed 1,500ft then dropped down to the port of Bermeo. From Bermeo back up even higher then down to the beach town of Bakio. Between these towns, in the mountains, the pastoral countryside felt wild, remote from the life in the settlements that fill the amiable spots at the edge of the sea.

Near the highest point heading toward Bermeo; a prehistoric burial. An information plaque might have told me it was a man, but I can't remember.

I see a low mound covered in grass and wildflowers whipped by wind that has blown for thousands of years. Sunshine. His family and friends stand on that high ridge after carrying him up. Or maybe he died nearby. Buried alone. Maybe the whole clan there that day.

Where is everyone else buried? Were they buried? Reasonable to guess some kind of notable figure.

Maybe it was a woman. Maybe I had misread the plaque, or just assumed it would be a man. It was probably written in Euskara so how would I know anyway? Women held leadership roles amongst some of the tribes of North America when European adventurers first landed. Why not here, thousands of years before?

In the mid-aughts I submitted a DNA sample to the Genographic Project. This wasn't a service to illuminate your modern family tree, but an effort to map the patterns of the earliest human migrations – deep ancestry. It traced my last common male ancestor to Africa 65,000 years ago, the Hindu Kush around 45,000, then northern Europe and finally the Iberian Peninsula around 10,000 years ago. The same era of this person's life?

It felt like finding the gravesite of a lost relative. Why not the resting spot of a great grand ancestor, a far distant cousin, or family friend? I stay by the grassy mound for a while. The feeling of connection is real. Not family connection, which can convey a sense of exclusivity. But connection to humanity, a much broader sense of sharing, of solidarity. A connection to the individual lives of all of us over hundreds of thousands of years. Though the world we fashion around us can change dramatically, we stay fundamentally similar through the ages. It's good to remember this.

The flowers are vibrating like second hands on the clock of human deep time.

The caves I passed in Brassempouy, in France, just before I met Isabelle and the rabbit, were described as Paleolithic sites. The Paleolithic, commonly known as the Stone Age, covers about 2.5 million years and includes our earliest hominid ancestors and relatives, up to about 12,000 years ago. Is this grave from the Upper Paleolithic, like some of the artifacts in Brassempouy? I ask myself. How old is the Industrial Revolution that has so radically remade our day-to-day life? And we take this way of living as the norm of the human condition, if not the apex. What of the tens and tens of thousands of years before that shaped us, from even before we made our first art on the walls of caves? Material progress is not a measure of greater wisdom.

Standing around this burial, the grief and sadness and uncertainty would have been the same as we experience now. The love and hope too. We may have better physical health as moderns. But mental health? I bet those ringing the fresh grave might consider us the suffering savages.

To the west past Bermeo I can see another high ridge. But its sunny face is smothered by a roiling grey cloud, like an enormous, never ending barreling wave. It seems far, but I wonder if the path will lead me there later today.

Down in Bermeo I sat outside a bar alongside a park bustling with pedestrians, just across from the drydocks. I was having a *tortilla* and *café con leche*, fast becoming a daily staple. When someone first mentioned tortilla to me, I envisioned a round of flat, unleavened bread, Mexican style. It didn't sound that appealing on its own. But a *tortilla* in Spain is anything but. It's essentially a potato and onion pie bound by egg. No crust, but it always comes with bread. Even that may not sound so appealing, but I found them fantastic. Sold by the slice, they were on the countertop of nearly every bar, freshly made, usually inhouse. Inexpensive, tasty, nourishing and filling. Sometimes I'd stuff in two portions.

Hours later I approach the top of the occulted ridge I had seen from the gravesite. The cloud billows over the edge, looking from below like smoke from a fire raging on the far side. I leave the warm sunshine and am soon pelted with freezing bits of condensation. On top the grey vapor scuds low through the trees, sucked over the edge by the drop in pressure.

In the reduced visibility it isn't clear which way to go. I follow a wide trail that runs along the ridgetop.

The wind is steady, but beneath it I hear an odd sound, something not part of the swaying, cloud-filled forest. I stop, but it doesn't repeat itself. I start walking. My vision remains restricted by the thick cloud flowing around me. I hear the sound again. Like a rock being kicked. Stopped mid-step I peer intently into the woods. The trees are grey outlines, then disappear altogether. I think of sunny, friendly Bermeo behind and below. I resume walking, slightly tense, my senses heightened. But nothing.

Then again, a muffled sound, keeping with me, I'm sure keeping with me, and now, I swear, a fleeting shadow. My heart pounds. The trail narrows. The trees draw close. The viscous clouds thicken. My eyes have limited value so my ears step in, reach as far as they can, tingly with effort.

Only the monotone of wind.

Then, there, directly in front, filling the way, an enormous, thick-bodied shadow. I freeze. The shadow jerks and snorts. A horse! She wheels and disappears, and others crash through the forest around me. I am surrounded, then they are gone.

Pellets of icy precipitation flick the blue jacket Corinne had given me. I pick up my pace and finally break out of the cloud wave. The afternoon stays grey on the far side of the mountain.

Down, down I went toward the coast, to Gaztelugatxe, a rocky islet connected by a foot bridge then a 200 stairstep climb.

"Our sailors and fishermen have sought blessings from the chapel there, for hundreds of years, before setting off on long voyages. And given thanks on return."

Joxe had told me about it. The site is over 1,000 years old. I wondered if Elcano had done so in 1519. Perhaps it's what brought him safely back to Getaria? And had he forgotten before the next voyage?

I dropped a 5-peso coin in a small donation box on the wall of the stone chapel on the top of the islet. The coin wasn't worth anything monetarily, but spiritually it meant a lot to me. Emily had given it to me when I left the Philippines for good in 2014. We had worked together on a project from scratch. She had blessed the coin, so that I may be kept safe in my journey away. In dropping it in the box, I asked that the warm wish of goodwill return to her and her family, and for anyone who passed here who may need it.

Back on the mainland, I was struck by the grave markers in the Basque cemetery next to the 12th century chapel of San Pelaio. They were unlike anything I'd seen. Imagine the empty space of an old-fashioned keyhole, with its triangular bottom and round top. Now fill in that empty shape with heavy stone. Like in France, these graves were tended with fresh flowers. It felt intimate. Still part of life.

Before coming here I had only known of the Basque vaguely, as hearty sheep herders on the high plains of the American west, and from the occasional reports of separatist violence a few decades before. Now at least I knew them as great navigators, skilled shipbuilders and manufacturers, makers of delicious *sagardo* and *pintxos*, gracious and proud and tied to their land and history. I would only be 10 days in Euskadi by the time I reached Portugalete, so I wasn't doing much more than skimming the surface. It took me almost that long just to learn how to correctly pronounce thank you – *eskerrik asko!* But I was glad to at least have that much exposure.

Unlike Bermeo, which was sunny and bustling, Bakio was grey and deserted when I walked into it late in the afternoon. An offseason beach town of boxy buildings covered in what impressed me as cheap bathroom tile. I had never seen such wholesale tiling of external walls. Was it cheaper than maintaining paint? Better insulation?

Later, in Portugal, I came upon what may have inspired this style – the beautiful azulejo tilework that covered many buildings, both inside and out, a craft that dated back centuries to the period of Arab rule. Alas the modern version in Bakio, and in the towns I'd subsequently cross, was not a success. It was made worse because the buildings started off without character in the first place.

That was another striking difference I'd find between France and Spain, the architectural heritage. Judging by the ubiquity of traditional buildings in France, it seemed the French went to great lengths to preserve them, even the simplest structures. At least that's what it felt like walking through, for instance those solid trusses in Aubazine. The French do value their *patrimoine*, which I think is reflected in the vibrancy of the *Compagnons du Devoir*, the program to apprentice in traditional techniques. I was unaware of a similar program in Spain, or at least one as popular and widespread. True, the charmless buildings of Bakio were not that much uglier than the apartment blocks facing the beach in Saint-Jean-de-Luz, but I'd find modern building the rule in Spain, at least in my sampling. Granted, most coastlines are overbuilt, and I was walking primarily along the coast. And I would come upon many exceptions to modern and ugly on the Camino del Norte. But someone told me the Franco dictatorship had a lot to do with the proliferation of ugly – an urge to break with the past and modernize. Plus, construction was a lucrative business for those close to the regime. There was profit in getting the patrimony out of the way for new projects.

I was the only occupant in a surf hostel. In spite of the hollow feeling streets and the rubberized mattresses, Ibon and his Australian wife Kim exuded welcome. He talked at length about all the real estate speculation in the runup to *la crisis económica*, the 2008 financial collapse, which in Europe they consider extending until 2014, at least.

"It's started coming back, finally. I think the mayor is going to get three years in prison. Just wait. Some people made a lot of money before it all collapsed. I think it'll happen. Yep. Three years mate. You want another beer?"

"They assassinated the chief engineer, and then his replacement." Joxe again, talking about the Lemóniz Nuclear Power Plant. I came across its carcass the day after leaving Bakio, before reaching the tiny port village of Armintza. A number of people had been killed in the late 1970s early 80s in protests and attacks on the site. It was finally scrapped, and now sits fenced and decaying, tucked in an isolated hollow facing the Cantabrian Sea. A monument to technological brutality.

Coming into Armintza I passed a group of English

motorcyclists in unzipped leathers, and asked a man pushing his sick child in a stroller where I could find lunch. He pointed me toward the small marina. I resisted most of the bottle that came with the *menu del día* because I wanted to walk for a couple of more hours. I followed a dirt road up out of town.

The forests were changing. With the sun and higher temperatures, it was the smell I noticed first. Disagreeable, kind of a sharp menthol about it. Not fresh or woody. In fact, aggressive, as if I wasn't welcome passing through, as if the woods were trying to repel me. The second thing I noticed was a lack of sound. Then the lack of movement. Where were the insects and birds and other creatures? Where was all the hopping and chirping and scurrying and buzzing and fluttering? Jean Louis, it's like what happened to your boyhood fields!

The forest was eucalyptus. I had seen a few stands of eucalyptus before, but this, coming up from Armintza, it had taken over. A monoculture. Like the colza in France. Complete domination. So alien and hostile all other life seemed to have fled. I love the quiet of the woods. But even in the quiet there is sound. This was unnatural. *"this biodiversity is falling down."* – Jean Louis. I lost my way several times on the crisscrossing logging tracks. These were not roads that took you anywhere. They were only for extraction.

Reassuringly the sea was still near. But falling further and farther below. Falling down.

Mostly natural forest returned as I reached the highest point along these coastal cliffs. I couldn't leave the eucalyptus fast enough. This crest was Ermua Mendia. After it I'd drop toward Plentzia and the flatter, more open clifftops that ran to Portugalete, the ones Miran had described.

More settled areas were coming:

Stout horses with the thick wavy manes of mermaids, their fetlocks covered in glossy pompoms.

Shattered gun emplacements from past killing sprees, surveilling the wild Cantabrian Sea.

Jogging, dog walking and bike riding.

Before descending to all that I set down my pack near a broken ruin on Ermua Mendia and pulled out a *nectarina*. Its juice dripped from my chin.

I stood.

A tuft of cloud rolling, catching in treetops shorn by the breeze. A white sail, far below and far out, leaning full. The horizon, an endless fogbank, waiting, wailing, hungry.

Who is it following me, skulking and unsure?

Yes, I see you. Come out!

I did not start the Camino to finish it

I started to walk it

And on the Way I've met many, decent and good

But you there, stalking in the wood

little man, small man, wishing you always could

I hoist you now and let you fly, away this wind

Let that torn cloud take you then

carry you to that cold grey bank

where you will still, until you learn to love again.

CANTABRIA

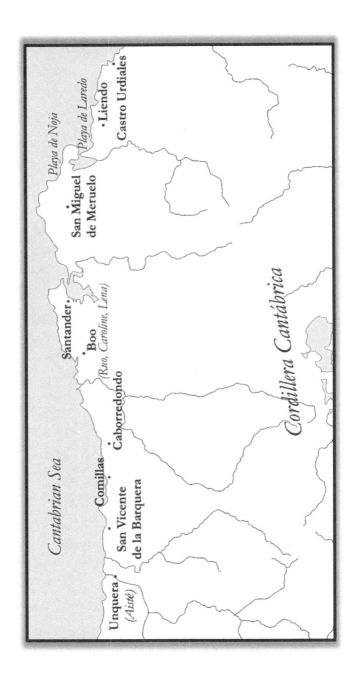

Cantabria 15

The final two nights in Euskadi I stayed in early 20th century *pensións*, worn wooden stairs and rails with iron stiles, high ceilings, enormous windows, brass peepholes, creaking floors, temperamental plumbing and retrofitted showers so constricted woe to thee who wants to bend over to wash thy feet. The matron of the first place tucked my euro bills into her brassiere. She later patrolled the dining room with a hawk-eye – the waiter bent and whispered, "We call her the sheriff." In the room an automatic air freshener sprayed a scented mist every nine seconds until I found the switch. I hoped the sheriff wouldn't mind me fingering her apparatus.

In contrast, at the place in Portugalete the amiable manager didn't seem concerned whether I paid or not. The room smelled of cigarettes from the floor's long-term residents. I couldn't decide if the indelible scent was better or worse than the automatic air freshener.

The first two days out of Portugalete and into Cantabria was too much pavement walking and my feet began to grumble again. The sun was strong. I was happy to have the Peyrehorade umbrella to pop open. The A-8 motorway pressed close, and its near constant hiss was in stark contrast to the wind, sea and forests of coastal Euskadi. Cantabria felt more crowded, more settled, busier, even a little more contemporary. Initially this was the effect of the densely populated corridor of Bilbao-Portugalete, which is actually still Euskadi. But it was also partially a result of the more accessible landscape along the coast. The shore was still rocky and mostly cliffs, but on top was wide and approachable. The ruggedness of Cantabria was further inland than on the riven Basque coast.

But even with the A-8 writhing like a snake, there was plenty of good walking country, especially when the trail broke away from paved roads. I don't mean to imply that the Cantabrian coastal landscape was open or flat. The land was still deeply quilted with watercourse and hill, forest and field. There were handsome old farmhouses with tiled roofs, the hewn stone of their corners and windows left free of plaster, giving them a solid, multigenerational feel. They reminded me of the sturdy houses I'd seen in Gascony and the Pays Basque, in France. And some had the wide arched doorways on the ground floor like Isabelle's grandfather's barn near Amou. Certainly livestock and wagons must have passed through these doorways?

In a rich pasture backstopped by eucalyptus I came upon blue bulls, taking their ease in the shade. Now these are regal beasts, I thought, with wide sweeping, black-tipped horns. Gunmetal blue-black coats. They regarded me impassively. Disinterested. *Tudancos*, the cattle of Cantabria. First those curious, butter-white *Charolais* around the Loire. Then the auburn herds of *Limousine* dotting the hills on the western flank of the Massif Central. Later that shaggy ochre band, half-hidden somewhere between the Dordogne and Lot rivers. And now these, with their sleepy eyes. Gorgeous eyelashes. In these animals you could feel the echoes of the wild aurochs who once roamed the Eurasian landmass, especially in the blue *Tudanca* before me and that shaggy band in France. I could imagine them grazing near the gravesite on the ridge above Bermeo, wary of the spears of men.

It wasn't until Liendo that I was able to reenter the stream of *peregrinos*. The time alone through the western part of Basque Country had settled me and I found myself looking forward to more company.

Liendo sits in a wide vale ringed by hills and the A-8. The municipal *albergue* is beyond the bar and church.

"You better claim a bed," said a German fellow. "I think there is one left upstairs."

Fortunately, there was. I was surprised to find the *albergue* nearly full. It was only 3:00 p.m. Lucky for me a Dane couldn't resist stopping in the bar, where a foursome of elderly ladies prepared for a round of cards at the high table in the window. Probably Mus, Miriam later told me, a popular card game that originated in the Basque Country and then spread widely.

"*Ja*, poor man, the beer is so much cheaper than at home, that's why. I would do the same. Now he will have to find somewhere else to sleep."

Latecomers idled outside then drifted off. I didn't think there was another place to stay and wondered where they'd end up. Unexpected kilometers at the end of the day, and a late afternoon thunderstorm bearing down.

A young American couple shared my corner. She was typing away on a folding pocket keyboard that connected to her smartphone.

"I'm blogging our walk. It's fun, but sometimes it's too much, having to write something every day." He might have been a

minister. I wondered if that took away or added to her experience. The writing, not the holy man. I wrote in a journal sometimes. Certainly not every day. Many evenings I had neither interest nor energy. Maybe her blogging  neither added nor took away. Maybe it just made her Camino a different experience. Like whether you walked alone or with someone. Whether you stayed in pilgrim hostels or hotels. Whether you carried your bag or had it ported. I thought her keypad nifty. Clackity-clack went the plastic keys, creating a story for others to follow in real time. Maybe those reading along would not otherwise experience the Camino.

"The *albergue* where we will stay tomorrow takes reservations." It was one of the Germans. "Shall we add your name?"

"Sure."

The next morning the drone of the A-8 finally faded as it bent more inland and the Camino stayed close to the coast. I lost my way first thing trying to exit Liendo's bowl, not paying attention to the lay of the land. Eventually the inner compass kicked in and said, *those rising hills in front of you don't make sense.* Back on track, I waved at the Germans having breakfast at an outdoor table on the approach to Laredo. Then, for the first time, removed my shoes and walked a beach.

Laredo had a wide, curving strand of heavy brown sand, fronted with low, indistinguishable apartment blocks. More charmless, boxy buildings like Bakio, tiled and empty, but not completely a ghost town. I walked a mile  or so along the sand, umbrella deployed, my feet delighting, to catch the small ferry across to the more charming but almost as touristy Santoña. It was mostly locals in line waiting where the ferry skiff would beach and drop its gangplank, but there were a few of us *peregrinos*, distinguished by our packs, walking sticks, worn attire and odd hats. I'd taken to wearing my surf hat nearly all the time, even with the umbrella. The sun was becoming stronger and stronger as the end of May neared.

Then another long wide beach, Playa de Noja. Except this playa was mostly protected, not built up like the beach at Laredo. I pulled off my shoes again as soon as I touched the sand. People strolling, a few dogs, a kayak, a couple of campervans nestled at the base of the sloping green hills. These are bigger beaches than anything in Euskadi, another difference of the terrain. Playa de Noja was at least 2km long.

Walking, splashing along the edge of the cool water, I could get used to this, I thought. Our feet have nearly as many bones as our hands. Yet we stuff them into constricting, rubberized containers, turning them into a blunt clumsy object. Is it any wonder they protest? Perhaps if I had walked barefoot the whole way, I would have been more respectful of their capabilities. I thought of Zola Budd, the South African runner who raced barefoot. And the kid Kaiser in elementary school. He ran barefoot too, kind of pranced. But he was always out front when we did laps around the field. There's got to be something to it.

The next day more beaches, also protected from overdevelopment, and these with novice surfers enjoying the gentle waves. Nearly every place I saw I said, *I've got to come back here, I've got to come back here*, one place after the other. But I know it's packed in the  summer. I realize by describing something as *touristy* I give the impression of dismissing it. But one of the features of a tourist-focused infrastructure was I could always find someone selling an ice cream cone in the hot afternoon. There's no dismissing that.

Another long beach walk to a ferry, from Somo to Santander, Cantabria's capital and largest city. I sat outside a small place in a plaza, refreshing myself with a *café con leche* and *tortilla*. The city was busy with a good feel to it. People walking everywhere, shopping, socializing, going about their business. But according to the guidebook, the stretch exiting Santander was supposed to be one of the bleakest along the Camino del Norte – industrial with busy roads. The guide might have even advised jumping a local bus just to get it over with. The charm of the guides I'd had in Flemish and French was that I didn't understand enough to get caught up in such details.

Well, I thought, the last couple of days have been quite pleasant. I shouldn't expect it to continue without variation. In fact, I'd had more pleasant days than I could remember. A *bad* stretch wasn't really a bad stretch, it was just part of the overall continuum. *Vamos*, let's go.

Cars zoomed through the busy intersection as I stood waiting, uncertain what to do. Camino markings had disappeared in the jumble of the urban periphery. I'd seen a pair of what I was sure were fellow *peregrinos*. But they had borne off left, which didn't feel right to me. The flow, the momentum seemed straight ahead, but there were no markings. What did I know? They had seemed quite certain when I saw them turn left. No hesitation.

Now I watched them from the corner. Should I follow? They hadn't slackened their pace.

The light changed where I was, but I waited. I noticed them slow, then they approached a passerby, a woman I think. After a moment she pointed her arm to the *peregrinos'* right. Ah, so they had gone astray. I should continue straight.

About 20 minutes later along came Ruo and Caroline, swinging

 tallboy cans of San Miguel *cerveza* and sharing a bag of Doritos. *Pèlerins* from Le Puy-en-Velay! They were the first pilgrims I'd run into who'd started outside Spain and didn't have a fixed date for arriving Santiago. Immediately I could sense they were a little more at ease, a little more confident, a little less worried about how circumstances were going to play out.

I knew it could be an added worry having a firm end date looming. Maybe you jumped on a bus or a train to make up time. Maybe you walked too fast or too far for your body's good. But not everyone would feel such pressure. I imagined Ana and Miriam's walks would be relaxed, even if short and requiring a lot of coordination. And conversely, my long-distance walk didn't automatically make me easygoing. I had burdened myself with a firm (and unachievable) date leaving Hunt & Corinne's, and even now still caught myself mistaking the finish of the Camino, or even the end of the day, as the main goal. Ruo and Caroline seemed like they had achieved a nice balance of robust walking without the self-inflicted stress of a tight schedule.

What was supposed to be one of the worst stretches on the Norte faded behind the ease and good humor of these two. So much for the guidebook. They walked at a good pace. Not a rush, but the long stride of those who had forgotten what days without walking were like.

Why Le Puy?

"At first what I knew is only the Camino Frances way," said Ruo. "But when studying what is the Camino, I found a lot of different ways. My favorite country in Europe is Switzerland, so I tried to search a place near Switzerland and that's how I found Le Puy-en-Velay. I think, this one will be perfect to me." Like me, Ruo liked the fact that while walking in France you were closer to the French people and their culture. "I could stay in their house, homestay. Here it is always youth hostel."

"And you and Caroline, did you start together, in Le Puy?"

"No, we met here, on the Norte. But she knew me before because she walked with Jean Denis, a Camino friend of mine, before we met."

Originally Ruo was looking for different things to do with her boyfriend, to see how compatible they really were. Walking the Camino was one such thing. But she figured out the answer to the compatibility question early, broke up with him, and decided she wanted to go alone. After finishing the Voie du Puy-en-Velay, she decided on the Camino del Norte instead of the Camino Frances. Like a lot of us, the appeal of the Norte was that it followed the coast, would be cooler than the Camino Frances, and be less crowded.

"But also I want to know how hard it will be." The Norte has the reputation of being more difficult walking than the Camino Frances, and I sensed this was the biggest draw for Ruo, this sense of challenge.

Their plans were wide open. Caroline would meet her boyfriend in a week or so, and they'd bicycle the rest of the Camino to Santiago. Or maybe not. "Maybe another direction." She had recently endured a sudden divorce and was trying to make sense of life's new landscape. She spoke French and German, and only a smattering of English, so the content of our exchange was limited. But it didn't matter. We didn't need to converse to feel at ease in one another's company.

"We have walked together every day since meeting," Ruo said

when it was just the two of us, Caroline up ahead. "I like Caroline because she is so free. We are the same age, but she has already experienced a failed marriage. And she have started a new relationship. I admire that she has gone through a bad time and has a new life again. Caroline to me, she is a strong woman. Even we don't speak English well, we enjoy and are happy together. We think we must be sisters. And we both like to walk fast," Ruo laughed.

"No kidding," I said, having to hustle and skip at times to keep up.

Before the Camino Ruo had never walked more than 10 kilometers. "I am much better than at the beginning. Walking for six weeks. My body is good. Now I am crazy for distance. We want to do as far as we can each day."

The afternoon passed easily, and low clouds started to set in. In a light drizzle I veered off toward an *albergue* in Bezana and they kept straight for Boo. I would have loved to follow along, but was mindful not to thrust myself on them, especially since they had such a natural bond and routine. Plus, I was already at around 30km for the day, starting well before Santander. Prudence dictated I take the closer *albergue*, as planned.

In Bezana I swung open the door and stepped in out of the heavy rain that had caught me, shaking out the umbrella. Warmth and the aroma of the communal meal being prepared greeted me. But then I noticed the little sign on the door that said, *completo*. Even I could understand what that meant.

There was no possibility, the host said, they were completely full. "Some will sleep here, in the common area."

As busy as she was, she took the time to call other places to see if they had space. Though the one in Boo was the furthest, it sounded like the surest bet. Those calls made a world of difference to me. It would have been easy enough for her to say, "Sorry, good luck." There was no obligation to do more. But she had done more, and willingly. She even sketched out the way to Boo for me, to make sure I'd get there.

Her *albergue* was *donativo*, which meant there was no set rate – you gave what you could. I hadn't run across this in France. The

Hospital de Peregrinos in Pasai Donibane, my first *albergue* in Spain, had been *donativo* too, though it didn't offer a shared meal so it didn't exactly have a communal atmosphere. Plus, the host didn't believe me when I told him, via gestures since we didn't speak a common language, that I'd slipped €10 in the box while he was outside – every time I walked past him he poked his finger at it and made a face. It felt like a shakedown.

The host in Bezana wasn't caught up in any kind of exchange. You can sense that in people immediately, can't you? They aren't trying to get something from you. She reminded me of Jean & Jeanne in Belgium, Seamus & Claire in Compiègne, M. et Mme Chenu south of Paris. They just give, having discovered the secret that they will never run out. If they receive anything, it is through this giving.

"Ah, it's you!" exclaimed Ruo. "What are you doing here?"

It hadn't been a great feeling to step out of that cozy *donativo* in Bezana, and mentally switch from the idea of a hot shower and hot meal to walking in the rain, but the prospect of seeing Caroline and Ruo again lightened my step. Sketch map in hand I arrived in Boo an hour later.

"You want a beer?"

Did I want a beer.

The next morning the three of us stood at the Boo de Piélagos stop trying to figure out the ticket machine. It was frustrating enough we considered not paying. We were only going one stop anyway, to Mogro, a ride of minutes. Just a hop across the river. Supposedly *peregrinos* in the past would regularly hustle across the trestle between trains, but this was discouraged, not only for being against the law but for being unnecessarily risky. At another age I would have blown off such considerations, but that attitude was mostly behind me. Plus, there was that incident with the coal train on the fatally high trestle in Virginia, the one I had recalled when Geneviève pointed out the medieval *pont* in Orthez. I had told that story around the table over spaghetti last night. But, trying to keep the English basic, I didn't clarify that when I swung down through the wooden ties there had luckily been a support pylon where I could just reach my toes. In the minds of my fellow *peregrinos* I had painted a picture of me swinging in the air as the train thundered to a shuddering stop above me, like some cartoon character.

"No."

"Aw, come on."

"That's not true!"

I'm not making this up, I swear! A state trooper, the police, came and got me. I climbed up on a ladder of a boxcar and the train backed up. He was waiting. My sister still has the news clipping!

But it was too late. My oversimplified version was too hard to believe. I was spinning a tale and they weren't going to be taken in as fools. It was like having shoes and tomatoes thrown at you before your song even ended.

Another *peregrina* arrived as we waited. She hesitated when she saw us, the only ones there, but soon we greeted. It was impossible not to since we were all doing the same thing, taking a shortcut. Ruo was going to show her how to use the ticket machine, but she had come the evening before and bought a ticket, to make sure she didn't have any problems in the morning. She looked a little ambivalent about joining the three of us, but by the time we hopped off at Mogro, we were four.

The ride was an odd whoosh of sudden, rapid movement and arrival, like using a sci-fi teleportation machine.

Now I could add a railcar to my pilgrimage mural; container ship, walking stick and shoes, a car and *utilitaire*, various small ferries (five so far), a gondola (the Vizcaya Bridge transporter across the river in Portugalete), and, I confess, an escalator – some of the steep streets leaving central Portugalete had moving sidewalks and I couldn't resist. And now the railcar.

The sun broke through a few times while it was still low, but finally it was locked out by the weather that had settled in yesterday late afternoon. Some type of industry ahead of us in Requejada pumped out enormous columns of smoke or vapor that merged with the grey ceiling, as if holding it up.

We moved steadily, but in no rush, sometimes close and talking, sometimes spread out, lost in our own thoughts. Lena, the *peregrina* who had joined us, wore a dark blue shirt that matched her eyes. At a loquat tree, heavy with fuzzy golden fruit, we descended like a flock of excited birds. We pulled and plucked and peeled, devouring the juicy flesh, spitting the large, dark brown seeds, slick and shiny as if coated with oil.

Lena was quiet. But she wasn't shy or uncertain. It was more a reserve. A kind of calm self-confidence. I asked her how she'd ended up on the Camino, the Norte in particular. She said she enjoys time on her own, especially in natural surroundings, and having new experiences. So it wasn't the Camino per se that drew her. She'd read a book by a popular German comedian who recounted his walk along the Camino Frances. It had been a great hit in Germany, even made into a film. That kind of book wasn't normally her style, she said, but it did encourage her to consider the Camino.

"It was not the reason, it just inspired me, but the idea was born before, that I want to, to have a walk, alone. Somewhere," she laughs. "That's the background. And, yes, the Camino is a very famous way, but it was not, was not important for me to do the Camino, especially the Camino, but the Camino is in Europe, it is close to Germany, and it's a way where you have signs everywhere so it's easy to walk this way if you're not a very good outdoor person. It's an easy way. So it fits perfect for me, yes, it was not a spiritual, spiritual? Is this the word? It wasn't a spiritual thing that it should be the Camino. It was more, okay it's a way that is next to Germany and things like that, no? The spiritual thing was that I wanted to have a lot of time for me, walking, being outside, meet some people, but not too much you know. And seeing what happens to me if I do this."

And why here, the Norte?

"It's much more cooler than the normal Camino, the most famous Camino, and I prefer cold weather. Not very cold, but not too hot, so. Oh, and also I didn't want to meet too much people. I know that the normal Camino is very full of people, so the Camino del Norte was my choice. Because the weather and the hope that there are not too much people."

Tereza, Ruo, me, Lena, we all shared similar reasoning for the choosing the Norte.

We followed Camino markers, sometimes confused about which way they were pointing. Supposedly they'd flip in Asturias and use the fan of the ribs to indicate direction, rather than the hinge point of the shell, which had been the case since Belgium. Mostly, I think. Honestly, I couldn't remember.

Ruo liked to use her smartphone, holding it aloft like a radio antenna. Sometimes we had to call her back as she followed its directions.

"It says this way," she'd say, wandering off.

Caroline, who must have seen this a few times before, just kept on, picking out the markers.

Ruo finally laughed and shrugged and put away her phone.

By noon it was raining again. Lena pulled a purple jacket over her blue shirt. Ruo sweated under a heavy-looking green poncho that also covered her pack, and Caroline used a sheet of transparent yellow plastic. I thought I was lucky with my gypsy umbrella, which allowed me to forgo raingear in the warm temperature and stay in my t-shirt. But all three kidded me about the umbrella. I think they were jealous.

Ruo had quit her interior design job in Taiwan. The middle child in her family, she was under some pressure to marry and have children.

"I want to make my parents happy, but I don't know if this is what I want. For my life."

She shared the story of a friend, also in her early 30s, who had been in a steady relationship for ten years and they decided to marry. But then the friend met someone else and hastily decided to break up, just before the wedding day. Unfortunately, after a brief affair, this new lover left. Ruo's friend later fell in with a married man and was still waiting for him to get divorced so they could be together.

"She is not happy. But it is too late now. I told her she need to wake up to see how stupid she is, but she refuses. You can see the same situation on TV. She broke everything and now has nothing.

She is waiting for this man. But he will never get divorce. She must make her own decision. If someone want to sleep, no one can wake them up. In the end, she is the only one who is hurt."

Ruo was determined to make her own decisions in life. This is what she was thinking about as she walked.

"I want to be in charge of my life. I should think things deeply to know what I need and what I don't want to be. Sometimes to make a choice, it is easy to not change the mind," she said. "I am still learning. I know my family, they might want me to get married. But the important thing is to marry with right one. If that one have not come yet, just wait. I should not rush because I'm the only one in the situation to face it. I should in charge of it not someone else."

We ended up in Santillana del Mar, everybody hungry. A gorgeous medieval village of yellow sandstone, but it quickly revealed itself as Rocamadour-like; prettified, everything turned into a boutique or giftshop, bar or restaurant. And despite the name, it is not on the sea. But we found a place that served pretty good food. My companions hadn't tried *rabas* yet, the Cantabrian fried squid I stumbled onto when I saw an order being served in Castro Urdiales – I'd pointed and the waiter brought me my first serving. The four of us sat at the corner of the bar and ate a heaping plate, tender and lightly battered. Ordered some *sardinas* too, strong tasting but fresh. In the back there was an open grill with giant slabs of meat – perhaps the flesh of the blue *Tudancos*? But we didn't go that savage.

I'm not sure who set the destination for the day, but by late afternoon we arrived at the quiet Albergue Izarra, in Caborredondo. It was my first experience with having to leave your backpack in a locker, and only take what you needed into the interior. No, Pascale in Gourdon asked me to leave my pack in her storeroom, before I went upstairs to that dreamy, all white bedroom. Her concern might have been mostly about dirt, but along the Camino del Norte, and

I guess all busy routes, the concern was bedbugs. Even if the sorting might be a slight hassle, and the feeling of the rubberized mattresses and pillows was weird, these inconveniences were way better than picking up a party of bedbugs for the ride to Santiago. Think about it. A different person in the bunk every night, for months on end. What is that, potentially 150-200 bodies a season? And not bodies coming from a tidy home, but from dozens and dozens of previous beds. In my case around 80 beds to date. Yuck. Better not to think about it too much. To be fair, I was mostly impressed with how clean and tidy the *albergues* were, especially the smaller ones.

There was only one other person in the upstairs room, so I claimed a bottom bunk there. Lena soon joined on an upper. Though the larger ground floor room had a view of the garden, the upstairs felt more spacious with just the three of us. Sleeping in proximity to strangers is an odd thing. You're at your most vulnerable asleep. Somehow you've got to make the determination your bunkmates can be trusted. And not most obviously regarding injury or theft, but also regarding disturbance. It's a compact you all agree to, yet without speaking it. Your arranging and rummaging, or talking or reading, or restlessness or snoring, things you normally think only concern yourself, they could be hyper disruptive to someone physically worn out, or perhaps carrying an emotional burden, trying to sleep in an alien setting.

As you select a bunk, if there is in fact a choice, you're interrogating those around you. What's your level of restlessness? Are you settled, calm, or agitated? Are you yourself interrogating me? How am I acting? Somehow you sense others on the same wavelength, and this is reenforcing, reassuring. Maybe this is why Lena came up. The three of us certainly enjoyed a tranquil night. We were all, it seemed, on the same wavelength. Plus, there were no men with big bellies in earshot.

Lena had graduated top of her class, maybe even number one, and started a prestigious career in Germany, on track to a judgeship. In spite of being in an enviable position, she finally admitted to herself it wasn't for her.

"So I quit. I don't know what I am going to do now. But it doesn't matter. The important thing is that I quit. It was my decision. Of course there was a lot of pressure not leaving the job, and all the things, but I couldn't do any other decision. At the end it was absolutely clear."

I could tell it had been an ordeal for her. Arriving where you had worked so hard to get, where everyone else thought you belonged, and then realizing it was false. To stay would be to live a lie. Yet how many of us do exactly that?

"My parents, my colleagues were upset that I quit. My boss offered me, how do you say it, a leave of absence? So I could come back. But I said no, I want the decision to be final."

She said she had been on a trip to Switzerland, where she struck up a conversation with an older man, staying at the same place. "You remind me of him a little. He told me, Lena, take off your glasses. He meant so that I could see. So yes, I took off my glasses."

She didn't go deeply into what must have been months, if not years, of pressure and self-doubt and struggle, but underneath her words I could feel it.

"I don't like sitting in front of a laptop or something like this. My eyes don't like it, my body doesn't like it, it just, the working place, this work is in a room the whole day and you don't have fresh air, you are looking to this laptop all the time, your eyes are tired, I just, I feel sick every day when I'm going to work and working about eight to ten hours, at least. That's just too much and the working place with the chair, the laptop and the room and the smell and the not so nice air, yeah it makes me sick. And, also, it makes me suffer being just in my head all the time. It's nine or ten hours at least just work in my head, just thinking, making decisions, writing down some things and whatever. I hate this. It's just too much mind fuck. Sorry for this word but it's so exhausting for me."

It wasn't that she felt sorry for herself. And she knew she was lucky to even have the option to walk away.

"I guess there are people they really like it, and it is easy for them, just being in the head making decisions and things like this, writing things down, but for me, being just in the head in this boring room, it makes me sick."

Too much stress, too many expectations?

"It's a mix of everything, but at the end, the reason is I guess I'm not made for this work. It's just my body's not made for this. I don't know what I'm made for, but this makes me sick. The whole day mind fuck."

The *Whole Day Mind Fuck*. How many jobs and careers perfectly fit this description? What about yours?

By late morning the following day the intense blue sky had returned. We moved loosely over the lush green land and its deep red soil, having been joined by a couple more *peregrinas*. We gorged more loquats and pulled at leafy boughs full of cherries. Lemon trees bent heavy. Shop windows displayed jars full of garden snails. The land seemed to ache with bounty.

Knowing Lena valued time on her own, I asked her if we had disrupted her plan when we met the day before in Boo.

"You didn't exactly look excited to see us."

She admitted she'd been looking forward to walking alone these days.

"In a way I'm very organized and strict, but in another way I'm very spontaneous – I don't know if this is the word for it. It's both inside of me. Sometimes I know in that moment, okay it's okay now, I just have to say stop if it's too much, but most times it's okay, when there are some spontaneous things. Yeah but normally I prefer to walk alone. I don't know why that's just the reason how my personality is. It's not a special Camino thing, it's a special Lena thing," she laughed.

I remembered all the miles alone in Belgium and France.

"To be honest, I thought, oh no, a group of people that I could like and then, that's it, I'm not alone anymore," she laughs again. "Because my idea was the best for me, that's how I know myself, for me every time it's good and it's a healing way for me being, not being alone, but having a lot of time for me and myself. I also like to join people, but not too much. It's too much to have people around me the whole time. I need a lot of space for myself. But I know if I like some people, then, how can I describe it? Then I forgot myself and my plan, and that I know what is good for me I forget it. And then I stay the whole time with the people, and afterwards I'm very exhausted."

I told her I'd become the same way, especially in these last years.

"It's the same since I'm a little child. My mother told me, it was every time the same with me, I always, okay, I make an example. My birthday, always my mother wanted to celebrate my birthday of course. When I was very young I did it like my mother wanted to do it, that's normal. But when I was eight or nine years old, old enough to tell my mother what I really want, I told her I don't want to celebrate my birthday like a birthday party. And she thought that I wouldn't know what is good for me because I'm a child. And then she did the same and she made a party for me because she thought it's important for me. And it ends in a way," she laughs at the memory, "that I, I remember I was at the toilet, I locked the toilet, my guests, about five or six other kids, they were in the living room, and me at the toilet, locking the toilet and crying inside the toilet saying I don't want to see anymore people. I don't want to see people. I'm coming out when the people are gone." I'm smiling, imagining her as this very determined little girl.

"You know? Of course a couple of minutes later I went out the toilet and the birthday party, it's, it ended like normal, because I thought I have to do it, but afterwards I said to my mother," and here she annunciates each word like she must have as an eight-year-old, "I-don't-want-to-have parties on my birthday anymore. I don't want to have people around me looking at me, talking to me and I'm the person in the middle. That's very bad for me. Too much."

I know the feeling exactly.

"And when I met you and the others I thought, okay, it's possible that I like them," she laughs. "But at the end, maybe I'm stressed, if I'm not, um, what is the word, if I'm not, brave enough to say okay it's too much for me, or going away on my own again. Afterwards it was very nice to meet you, I want to say. But that's the reason why I was not just happy when I met you. Yes, hopefully you understand what I mean."

I did, of course. And I marvel at the ability of non-native English speakers. I can feel their years of serious study, their determination. Even when their words are not exactly right, their effort at precision is such that what they are conveying feels crystal clear. So clear sometimes I feel they know the mechanics of English better than I do. I appreciated Lena was making the effort to share so much. It was a nice surprise to feel so much in common. Perhaps she was tapping into my German roots.

Our way wound into Cóbreces, where we passed along a salmon-colored *iglesia* with twin spires and a baby blue Cistercian abbey.

Lena told me about her encounter with a snake, on her fourth or fifth day of walking.

"My body was exhausted because I went up the hill in the forest, so I was sweating and just had to sit down."

She did some yoga. "And then I decided to lay down on the ground to be, to feel down to earth, you know."

Then she started a kundalini meditation, a type of meditation that focuses on coiled energy at the base of the spine.

"It was just spontaneous."

After some time she heard a girl say, "Oh my god, a snake!" And Lena opened her eyes and stretched out above her was a large snake.

"It was just a sign of, okay, you are on the right way. It fits, it fits perfect. You do a kundalini meditation and then there's a snake, and the sign. It was the perfect moment. I knew, okay, I'm at the right place. Everything's okay."

What a story. I thought of that big snake coming into Éauze.

"I don't know why I am telling you all of this."

After Cóbreces and its salmon church, Lena slipped off to walk alone and the other *peregrinas* followed a way that would pass a small beach. I stayed more inland and headed toward the quaint village of La Iglesia. In the distance on a sweeping bend, I saw a figure trudging along. A backpack with a pair of legs. Even at my easy pace, I knew I'd soon catch up. It was a young woman moving slowly, under a pillowy, heavy pack.

"I have too many things," Kemba said, wiping her forehead. We had stopped to rest on a low wall. "I must leave some things at the next hostel."

I hefted her pack. It reminded me of Rebecca's, overstuffed and unbalanced. Rebecca. Where is she? Is she somewhere here, along the Camino del Norte? She told me she planned to come this way, as we sat in that sunny plaza in Mechelen. Or is she in Taizé, having decided to stay on indefinitely? Did any pilgrims do that, embark on the Camino and find a place they decided they never wanted to leave? Part of me yearned for that, to know you had found your place.

"Can I carry anything for you?"

Kemba thought for a moment, then pulled out a thick parka.

"I don't need this anymore. But I don't want to throw it away. Or leave it anywhere. Please, maybe you can find one of those boxes for donation. You know what I mean?"

For a single jacket, it was indeed bulky and heavy. She was right to let it go. Where would I find a donation box? I hadn't noticed one since I started. Did they even have them here? I suspected I'd end up carrying the coat for a while. But I had plenty of room, which seemed a little odd – where had all my things gone? The Osprey's 50 liters had been nearly stuffed to the max when I landed in Antwerp. Even after unloading a few kilos in Paris it had still felt full. The pack was slack now. It was a mystery. I could have definitely made do with a smaller volume bag.

Kemba and I stayed together until lunch in Comillas, a busy, wealthy looking town right on the coast, full of elaborate architecture.

She told me that her time on the Camino had helped convince her she needed to pursue her dancing and choreography full time. The walking had helped clear her mind. "It is my only real passion. Now I must find the courage to go through with it."

She sat for some moments in silence, as if still processing the consequences of her decision.

"There is no money in it, how can you live? That will be their arguments against me. But I must try. Otherwise," she trailed off. Her struggle reminded me of Ruo's words, about being certain, and following through, or you end up only hurting yourself. What could I say, except offer words of encouragement that cost me nothing?

These women, I thought, pushing against the forces of convention and tradition, they must possess reservoirs of courage and determination.

Kemba ducked in the *mercado,* and I looked around town a little bit more. The buildings were so striking I later asked Ana and Miriam about it. "Yes, Comillas is a famous village," Ana wrote me. "The *Marqués* was very wealthy from business in Cuba. He built the palace and university and other buildings, and there are some from the famous Catalan architect, Gaudí." She said the *Marqués* was close to the Spanish monarch, because of all his wealth, and the royal household would summer there. "Because of the friendship Comillas was the first city in Spain to have electric light."

It was late afternoon before I reached San Vicente de la Barquera, a humbler town than Comillas. Looking for the *albergue*, I came upon a donation box, for clothing. I pulled Kemba's heavy coat out of my pack and pushed it inside. Someone would surely appreciate the thick jacket next winter. It was the only donation box I saw the whole Camino. My pack was slack again.

The Galleon *albergue* was halfway up a hill that rose behind town. In contrast to the nearby fine and airy, castle-like stone church, the Galleon was boxy, damp and packed. *Peregrinos* were everywhere, but they lacked a sense of cohesion. They were atomized, in their own worlds. Several slouched around the entrance, spent, lending to the enervated air. A woman in the kitchen gestured toward the tear in my t-shirt, where the pack was wearing through on the shoulder. With a sly eye and a heavy accent she said, "I like that." In Spain I had swapped the clean shave for closely trimmed beard stubble. Maybe she liked that rougher look too. I sensed she wanted me for dinner.

The large room where I was sent to find a place had the feel of a minimum-security lockup. Metal bunks with rubberized blue mattresses were tightly spaced. The light was greenish, and there was only one window, barred, at the far end. The air was humid and smelled of unwashed feet, of which there were many in view.

Where had everybody come from? After our pleasant night in the semi-empty Albergue Izarra, and the sunny miles where it was only us, now there seemed to be hundreds of *peregrinos*. There were only a couple of bunks left. One was an upper bunk across from mine. I wondered who would claim it. A snorer, a spreader, a rowdy? There was no carefully choosing your bunkmates tonight. You took what you got.

I couldn't be more happy than to see Lena walk in. I hadn't seen her since the baby blue abbey, midday. And she was relieved to see me atop my bunk. But the look on her face betrayed her more general feeling.

While there was another space deeper in the room, she didn't even consider it. "I didn't feel comfortable," she told me later. "The energy is very bad in that place."

Like me she preferred the small *albergues*. "I avoid the big ones, normally," she said.

Ruo and Caroline ended up having to spend for a *pensión*. I ran into Martin, Sascha and Tony, the three good-humored Germans I'd met back before Santander. They were searching Booking.com for a place. My notion of the Camino as walking along, finding your way with the markers and asking directions, then bedding down where you could, was taking a beating. Smartphones looked more and more like a necessary tool with the swell of pilgrims. I couldn't help but think this removed, or at least diluted, the essential aspect of human interaction. Instead of having to rely on your fellow man or woman, all you needed was a battery charge and good connectivity.

But really, wasn't this a natural evolution? I'd used my Nokia to call ahead and secure a place – recall Jean & Jeanne, Father Giuseppe – and I'd used my laptop to scope out the next day's landscape, for instance abandoning the Camino for the GR 123 after Deba. And now I had a guidebook providing me with all kinds of information and instruction. What, every day had to end up with M. Celo, baguette tucked under his arm, taking me by the hand for the experience to be authentic?

I guess there's a balance to be had, where there is still enough uncertainty to keep you open to unusual opportunities. Whether you've prebooked a package tour or you've set off not knowing a thing, it doesn't matter. Mentally you want to be somewhere between hairshirt and automaton. That's a lot of room for different approaches. Afterall, you could just catch a flight to Santiago, if arriving there was your only objective.

It was the Germans' last night. Seven of us gathered for a few late beers and dinner. Though around 9:00 p.m., it was still light. And there was no rush to get back to the thick air in the Galleon. San Vicente de la Barquera was as far as the Germans had gotten in the time they had off. "We'll be back on our next holiday." Though I'd only bumped into them a handful of times, the three were always helpful, and I liked their carefree spirit. You never knew when they'd pop up with a smile and a laugh.

Scattering **16**

The Cantabrian Mountains were broadening, and their ripples pressed a little closer to the sea. With them came the A-8 motorway, reapproaching the coast and rejoining the soundscape. We were leaving Cantabria and entering the Principality of Asturias, a larger, but slightly less densely populated region. This was the trend walking west: Euskadi, Cantabria, Asturias and finally Galicia, each larger than the preceding, but less populated. It's hard to overstate the lushness of this stretch of Spain – I hadn't fully appreciated it before arriving. The Cordillera Cantábrica traps the weather coming in from the Bay of Biscay and Atlantic, keeping the climate moist and mild. Once, flying south to north over Spain for the first time, I was startled by the transition from dusty brown central plateau to the green lands over the mountains. South of the range it looked like I could have been flying over parts of the Middle East. While the sun was at times strong along the Norte, I could only imagine how hot it would be on the other side of the mountains, along the Camino Frances.

I had become proficient at spotting fruit trees. In Unquera, just before crossing the Deva River into Asturias, I found a narrow grove of cherry in a park as you entered town. Pack off, I roamed the shade beneath them, eating my fill, using the trekking pole to bend down the higher branches. On the other side of the street *peregrinos* streamed by, alone, in pairs, sometimes larger groups. They followed the markers. The cool shade and sweet fruit was so close, but they did not see. I felt a little selfish with the bounty but was happy to remain undiscovered.

It was the last day of May, and the summer holiday season in Europe was picking up. Though August was the peak, June, and especially July could get very busy. By now I shouldn't have been surprised at the number of *peregrinos*, but I was. The morning had started early back at the Galleon, some *peregrinos* up at dawn, trying to be quiet, hurrying to get underway. There seemed to be an urgency, an anxiety governing their movements. It must have been concern over finding a place to sleep. Trying to get to the next *albergue* early, before it filled up, especially the big public ones. I didn't like that feeling of being rushed, of worrying about where you would end up. It seemed self-imposed, like that sense of urgency that sometimes overcomes you in life, of trying to finish just one more item on your punch list, so that at the end of the day, or the end of your existence, everything is exactly how you want it. This moment never arrives, but it's easy to convince yourself that with the proper exertion, it will. *I'll get the perfect bunk if I beat everyone else there.* But what about the walk itself?

After crossing the Deva River with my cherry-stained fingers, I climbed a long hill with a German fellow who had met a woman while walking the Camino a couple of years before. They married. She was from Bulgaria. He had left her at home with their young child while he did a short segment on the Norte. "I love the Camino. I love Spain." They had moved to Spain because he loved it so much, though he still worked for his German company.

"Technically speaking, I am on *Elternzeit* right now."

He's on paternity leave, on the Camino, and *she's* at home with the baby? We parted before I could get the rest of the story.

And that's what the Camino in Spain had become:

The stories.

Everyone celebrating their stories. Or wrestling with them. Or chasing them. Or trying to decipher them. Stepping away from them, sharing them, going beyond them. Through the individual stories connecting with each other and maybe finding understanding and insight, or the courage to go deeper, or to escape. Or merely to create the space in order to allow yourself to shake loose and metamorphosize into the next lifecycle.

Yet mostly we hide inside and cling to our stories, tenaciously, whether they're true or representative or not. We are stubborn. Reluctant to change or admit failure. To take risks or evolve. To let go. I say we, but of course I mean me. I must admit, I was getting tired of hearing my own story by this point – where I was from, what I had done, what I knew, where was I going.

Richard Rohr, a contemporary Franciscan friar, points out it usually it takes a force as powerful as loss or love to reveal a new way of being, if we are open to it. The catalyst can also be something more meditative, like the Camino, where you start to repeatedly bump up against the limits of your self, both mentally and physically. This constant force, like river on rock, wears down your rigidities and the narrative notions of who you are, who you have to be, and allows you to drop deeper and deeper into...what?

I don't know.

This is where I reach for one of my favorite phrases of Rohr: *Faith is patience with mystery.*

For some faith is a kind of certainty, an explanation for everything. This kind of faith can absolve you of responsibility. I prefer Rohr's perspective, where faith is more of a sense of peace and acceptance that at the same time requires action. It requires patience, which implies a willingness to constantly examine.

I don't know where you end up, through prayer, through meditation, through walking, through love, through pain, through death. But having the faith to embark on the mysterious journey in the first place, with genuine openness of heart, that, to me, seems a good place to start. A good place to start writing a truer story.

As long as you aren't obsessing too much about finding a bed.

Somewhere that first day in Asturias one of our gang had introduced me to Aistė.

"Let's have a *sidra*, yes?"

I readily agreed and followed her into the roadside bar, near La Franca. It was midafternoon, fairly warm, and I hadn't had a *sidra* since the night with Joxe in Donostia, two weeks before. And we could relax. Ruo had called ahead to an *albergue* in Pendueles and put our names on the list. A prudent thing to do, I conceded, given the crushing tide of *peregrinos*. For the moment it was only Aistė and me, the rest strung out at their own pace.

"We have to take the whole bottle. They don't sell by the glass."

I shrugged okay. Someone else would come along. We sat at a table outside. I asked her where she had started from today.

She looked blank for a moment and then laughed. "I can't remember."

It was true. I too had drawn a blank many times when someone asked me the same. You stayed in so many places, night upon night, that it became impossible to remember clearly. The preceding days were a blur. The preceding weeks a blank. If I didn't have my *credencial* and its stamps, there's no way I could have recalled my particular route. To the reader, I apologize for all the strange place names that pass rapidly across the pages. I sympathize.

Aistė hadn't been with us in San Vicente de la Barquera. She had started somewhere well before. I now recalled seeing her pass in Unquera earlier, while I snacked on cherries, her legs striding out. This was a long day for her.

"All of them have something to tell." I was curious about her tattoos. "The story, emotion, fact, they each represent some kind of period of my life." Her right shoulder to mid upper arm was completely covered in solid color, like the dark green of a dollar bill.

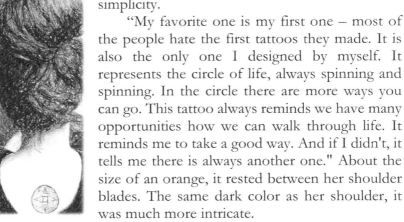

With a plain border, it was striking in its simplicity.

"My favorite one is my first one – most of the people hate the first tattoos they made. It is also the only one I designed by myself. It represents the circle of life, always spinning and spinning. In the circle there are more ways you can go. This tattoo always reminds we have many opportunities how we can walk through life. It reminds me to take a good way. And if I didn't, it tells me there is always another one." About the size of an orange, it rested between her shoulder blades. The same dark color as her shoulder, it was much more intricate.

"For me, this is an opportunity to turn my body into a work of art and in this way feel great about the body I have. With the tattoos I feel much more comfortable with myself than before. I already have many and I want more. I know, some of the people can tell that you have some psychological problems. I believe if the person finds a way to feel better with himself, the person should take and go that way. I found mine and I'm happy about it." She would get a tattoo of a shell after she reached the end of her Camino in Finisterre.

Aistė was good company. Sociable and gregarious, curious and openhearted. From Lithuania, she looked like she could have been a member of the national volleyball team – tall and fit, cheeks flushed, she was the picture of youthful vigor.

Aistė turned 19 just before starting the Camino.

"After I finished school, in summer me and my good friend Jurgita did the Euro-trip. We travelled from Lithuania hitchhiking to Germany, and from Germany we started to travel by trains to Portugal. My first journey inspired me, and I knew one thing – I want more. More to explore, to see, to experience, go alone, be free. Before the Camino I worked a lot in Vilnius, my hometown. During the week as a waitress and on weekend nights as a ticket seller on the doors at a techno dance club, Kablys. I knew I will walk the Camino, so I tried to work a lot to earn some money. Of course it didn't work that well," she laughed. "Before I started this walk my life was very intense emotionally. I was fighting with myself a lot. But every day I knew that I will walk and something will change. But before starting it was all about work, parties and dealing with myself. The only thing I remember doing is dancing with loud music. But I have a really bad memory," she laughed some more.

The green *sidra* bottle came with a shiny metal apparatus I had no idea how to use. Aistė was expert. You slid the bottle neck up a tube and fixed the bottle bottom in place, then put a wide-mouth glass in a cradle about 18 inches below the outlet of another tube. Press the button and out came a stream of *sidra*, like from the keg at the *sagardotegia* in Astigarraga. The jet aerated it. Perfectly refreshing on the warm afternoon. A little more fruity than the Basque *sagardoa*.

"Some of the people from work didn't believe that I will go to do the Camino. They said I will not make it because I wasn't prepared at all. I didn't do sports or walking. At times I questioned whether I could do it, but I always believed. I had and I think I still have some strength in my mind that kept me going that time and it keeps me going now. Anyway, when the time came, I quit my job and flied to Paris and took a bus to Hendaye. I started to walk from Hendaye. My first solo travelling journey started."

"Hendaye, not Irun? Did you take the little ferry across to Hondarribia?" I hadn't met anyone else who had done that. "And the GR 121 along the coast?"

"Yes, the ferry, to Hondarribia. It was a pleasant moment to cross the river with it. I think I walked also along GR 121, but I can be wrong. I got lost somewhere there. It happens a lot of times because I don't have a map and my smartphone is broken, so I only follow the yellow arrow. Most of the pilgrims at least have a physical map or Google Maps. I love not having all that! We are so addicted to our phones, maps, GPS – we all should go somewhere without any of it. Follow the road, the signs, symbols, rely on intuition. It's a better way how you can meet people. You ask people where to go, and sometime they can become your friends on that day of the road. Who knows? You can be more open to the world that is going on and its surprises. But I think I am bit too strong about this."

"No, no, I agree completely. I don't have a smartphone either. I do use maps. But you still have to ask. And you can still get lost. I remember helping my uncle get around a new city, Albuquerque, for a few days. He drove and I read directions off the car GPS. One afternoon it stopped working. I looked up and had no idea where we were. We were helpless. I mean these are great tools. I'm sure I'll eventually get a smartphone. But they can make you stupid too, if you become too dependent on them."

I asked her what she thought about the Camino del Norte, why she wasn't on the Camino Frances. Like I asked everybody.

"My older sister with her friend walked the Camino Frances. I asked her which road should I take if I walk alone. She said North. And that's it. I was looking for the road which is not much crowded, where I can meet more solo pilgrims, where I can walk alone. I think Camino Frances it is way different from what I was looking for. It is a popular way, many what we call *tourigrinos*." I laughed, having not heard the term before. "It is a way more for a group of people or friends, but in my view not for a solo-traveler. I believe you can't find much peace and silence there as you can in Camino del Norte. Again, I can be wrong. I believe in any Way you can get an amazing experience. It is your decision if let yourself immerse in that experience or not, and how much open you are for things to happen on the road."

The cool *sidra*, the balmy afternoon, I was thoroughly enjoying sitting there with Aistė. She was quite self-possessed and reflective. Way more than I was at 19. Way more than I am now.

"In Camino del Norte it is a lot of time and space for you to think, to release, to heal without distractions and chaos. And the way is sooo beautiful."

I could feel the intensity in the way she said beautiful. It wasn't a platitude. She truly meant it.

"Sometimes I'm talking with myself, singing or dancing, crying or laughing. Sometimes I walk a very long day and I am exhausted. But when walking it is a pleasure, and that is why it is hard to stop. Basque Country was very difficult for me physically and emotionally. It was the start. I didn't have good socks. I got a lot of blisters, blood blisters and pain. At one moment I got around 10 on both feet. A few Spanish guys, in a beautiful monastery I stayed, were my doctors. They thread the needle with thread into all of my blisters and healed me."

The image made me shudder. I remembered when I first saw such a thing, in La Romieu, France. But I don't think that young woman continued.

"I stayed in that monastery for couple of days more to heal my feet. One of the pilgrims from monastery gave me his very good socks. I think I will finish the Camino with them. Now I understand the most important thing for the Camino is a good pair of socks! But you know, I was always asking myself, why I am walking, why I'm doing this? I'm still asking myself and will probably keep asking all the way to Santiago," she said. "I called my mother, from Basque Country, and asked her maybe I should stop and go back home. Many thoughts were crossing my mind then. But now, more along the road, the mind becomes more still. Not too much wandering or overthinking."

Like meditation. A walking meditation. Not focused on your steps, but your internal flow.

"The nature is always changing along this Way. I love that. I feel like every region I'm in another country. In Basque Country, where it looks like only nature exists and only few pilgrims, then Cantabria was different: finally meeting more people, walking with them but not all the time."

Then she laughed at a memory.

"I don't remember where it happened, but I fell down from a hill near the coast. I was walking, up to the hill, I saw a beautiful view, and suddenly my mother called me. I was talking with her on the phone, telling her how beautiful is the place I am, and at the same time walking down the hill to the other village. And I slipped on a rock and rolled down the hill. The phone flew away from me into the bushes, and I just fell down rolling from the hill. The woman from the village down the hill was shouting are you okay. I said yeah, but I look at my legs and I thought, *I broke my legs*. But I stood up and took my phone. My mother was still speaking, in the bushes, asking what's happened. I was so surprised because I didn't get any injury, no blood, no broken leg, nothing. I was just thinking, someone is watching me and saving my life, really."

Aistė waved at another *peregrina*, Chloe, who joined us. She took a big *café con leche*, and Aistė and I finished the *sidra* on our own.

When we finally got to the *albergue* in Pendueles, I was grateful Ruo had called in our names. The place was nearing full and a few other *peregrinos* were waiting outside for the 6 o'clock reservation deadline.

The American woman whose toes were suffering on the downhills after Donostia was there, waiting to see if a space opened up.

"No! They're still killing me. Everything's killing me," she laughed. "I've taken the bus a couple of times. I'm too slow and I'm running out of time."

"Just stop wherever you end up. You can always come back," Corinne's wisdom, not mine.

"I want to finish. I might have to take the bus again, but I'll get there. What I really need is a massage."

"When you find a good place, let me know." I was serious.

She said she would, then headed off in search of a bed.

Upstairs looking for a bunk I spotted a familiar profile.

"You! Tereza, right? The first time we met you were in bed too."

"Yeah, I go to bed rather early," she laughed. "Deba, yes?"

"Yes, and how are you, healthy, well?"

"Only one blister. And no more runny nose," she smiled.

Tereza had answered her doubt about whether she could walk *so many kilometers in one journey*. She had come over 300km since Irun. Later we talked about what walking meant to her.

"You know, I came on the Camino to have some time to think about my life. To find my priorities, and what I would like to do. This walking, for my mind nature is like a medicine. I have always liked hiking. But I now know walking is a way of life for me. It is the thing what I absolutely love. Something what I can't imagine living without. Absolute freedom. Time to think more deep. A way to be in nature. A natural way of move. Something that makes me alive. I don't want to stop. But I have to work too," she said glumly.

Even though Tereza had what sounded like a dream summer job, guiding kayak trips in the Šumava, the national park that straddled the Czech-German border, she wasn't looking forward to going back after she reached Santiago.

"Can you believe me that I'm very lazy person? But I don't want to be, and I know what is the best against it. It's still doing something. Have a bucket list. Have dreams. Have hobbies. I'm strict to myself. Maybe sometimes too much. I want to avoid doing nothing, spending my time before TV, wasting my time on social media, you know. I am in love with hiking. Especially long-distance walking. My next dream is the Pacific Crest Trail. Do you know it, have you walked it?"

I told her I hadn't. She wants to do the whole thing, a through-hike, over 4,000km.

"But I can't tell my parents. Or boyfriend. Not yet. They will think I'm crazy. Walking for me is like a drug now. I know it. It started here, on the Camino."

The *albergue* was *donativo*, and our host provided a communal meal. Fourteen of us crowded the long table and shared a stew of lentils, bread and wine. A group of animated Italian men kept us laughing and entertained – they had spent a little extra time at the bar up the hill. Their energy was great, either full on or off, and I imagined them talking, joking and singing their way to Santiago. Aistė affectionately called them the *paperellas*, the little ducks.

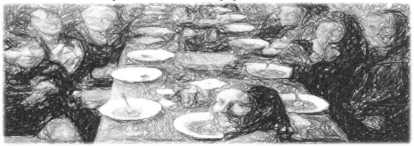

The next day was a bit melancholy for our loose group. We knew we'd be scattering. Caroline would meet her boyfriend in the next days. Ruo would leave the Camino del Norte and veer off inland on the Camino Primitivo.

The Primitivo is known as one of the most challenging Ways in Spain, if not the most challenging. Fewer towns and villages, less availability of supplies, longer distances between *albergues*, and more demanding terrain. It breaks off from the Norte around Oviedo and cuts through the mountains to link with the Camino Frances in Lugo. Ruo wanted to challenge herself further.

"I don't want to follow the herd behavior," she said. After Santiago Ruo planned to continue to Finisterre, the famous cape three days on that juts into the Atlantic, but, at her pace, she'd still have a couple of weeks left before her flight back to Taiwan.

"I need a extra plan."

"You could walk to Porto, in Portugal. I'm even thinking about it."

Ruo thought for a moment. "How long does it take?"

"I hear about 11 days. Less than two weeks." I was thinking about it but that was all. I wouldn't do it. Couldn't do it. But Ruo, sure enough, would end up walking *back* to Santiago from Finisterre (most people take the bus), and then continue to Porto. She was unstoppable. But despite all her energy, I could tell she was sad about separating from Caroline.

"I will lose my good walking partner."

Aistė was subdued too. Maybe a little tired from her long day yesterday. Maybe the effect of the greyer sky.

"When something happens, you become so self-concentrated, you start to think that it's happened only for you, and that only you are the one who suffers. It looks that the whole world stopped and you're dying with it.

"The Camino shows you differently: it shows you you're just one of the millions and billions. It shows you that the whole world is still living its life, is still moving, and there is soooooo much to see, experience and feel. Yes, sometimes the world is full of shit but it is still incredible.

"Last year, in 2016 my boyfriend committed suicide. After that I knew I have to walk the Camino. It was the first thought that came up in my head. There is not much to share. It happened, I had to leave. I felt it will help me. I didn't know how and why. But somehow. I started May 16th and I haven't stopped. I won't stop until I finish.

"I want to answer something, but I don't have questions. I am walking to release emotions, to understand more about myself through the other people, to understand how the world works and to see the world, the true world, not the little one I see only through my eyes.

"I was dealing with the situation that happened to my boyfriend. I was really scared I can do bad thing to myself also. Because I didn't see much motivation to live this life, I didn't see what is the purpose to live. Nothing made me happy. I felt like I'm dead, but I was still alive.

"It's like the Camino gifted me to meet people with really tragic or sad stories. After meeting them, more and more of different people from different countries with different whys, hows and life stories, I understand. I am not alone dealing with something. There is the whole world dealing with something all the time, the same second, the same moment.

"It is evolving every kilometer. I think it will keep evolving. My mindset changed a lot already. Walking more and more kilometers the mind stops wandering and asking so many questions, the feeling inside is more pure, like everything what it is unnecessary in life just walks away while I am walking.

"I can already say the Camino helped me a lot. It has opened my heart. Inspired me to live, to enjoy, to be happy. It reminds me that I'm not alone. To accept things, which life gives you, bad or good – whatever. It happens, and if you want to go forward in life you need to accept it and not get stuck with it. No one will wait for you. You live your life, and you alone are responsible for your own life and what you have in it, and what you feel in it.

"I think the most difficult is to choose, whether you want to stay unhappy or not. And then take an action and do something about your life. All the things that life gives you are lessons and experiences. If you let them happen, they can make you a better person."

I shared with Aistė a little about the suicides that had riven my family, 30 years before. "Though I don't think about it every day, it is still with me."

"Perfect words to describe everything," she said.

As part of the scattering, I would be flying back to the US for my twin nephews' graduations.

Yes, that day was upon me. I remembered Corinne's practical advice offered a month earlier, unvalued in my obtuseness. It took the excruciating pain on the roadside after Aire-sur-l'Adour to realize its simple truth. I'm indebted to both Corinne's words and the pain, for without them I would not have spent the awestruck afternoon at the *course landaise*, would not have lingered in the Basque Country, and would not have shared these rich few days with these special *peregrinas*.

We stopped to rest at the Bufones de Arenillas, karst cliffs famous for exploding jets of seawater during rough weather. But the day was muted, the Cantabrian Sea beyond misty and calm. We idled among the rocks and brush, shared snacks, delayed our inevitable parting. Someone made a comment about how odd it was that I, a male, had been a part of this informal group. Maybe she didn't use the word odd, but she meant that we all had felt equally at ease with each other. Someone else agreed, suggesting normally it was best to remain a little wary of male intention, especially while traveling alone. It was a brief, slightly awkward exchange, but I said I genuinely valued their trust and ease with me. My intention, if there was any at all, was only to share in their experiences and stories. A few hours later in Llanes, we half dozen scattered.

The hours on the ALSA bus from Llanes to Santiago yesterday, the all-night noise and light at the hotel in Labacolla, waking with an alarm, the tension at the Santiago airport as the minutes tick away – apparently I have no ticket. Maybe a payment problem? Over to the bank window. No. Back to the Iberia counter. Two American Airlines flights to Madrid  cancelled yesterday. What's the chance of picking just that date? In turn my flight to the US cancelled. Only a carry-on? They send me to Madrid, uncertain. In Madrid, waiting in line at Iberia. Told to go to American. Waiting in line at American. The line doesn't move. A woman needs a wheelchair. Rerouted. Back to Iberia. Waiting in line at Security, at the underground train, at Immigration, at the food bar. Rushing the concourse. Tension and anxiety heavier than any backpack. Maybe this is inevitable when time becomes the sole arbiter.

Small blessings; an aisle seat and no seatmate.

Chicago O'Hare smells of fried food, ketchup, human breath. It sounds of TVs, smartphones, and talking, talking, talking.

But I've made it.

About a week later I sit in the audience of the second graduation, smaller than the first.

"He immediately jumps up and, with his ear-to-ear smile, he fist-bumps me! And I thought right then and there, I am really going to like working with this student."

Each of the dozen graduating seniors got to choose whomever they wanted to "present" them at graduation. My nephew Mac had chosen Mr. Schneeberger.

"I spent, by my loose calculation, about 500 hours in the classroom with Mac." I think he meant one-on-one hours.

Mac had spoken fondly of Mr. Schnee, as he called him, over the last year, and listening to the teacher's words it was clear he in turn genuinely cared about the development and wellbeing of my nephew. Knowing that was somehow reassuring. The school was for kids who learned differently, for one reason or another. Mac had suffered a prenatal stroke. While he could tell you just about anything you'd want to know about a professional athlete, it was a longshot he'd ever pass a driving test.

Mr. Schnee talked about Mac being prepared for class, ready to learn, and willing to work until his assignments were completed correctly. He talked about Mac being Prom King, to which Mac, on  stage, grinned broadly, and he talked about basketball. There were no girls in the class, so no Prom Queen.

I remember one game where Mac sunk a half-court shot at the buzzer. "Like LeBron Uncle Jerry!" His team was behind by 30 points, but he reacted like he'd just clinched the NCAA championship; jumping up and down, waving his arms. And we did too, everyone in the gym, even the opposing team.

It wasn't the winning. It was the playing.

Mr. Schnee talked about Mac's compassion, about his day-to-day willingness to help other students. "He never criticizes or chides anyone else. He only offers words of encouragement."

It was odd to listen to a stranger talk about someone you think you know, close family, and realize they know them better. But it was reassuring too, to know that others could realize Mac's essence, his qualities that maybe those closer to him took for granted, or even overlooked.

"Mac is honest. He actually doesn't know how to not tell the truth."

This struck me. So obvious, and yet so singular.

Mac may get frustrated and angry, or overwhelmed and anxious, or impatient and obsessive. But he doesn't lie and manipulate. His truth, and his love, flow forth unabridged.

"Mac loves his family. How do I know? He told me so. Every day."

The emotion began to get Mr. Schnee. He tried to maintain his composure behind the lectern, but he was unsuccessful.

"Sometimes I would wonder, who is teaching whom? As the saying goes, what comes from the heart, reaches the heart."

We were all crying in the end. It was joy, joy for each of these students to have made it this far. Tears of relief and hope too. But also, I think, at least for me, tears of sadness. Sadness because of how tough this coming life of adulthood would be on Mac. Tears over a world that chews up those who love so freely.

I think about his parents. How they will always be parenting, how, no matter how well they prepare him and arrange things, one day they will be gone. Even knowing his two brothers will do everything in the world for him, I know it's still an insatiable worry, that it will be their last thought at their passing.

An Asian woman next to me on the commuter flight tells me how much she enjoys visiting the States, the first time in 2008. That it feels like coming home, that people are so open and genuine, that she and her husband would like to move to New York City for a year to experience the US more fully.

"I feel like a visitor when I come back," I tell her. That I feel alienated from the distracted culture where marketing, militarism and entertainment have fused into "a mind-numbing juggernaut."

She is quiet for a while and I feel like a jerk, answering her heartful enthusiasm with a harangue. Where to stable my high horse? But we resume our conversation and talk of other things.

After we had deplaned, in the busy gate area of JFK, she turns and hugs me. She hugs me. A complete stranger. And wishes me well on the rest of my Camino.

Back in Llanes I sit at an outdoor table, near the *pensión* where I'd left my backpack.

I'd passed the test of submission to US airport security and its threat of public humiliation. I'd successfully endured the penning inside the fuselage, its borderline captivity where if you think too much about your circumstances you risk being overwhelmed by the sensation of being buried alive. I uncharacteristically watched two movies and pretended the heat of the man pressing against me was somehow reassuring. Finally, fresh sunny air at the airport in Avilés, and in disembarking the ALSA bus here in Llanes, the end of the rushing sound and motion.

I was back.

Was it indulgent, wasteful, flying back like that? Shouldn't I have just gone back and stayed, picked up where I left off on the Camino another time? Or even ended it altogether, since I claim the going is more important than the actual arrival?

Going back for my nephews' graduations had become part of the Camino. At Hunt & Corinne's I had wrongly placed it at the end, as something to get back to, something separate. But the graduations were more appropriately part of the walk; from the pride of my nephews and their friends, to the words of Mr. Schnee, to the hug at JFK, even as part of the dissolution of our group the week before. In spite of how much I complain about air travel, I'm also grateful for what it allows us to do.

I'm a zombie but I don't want to get up and leave. It's almost 9:00 p.m., still light, and the outdoor tables are full at all the bars and restaurants. The first week in Belgium the sun set before 7:00 p.m. Here, people drinking, talking, mostly not even eating yet. The sun, which wouldn't set until almost 10:00 p.m., breaks under the ceiling of dense cloud that had lodged on the Picos de Europa, abode of some of the highest peaks along the Cordillera Cantábrica.

The rooms, with their big bay windows glowing orange, are all empty. Everyone is in the streets. Groups in funny hats, chanting. Shouts and laughter. The women beautiful, in their contouring white pants.

I spoon *fabada*, a white bean soup with smokey blood sausage and chunks of cured pork belly. It's way too heavy to be eating this late, but it smothers the travel meals. Men pour green bottles of *sidra* from above their heads, behind their backs. A passing dog snatches bread from the hand of a little girl at the next table and she cries. Her parents laugh and so do I.

I don't want to leave this spot, but I smile at the prospect of my backpack, of walking tomorrow, not knowing where I'll sleep or who I'll meet. Finally back in the room I open the heavy shutters to the fading dusk. Songbirds, gulls, adults, children, all the voices rise in echo, saying we're okay, *it's going to be okay.*

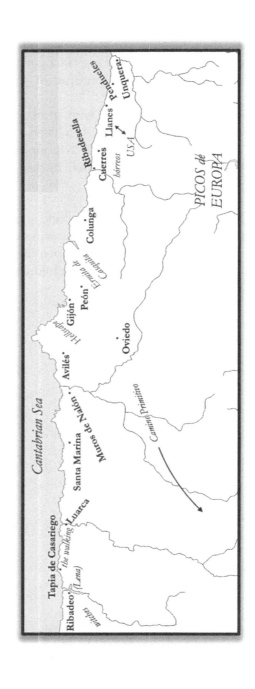

ASTURIAS

Back in Asturias **17**

Bed bugs. I thought I would make for the *albergue* in Ribadesella but learned it had recently shut due to a bedbug infestation. Seamus's words about Rue Lazare came back to me. We filthy pilgrims. I counted my blessings for the near miss, but shuddered thinking about all the downstream mattresses, teeming with dispersed colonists.

I left Llanes early, eager to be walking again, not sure where I'd stay. When I pulled on my backpack, it gripped me like a koala bear. I missed it too.

It was drizzly, pleasant, rural terrain, bumping along the coast. Rocky coves and muddy inlets, tiny beaches of yellow sand, smelling of life in the cold, intertidal zone. Narrow country lanes that passed broken-down *monasterios* and churches of Our Lady's Sorrows. I began to notice small, isolated structures that I assumed must be a kind of traditional raised granary. Indeed, I later learned they are called *hórreos*, and are meant to keep the grain protected from moisture and rodents. They are simple structures, usually square, made of wood with a hipped roof of tile, sometimes with an exterior walk. They sit atop tall – and this is another term I learned – stone *staddles*, kind of a mushroom shaped support with a tapering column and wide cap to keep creatures from crawling up.

The A-8 zoomed in the distance. The *hórreos* held their grain in silence, as they had for centuries.

I wasn't encountering any other *peregrinos*. It was as if they had all passed through this area while I was back in the States. I was alone again. The bartender in Celorio, where I'd stopped for *tortilla* and *café con leche*, suggested I see Playa de Gulpiyuri. A man walking to catch the bus guided me to Villanueva and Bufones de Pría. At a late lunch in Graña, avoiding a heavy downpour, a patron sent me here, Casa Belen, a small rural *donativo albergue* in Cuerres.

Established by a pair of retired teachers from Bilbao and surrounded by the sound of cowbells, it was unexpected and delightful, the best way to be. The couple was away, and three young volunteers were running things. After a dinner of homemade spätzle, we repaired to a small outbuilding and sang songs of Taizé by candlelight. Echoes of Rebecca again.

I had a bunkroom to myself, and two couples from Mainz shared another. One couple had met in Burgos, on the Camino Frances, a few years before. Not only were they from the same country and city, but also the same street. It took the Camino to break them out of their routines so they could fall in love. Now they walked again, and said they would keep doing so, the Camino the reason for their coming together.

More than once I'd been asked, "Is this your first Camino?" The first couple of times the question didn't make sense to me and I attributed it to a language quirk. That dissonance reflected my understanding of the Camino as a singular event. Just as there was no single path, the Camino can be walked as many times as one needs or desires, whenever you feel the pull. Not only did each *peregrino* have their own motivation, their own reason for stepping off, a single person could feel the pull at different times in their lives for different reasons. One of the Italians at the *donativo* in Pendueles got a tattoo every time he walked. He showed me six. How many would Aistė end up with?

Restless cowbells in the predawn drizzle, then bells from the Cuerres *iglesia* at 5:00 a.m. It has been a long time since 5 o'clock bells I thought, lying there in the stillness. What, Bazoches-les-Gallerandes with Father Giuseppe, then La Romieu? That seemed another world, France.

My toenails were protesting. I'd been so eager to get walking yesterday, I'd walked with my big toes pressed into the top of my shoes. Why on earth had I done that? Now they are tender. *Calma.* Relax. Be aware. *Be Here Now.*

There's a small bird who likes to perch on the barbed wire fencing; black head, maybe a cowlick, white collar, russet chest. He sounds like an old manual typewriter, slow raspy chirps – *cshk, cshk, cshk.* It's an incongruous sound coming from such a little creature, but he seemed fine with it. One swooped from a higher limb and inhaled a racing insect. Just like that. Gone.

The Ribadesella *playa* was the first large beach since San Vicente de la Barquera. It's built up, like Laredo was, but not with boxy tiled apartment blocks. These were houses, some quite grand, of varying designs and colors. I don't know architecture well enough to know if these were 19th or early 20th century homes. But I'd read that many Asturianos had gone off to Spain's colonies at the time and been quite successful. Known as *indianos*, they came back and built ostentatious homes to show off their wealth. I'd come  across such buildings regularly traversing Asturias – clusters of antique grandeur, the source of prosperity from somewhere far away.

"Look for ones with palm trees," Miriam told me. "It means it's authentic *indiano.*"

Leaving the strand I broke off the marked Camino and climbed the headland to keep the view of the sea. Halfway up I was rewarded with the most laden, luscious and accessible loquat tree. I'm drawn to Vega by the name, one of the brightest stars in our heavens. It's another large beach but facing northwest, open to the swell. I've learned how to ask for my *café con leche* in a glass, like I've seen the locals take it. And *tortilla por favor.* Lush, green, well-watered, mild climate, full fruit trees, good surf, uncrowded, mountains and sea, it's good country along the Cantabrian Sea. Good country.

Following the trail along Playa la Vega to the next headland, a VW van, wetsuits drying, a young couple eating from bowls. There was no one else around. Another day with no pilgrims.

In Colunga, where I end up for the night, *peregrinos* reappeared, dozens and dozens of them, as if conjured from the karst blowholes. They are all older now. Like me. And up. One pointed me to an inexpensive *pensión*. I take a room, small and clean with no character. Perfectly functional. The shower less so. The standard constricting cylinder, so narrow I can neither squat nor bend over. I am hyper careful to not bump the water control, which I've learned can result in instant scalding or an icy douse. I content myself with letting the soapsuds run down to my feet, then rub one with the other.

At dinner the small restaurant was crowded and noisy with only us. How many of these places prosper only because of pilgrim traffic? I squeeze into a table with a German couple already eating. This was his second Camino, her first.

"My daughter is in Texas."

I assumed he meant temporarily and asked what she was doing.

"She is married now, to an American."

The woman didn't say anything, kept on eating, looking at her plate.

I sensed something awkward about this subject, but he had opened it. I plunged forward.

"Oh that's great. How did they end up there? Does she like it, have you visited?"

He answered the last two, but not the first. Yes she likes it very much, no I haven't been able to visit yet.

Had the husband been working in Germany, had his daughter been working in the US? Or maybe they had been in university together somewhere? Why Texas? His reticence made me more curious.

"She returned to marry and start a family with her host father."

That was unexpected. It took a moment for it to sink in.

I see.

But I admired the gentleman for coming right out with it. I thought about it. Her parents send her away on a high school exchange program, to give her every opportunity, and she falls in love with the guardian. I didn't ask any follow-up questions, feeling it would be merely gawking, but I couldn't help but wonder how difficult it would be to build a new family among the wreckage that relationship must have caused. But it is only my assumption that there was wreckage – the former wife, the kids, the community. Maybe there was no wreckage. But when has love and passion ever been free of wreckage?

His daughter was now 24. His partner, not the mother, hadn't said a word, just kept on eating, even taking portions from his plate.

"That's why I walked the Camino the first time. The Camino Frances. I was very troubled. Finally, one day, I realized all I wanted for my daughter was her happiness. And she is happy."

An American, Rick from Arizona, approached the table on hearing my accent. He told me his whole hiking history, even though I hadn't asked.

The *peregrinos* all disappear, and I am alone again the next day. Am I missing the main Way? I scoot under the A-8 and enter countryside that feels forgotten. A lane leads me along a ridge through three quiet villages: Pernús, La Llera, Priesca. Green pastures with black and white dairy cows, corn fields, *hórreos*, stands of eucalyptus, steep hillsides. It's misting rain, but warm. A dog bark, a cockcrow, the caw of a crow, a man working unseen, a whiff of woodsmoke. More loquats, plump and juicy, these without even brown spots. How much is unchanged in this fertile land from over the centuries, even millennia? The name Asturias supposedly has Celtic origins: Astyrs. Even the Basque symbol, the *lauburu*, had struck me as Celtic. What had life been like in those times here? How far had the world extended?

Asturias is known for its dairy production. The heavy beef cattle, like those majestic blue *Tudancos* of Cantabria with their sweeping horns, had been replaced by mellower milk cows, their bells and lowing floating over the landscape. I'd pass small barns with animals hooked to stainless steel machines sucking away their milk as they chewed feed. The occasional bull seemed well-behaved,

waiting patiently alone in his paddock, staring longingly at the brown cows with their long dark eyelashes across the road. More cows than people on most stretches.

The clouds are breaking up by Villaviciosa. In the place I take a *café*, the sign says *baño*, the word I finally recognize. It's been *aseos* and before that *servicios*. In Basque Country, *komuna*.

My feet hurt. My big toe toenails are not as sensitive as yesterday, but my feet hurt generally, and they will for the duration. I didn't want to admit this. I hoped they'd get better, but they won't. I don't really worry about the discomfort per se. It's the persistence that bothers me, the fact that my feet are probably changed forever and not for the better. The ache is part of the foot. I only watch for swelling now.

Maybe I should have gotten a new pair in the States, I think, examining my Oboz lowcut hikers. They certainly lacked any cushioning by this point, though they were never very padded to begin with. I'd replaced my shorts with a size smaller, because they were slipping off my hips. Why not shoes? No, this pair has been with me from the beginning, almost three months now, and what, at least 1,000 miles? Might as well finish with them rather than risk breaking in something new. Where did I see that young guy walking barefoot? All the way from Germany or Switzerland. Yeah, barefoot. Probably not as outlandish as I first imagined – natural stride, careful stepping, cool and dry. Imagine wearing thick rubber gloves all day. What would it feel like to pet your dog? How well could you prepare dinner or get dressed?

Marching along, actually marching, heel-striking through France. Ridiculous. Next time, if not barefoot, then at least not much more than sandals, like the waif. I bet I'd be way more careful with my feet and in return they'd be much happier.

Shortly after Villaviciosa I came to the cutoff for the Camino Primitivo, an unremarkable road junction by a simple chapel, Ermita de Casquita. This is where Ruo most likely would have veered off.

I stop for a moment at the concrete post that marks the split. Has she finished the Primitivo by now? Reached Santiago? On to Finisterre? She's full of energy, full of searching. She wasn't going to stop until she found the answer she needed to return home and enough commitment to see her decision through, whatever it was.

Did Tereza tell me she was taking the Primitivo too? Now I can't remember. Maybe she said she still hadn't decided. Two of the most determined walkers I've met. Ruo her searching, Tereza her going. These are journeys that have no end.

There are clouds on the high hills. Standing at the junction, in the last of the warming sunshine, I feel a deep sense of contentment wash through me.

Physically wash through me, as if it is substance. It's arresting.

I've experienced general contentment after achieving specific circumstances. But for such an intense version to well up here, unsought, while pausing alongside the marker and wall? Why here, why now?

But it is contentment no doubt, a deep satisfaction and peacefulness. It's as if I've slipped into a meditative state and yet I remain fully conscious and ambulatory.

It's not this specific spot along the road, I don't think, but more of an accumulation. But an accumulation of what? Don't overthink it, I caution myself.

As the sensation first began to well inside me moments before, I ignored it, kept thinking my thoughts. When it persisted I dismissed it as impossible. Contentment? For what?

Why ignore and dismiss it? Afraid again, like with the dreams of poetry? Of having a door open and being afraid to step through? It's real, this sensation, this vibration. *Faith is patience with mystery.*

Dare I try and visualize the contentment, pinpoint it? But I know there is nothing to see. This is not a contentment of a specific thing. I let the sensation be, slightly bemused, unprepared, grateful I guess, though I kind of feel guilty because I don't know what to do with it. As if I'm wasting a special moment, a unique juncture. Someone has handed me a key but I don't know what it opens.

Yet. I don't know what it opens yet.

I finger the beads on my shoulder strap and head toward the clouds, following the climbing winding VV-8. There are no cars. There are no *peregrinos*.

Thank you for this body. Thank you for this fitness. Thank you for this health. I know it is unearned and passing. But thank you.

Wind and cloud pour through the 450m pass on the Alto de la Cruz. The A-8 burrows unheard, unseen, deep below in a series of tunnels. I devour a can of *sardinas* sitting on a stump under my ever-reliable black umbrella from Peyrehorade.

The Camino.

It's not to get to know myself. I've repeated the condensed version of the story of my life so many times to others along the Way it sounds to me stale and formulaic. Even irritating. *I'm from here, I did this, I do that, and I think such and such, that is me.* For all the events in life I have found so consuming, so defining, I can see how petty and inconsequential they are. No, that's a little too nihilistic. But being compelled to repeat my story so often I can see it is not all that I am. These headlines, where I'm from, the work I've done or do, the things I've seen and experienced and made, the people I know or have known, my beliefs and perspectives, the things I've yet to do but want to, I cling to them even as they turn to dust.

The telling and retelling, I've begun to see, ultimately liberates you from your narrative, if you allow it to.

The contentment I felt back down in the sunshine, it wasn't my personal contentment. It was a larger contentment, something shared, something not limited by time or circumstances. It is like love. Love is not transactional, e.g. I love you, you love me, or not. Love is the context in which something takes place. Like this contentment. It's not something to be possessed and parceled. It has to be embodied.

This Camino is not for me to know myself, to delve more deeply into my story and try and understand it. No. Clinging to my story, reenforcing it reveals its insubstantial nature. It's not that my story is limited and meaningless, but there is something beyond it that is more meaningful. In this way the Camino is not to get to know myself, as many of us probably conventionally think at the outset – some great adventure of self-exploration. No. It's more than that. The Camino is for me to *unknow* myself.

I've come here, I realize, for the unknowing. To get myself out of the way.

Ultimately there is no arrival.

There are abundant cherries on the way down the other side. The rain lifts. I think to stay in Peón, because of its name. But also because it is quiet, merely a crossroads in a tranquil valley. To go further I'd draw too close to Gijón, the largest city and port of Asturias. The Asturian countryside is too appealing to leave. Plus, to make me feel even more at home, a short-legged burrow at the junction flares his black nostrils through the fence, wondering if I've brought him a treat. And what a haircut he has. It looks as a monk's tonsure; his mane, back and flanks tightly trimmed, his belly and legs long and shaggy.

I sit at the bar next door to the donkey. The bartender is young and baby-faced. I don't ask until another patron enters and stands at the end of the bar. I want him to hear. After he's served his wine and soda, I say to the bartender, "*Necesito un habitación por esta noche,*" hacking my way through the Spanish, but they understand. He says he's sorry, but he doesn't know of any place to stay here, which is why I waited for the other fellow. Rafa, the man at the end of the bar motions with his phone, wait, I think I know of a place.

A farmer in shorts and rubber boots walks in followed by a small dog. At the counter he orders an espresso and what looks like a small glass of cream. He drinks both as shots, espresso first, then walks back to his work.

Rafa calls his cousins, Constantine and Mario. They have a new place, not quite finished, but yes, if I don't mind, I can stay there. It isn't 100m away.

The next morning I say goodbye to the burrow, back waiting at the fence.

The dense brush buzzes, at first only as background in my

head. Then, chipping away at my distraction, it pushes to the fore. It's not background this. This is the sound of all life, the pulsating energy of everything. The struggling and striving and thriving amongst the rich scent of blossoms where everything is possible, as long as you leap.

Then, on the far side of Gijón, coming over a hill, a pall of dull red covers over everything, choking the buzz, constricting the pulse, smothering the scent.

Mountains of black coal.

Great smoking mounds of refuse.

Conveyor belts reach to the other side of the universe carrying the guts of our planet.

Everything in view is tinted red, rust red. The concrete, the steel, the galvanized guardrails, the trees, the air. Deformed chickens scratch along the roadside, like maimed and homeless veterans. The sounds of engines, furnaces, alarms and sirens, trucks and trains. But not sleek passenger trains. These are contraptions groaning and shrieking, suffering with the earth we have exhumed and loaded into their bellies, so we can fill ours.

I am in Dante's *Inferno*.

I can't go faster or roll up the windows. I can't turn up the music. A great cosmic hand grabs the back of my head and rubs my face in everything around me. I am forced to acknowledge it. To bear witness. In my trekking pole. In my roundtrip ticket home. In the hot water of my shower.

In memory that brief stretch of hellscape looms large, dominates the day, annihilates the pleasure of waking in quiet Peón, petting the donkey, and walking through the vibrant metropolitan sprawl of Gijón. Maybe that's because, like Hell, we intuit it is everywhere, not just a remote hypothetical place. The industrial wasteland on the backside of Gijón in reality spreads just below the surface of everything in our sleek industrialized lives. We go to great lengths to compartment that reality away.

As if on cue, the green hills closed over the infernal vision and Avilés lay on the horizon. By late afternoon I was sitting on a bench in the pleasant grounds of a small church eating a simple lunch,

Avilés within striking distance. Albeit via a corridor of road and more industry, though nothing as stark as the morning.

"I'll stay here," he said.

I told him I was continuing into Avilés. "It's not so far. You can easily make it this afternoon."

"I don't like the big *albergues*. Here is more peaceful."

He had a point. There was a wide veranda around the church. Probably no one to disturb him. But it would be a hassle if someone showed up in the evening and told him he had to move on.

"I normally do this. There usually is no problem at these chapels." He pulled out a flute and started to play. He did look like a minstrel, with beard, bells and colorful clothes. He might have said he was from Switzerland, but I don't think his origins were important to him. He might have been barefoot too.

I felt a bit soldierish pushing on. It would end up being almost a 40km day, which was too much. But I didn't want to wake up and walk into the city. I had done that today. I wanted to wake and put the city behind me. Not to be critical of Gijón or Avilés, or Santander for that matter, just because they were cities. They are, in their medium size, quite decent, even if their margins are characteristically unappealing. I just preferred the small roads and trails to the large boulevards and highways that converged on these urban centers. It's a cost of their vitality I acknowledge but prefer to avoid.

Numbers for radio taxis were affixed to utility poles along the way to Avilés. *Peregrinos*, demoralized by the long stretch of barren, industrial road before them could choose to skip the unpleasantness. I empathized, especially for those walking only for a week or two. They probably spent enough hours traversing concrete in their home lives. I didn't like it either, but for me such stretches were a miniscule part of the walk. And there was nothing along the Camino del Norte like the expanses of Brussels and Paris. The agglomeration around Bilbao was the only thing to come close, and I had avoided it by clinging to the coast. So the taxi numbers didn't tempt me, and eventually I was able to divert to a bike path that ran alongside the channelized river. I joined the throngs out enjoying the afternoon and followed them into town.

In the municipal *albergue* we are packed into a large, fetid room of damp bunkbeds and anxious people using dank toilets. My wish of reaching the city was granted. I rue the words of the minstrel as I lie there, listening to the snores, farts and groans. The door leading out to the restrooms swings noisily all night, admitting stabs of bright light. I thought I had lucked out being next to a window, but the woman on the bottom bunk complained testily about the "cold" air. She roughly readjusted herself, then fell off to snore all night. Old women, I add old women to the list of certain snorers, right below fat-bellied men. Out of a sense of decorum I had resisted designating them so, but I can no longer suppress the annoyance. I imagine the minstrel; starlight, fresh air, and when he needs to pee, a flowering bush is at hand. I know, you get what you pay for. I should be grateful to the city for providing cheap pilgrim accommodation. I could have always found somewhere else. Maybe if the Germans had been along with their smartphone.

I feel the mass of the pilgrimage pressing against me. Get me out of here. The morning can't come fast enough. And even before it arrives, pilgrims are up in the dark, whispering hoarsely, rattling their bunks and getting ready to rush off into the day.

Between the industrial sites and the Avilés *albergue* it had been a grim day. But I was compensated the next day when I somehow stumbled upon a most delightful spot in Muros de Nalón: Casa Carmina. Small and family run, the bunk room was airy and immaculately clean. Large windows let light and fresh air pour in. The bathrooms were spotless and bright. There were a couple of private rooms out back and a large garden. But the best part was the common area with a full bar manned by the daughter (I think) and her equally vivacious friend. They prepared perfect espresso and offered me a shot of *orujo*. Like grappa, it's a kind of brandy made from the leavings of winemaking. The rust red pall and humid snorting was soon forgotten.

The elegant, ageless matron sat in the lounge, speaking with local patrons as they dropped in. This combination seemed key to the place's success: the balance between bunkroom and private accommodation, full bar and a kitchen that prepared an excellent plate, *peregrinos*, locals and other guests, the owner's personal presence.

Bob Dylan and Glasses of Rioja. I could park myself for a few days right here, I thought. There was a largish road running behind with the regular vehicle, and the now ubiquitous A-8 wasn't a kilometer away, but this didn't take away from the intimate atmosphere. Alas, refuges for pilgrims are one-night stays only, unless you are sick. That is the rule of the Way. But I'd be back. Stretch out in the private room out back, retrofitted *utilitaire* parked around the side. Another place on my growing list.

Luarca, a couple of days later, was in some ways just the opposite. There wasn't that much to the small inland community of Muros de Nalón – the ambience of Casa Carmina was the draw. But the small port town of Luarca was popping. I didn't know what to expect as I approached the town from the bluff above. Like a lot of places on this coast, it was nestled in where a river had cut to the sea. As I dropped down the steep streets, I could feel the energy steaming up from the central area. Restaurants and bars packed. Musicians on corners. Families strolling, young people carousing. The shapely white pants, a fashion I'd noticed since entering Cantabria, were out in force and the girls couldn't have been prettier – the young men's short-sided pompadours weren't as big a style hit for me. A Saturday afternoon on a beautiful day.

I wanted to drop my pack right there, but I hustled to the *albergue* to get checked in. It opened at 3:00 p.m. Initially we thought there was no need, but yesterday we decided I would walk ahead and sign us in, just to be sure. Even though the last two nights had been quiet, you never knew when the tsunami of *peregrinos* would suddenly surge.

I had been bumping into a pair of Danish women since leaving Peón. Anne Marie, my age, and Lizzy, 74. Lizzy was among the eldest pilgrims I'd met, but she wasn't the oldest. There had been a gentleman, 81, in San Vicente de la Barquera, whom we'd approached as if he were the pontiff while he sat at an outdoor café. If I only have half their vigor in 20-25 years, assuming I'm around, I'll be grateful.

Anne Marie was a teacher/administrator at a kindergarten and an enthusiastic traveler. Lizzy, who'd held a senior position in the same school, liked to spend time at her cabin in Sweden, which has  no indoor plumbing, and where she has to saw and chop her own firewood. They claimed they were slow walkers, but I knew better. They were steady, which is the real secret. I may have hustled past them that morning after Peón, but here we were, four days later, in the same place. And poor Anne Marie, on the way to the airport in Copenhagen to fly to Spain, she lost her wallet, or it was stolen, with all the cash she had saved for the Camino. Their return deadline was a flight out of Santiago July 3rd, because she had to be back at the kindergarten July 4th. It was the 17th of June that day in Luarca. Like Aistė, they didn't use map, guidebook, or smartphone. They just followed the markers, which occasionally led them on out-of-date paths. Once I saw them emerge from the woods red-faced with brambles in their hair, but they were laughing. They stopped when they wanted and stayed where they could.

Somewhere they'd collected José, 68. His parents had emigrated from Spain to Australia when he was 13.

"We went to Perth, but now I've moved to Melbourne, for the grandkids."

He'd walked the Camino Frances twice, once with his son and once with his wife.

"When I get a little down, I get the pictures out and start planning my next walk. You know, it gives you a sense of being a part of something special."

Community. It was something I'd heard from other *peregrinos*, and, to be honest, felt myself, especially these last weeks in Spain.

While walking the Camino you feel like you belong to something, something larger than yourself. It gives you purpose, shapes your days. There is spontaneity, the possibility of something new every moment. You feel solidarity with those around you.

If these qualities were diminished or missing in your everyday life back home, how intensely you would feel them on the Way. And how intensely you would miss them once it was over. You'd go through your pictures and look around at your routine and feel that hollowness of longing. Do you know this feeling?

Or maybe, just maybe you'd carry some of the qualities you'd rediscovered on the Camino back into your everyday world, for the benefit of everyone around you.

Anne Marie, Lizzy and José were an hour or so behind when I got to the door at 3:00 p.m. And fortunately I did. It was a scrum, but I was able to register us all. By 3:30 p.m., when I left after a shower and a change, they were turning *peregrinos* away.

I headed back to the full cafés and street music, strolling, light without a pack, taking it all in. It was hard not to. There's something compelling about such casual bonhomie. There's something to life in these places of plazas and narrow streets that doesn't flourish in cul-de-sacs and mown lawns. Instead of sitting by yourself inside your comfortable house, you're a mix of people sharing a rich moment of life in the streets. Do you know this difference?

Alva, the young woman in the town surf shop where I'd spend tomorrow night, said these towns were dead in the winter. True, but that only added more poignancy to this seasonal blooming.

I ordered an espresso at my final stop. The narrow streets were now deep in shadow. The nearest street musicians were packing up. Next to me was a large family. From under the table appeared two instrument cases. The boy and girl, confident smiles on their faces, pulled out an accordion and violin. They played. The afternoon continued.

I was coming to the end of Asturias. Galicia, the final region of the Camino and home of Santiago de Compostela, was near. It was hard to conceive. After so many nights and weeks and miles, and here I was, on the doorstep.

I thought to aim for an out-of-the-way, final Asturian night on the coast in Tapia de Casariego and let this wave of *peregrinos* pass. For that was my sense, that while there was always a steady stream of walkers, there were pulses that rolled through at intervals. Anne Marie, Lizzy and José were going to stay on the more direct route, so we hugged and said farewell. Yet we all knew we'd probably run into each other again.

It was 40km to Tapia de Casariego, but the day was fine and the terrain relatively flat. And I was ready to walk.

Not the walking of making miles, or trying to get somewhere, like I had done so desperately along that brief stretch in France, but walking for the walking. I had had moments during the weeks that rolled out from Antwerp where I found myself lost in the walking itself. I wasn't calculating distance or thinking about where I'd find water or a bed, but just walking. Going, moving, feeling. Like a meditation. A meditation of movement. Mostly, when I settle inward, it's the mechanics of which I'm aware, the locomotion. The swing of the limbs, the strike of stick and foot, the rhythm of breath. Especially the breath. A meditative concentration develops with the awareness of the physicality of walking, of staying with it. Kind of like the groove I sometimes experienced when I used to run long distances. Everything else around you fades into the background, and it is only you in motion. In that state I feel like I can go forever.

But I mean something more than this, something more than mere concentration.

I find that sometimes I unexpectedly drop deeper, beyond the locomotion and breath, to the more subtle underlying sensations. The sensations on and in this body that is me, that is walking. The feelings coursing through every tiny part of this body in their infinite subtlety. Forever becoming finer and finder until they reach levels that are linked not to the corpus, but the cosmos.

This kind of walking transcends itself. It dissolves boundaries. It connects me to a greater flow, the flow that is around me, that is passing through me, that I am a part of. In this state I am aware of the feelings I generate in response to the surrounding world. I am aware of the feelings I generate in response to the machinations of my own mind. If I sense something on or in the body, I know it's tweaking my mind too. And if it is in the mind, it is in turn manifesting in the body someplace. This connection with the body is the key. Sometimes we get lost, believing understanding  is only with our head, only in thinking, thinking, thinking. This is a dead end. Without the body, there is no mind. Without the mind, there is no body. We are a seamless entity. The body and its breath guide the mind through the apparent reality of day-to-day life, to the deeper reality which underpins this life, and ultimately to the quantum reality which goes beyond our lives.

There is a constant flow of sensation through mind and body, round and round, back and forth, on and on. If, through sustained body awareness, I can observe this fundamental flow, then I am beyond walking. Not experiencing it. Not thinking it. Not reacting to it. Only observing. Only perceiving. This is a true moving meditation. It takes me to the deepest reaches of the mind, and the broadest expanses of the universe. It is a great dissolution. A liberation. Out of the movement comes a settledness, a calm that continues long after the walking has ceased.

None of this was exactly clear to me that day walking to Tapia de Casariego, but I was intuiting it. I was on a path of fuller understanding. My comprehension has become clearer as I have reflected on these instances, whether they have occurred while walking, sleeping, or sitting. Progress on the path entails developing this kind of body wisdom; the body *as it is*, not how we might like it to be.

Why, why do this? Because when you experience this universal connectivity and ever-changing flow in your body, and not merely intellectualize it, you begin to instinctively let go of the self-centered behaviors that are so harmful. You sense their root of ignorance at the deepest levels. You become free of them.

Experiencing this quality of insight is rare for me. It's only begun in the last few years that I am aware of. It is not something I can conjure at will. At best all I can do is try and set the conditions deliberately, or have the conditions result unknowingly from something I am doing. Either way it is work. Physiologically it's as if I decouple from the intense reasoning and thinking processes of the prefrontal cortex and throw open Bai Hui point on the crown of my head. This point, well-known in Tai Chi practice, hums and vibrates, tingling with normally obscured sensation. Have you ever felt this? About the size of a silver dollar. I imagine the area aglow with the invisible, great cosmic flow.

These moments are fleeting. And to be honest, in the instant they are always unexpected. Like the poetry of Veix. Like the dreams of Gourdon. Like the contentment of Ermita de Casquita. I think being unexpected is critical to their authenticity.

When I access such a state, I am beyond the apparent world, beyond life, beyond death. I am unspooling into the realm of something beyond my comprehension. This mind state is the antithesis of the repetitive loop that captures me when I let worry take the lead on the Way, take the lead in everyday life, when inside my head sounds like a bad 8-track tape on continuous play.

It is a meditative state that manifests in the going, in the practicing, in the being. It is arrival where ultimately there is no arrival.

Entering Navia around noon, about halfway for the day, I think the streets are painted or chalked in bright colors, but as I neared I realize they are flowers. Thousands and thousands of flowers – blues and pinks and purples and whites. And gold and yellow. With green cuttings. Carefully arranged in patterns, covering the roads leading to a small altar set up in front of the townhall.

Little girls in white lace and garlands skipped along with their parents.

It must be a public confirmation ceremony, I thought. But Miriam clarified *comunion* is normally in May. "For the children, when they are nine. Then, in June they celebrate Corpus Christi's day for the boys and girls who did *comunion* in May. It's a big event in Navia, but in Zarautz, nowadays, we don't celebrate."

Navia feels buoyant.

Before crossing the river on the far side of town I stop for a lunch of *tortilla* and *café con leche*. I was still so full of fish and *rabas* from yesterday in Luarca I couldn't eat more. The place is packed with Sunday dressed families enjoying a meal, the conversations animated, children running and laughing. It's moments like these when I feel the absence of family. I'm grateful I was able to return for my nephews' graduations, but now it feels so long ago and far away, it's as if it didn't happen.

A few kilometers after Navia I pass a restored *lavadero*, reminding me of the *lavoirs* I'd seen my last week in France.

The long, out-of-the-way day paid off. While my mind didn't ultimately unfurl into cosmic bliss, there are only ten of us for 30 places in the squat little building overlooking the sea on a bluff at the edge of Tapia de Casariego. Write your name on the sheet of paper, drop a donation in the box, pick a bunk upstairs. Miracle enough.

Alva, in the surf shop, told me where I could buy a bottle of wine on a Sunday – the petrol station at the town's entrance. I picked up a bottle of *vinho verde* to share with whomever I found back at the sunny table outside the *albergue*.

Colin and Julia, he from England, she Madrid. The Czech friends Simona and Svatava. A very young woman from Moldova, Nadia, and the even younger Haeri from South Korea, studying in France to become a pastry chef.

What are their stories?

What is mine?

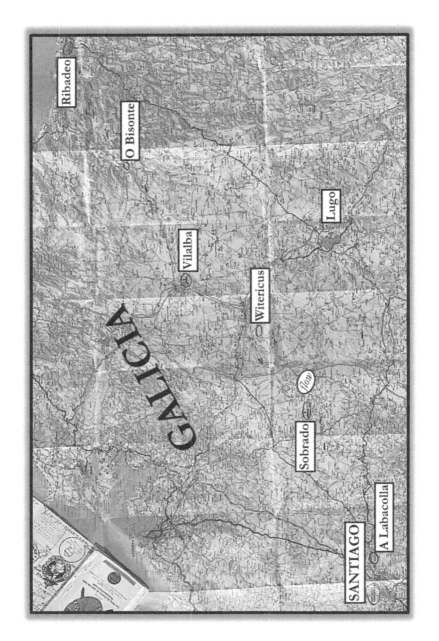

Flow of the Road **18**

I was done.

It had been a perfect night in Tapia de Casariego, maybe the quietest in an *albergue* yet. Only the sound of the gentle surf coming through a high round window all night. In the morning we were enveloped in sea fog.

Before uncorking the *vinho verde* the evening before I'd approached a guy pulling a surfboard from his car and putting it in a garage. He'd just driven a couple of hundred kilometers to surf the Atlantic coast of Galicia. The rule of thumb is surf the Cantabrian Sea side of Galicia October to December, then the Atlantic side spring and summer. He said he'd show me if I came back with a board.

I'll be back, I told myself again – I still remember where that garage is. The coast of endless coves and beaches, the *rabas* and *sardinas*, the green hills rising to snowy *picos*, the witches. Even though I had merely skirted through it, Asturias had touched me.

But I was done.

I was done with sore feet. With hefting the pack. With the race for a bed. With the snoring and smelly clothes and damp bathrooms. The stale air. It had been an easy walk into Ribadeo, the first town of Galicia. Past brown dairy cows. Past green corn. Past black and white dairy cows. Across the A-8 bridge high over the river. But when I arrived, I sought out the Oficina de Turismo, not the municipal *albergue*. I needed a *pensión* where I could park myself for a few days. I was at the brink of the impulsive decision to "just get it over with". Santiago was not more than 200kms, less than a week from here. Just keep going. Don't even stop in Ribadeo. You've got more than half the day left.

That's not how I wanted this to end.

I knew that what was crashing over me was just the accumulated momentum of three-plus months, of near constant motion, and now having the end in sight. But the more balanced part of me calmly stepped in; No, we'll stay in this nice town until you recover your frame of mind, until you feel like you *want* to finish these last days, not that you *have* to. It may take two or three days, but we'll not leave until you recover your open and eager attitude.

It took almost four days.

"Oh, it's you."

I turned around at the voice and there she was, Lena! At first I couldn't believe it. She should be long gone from here, long past Ribadeo, already in Santiago even. So unexpected her presence standing there in the street I doubted it. But the hug was real.

We weren't long-lost friends to be so happy to run into each other. But there was something more between us than just having walked together for a few days. A connection had formed, or more accurately, had been revealed. Our companionship felt very natural, maybe even long established. And while at one level I was surprised to run into Lena, whom I'd parted from in Llanes before I flew back to the States, on another level it almost seemed inevitable. She was still in Ribadeo for whatever reason, just as I was stopping here for mine. Our choices had synced, which in hindsight seems as if there was no way to avoid it.

Lena and I shared something the Camino had brought to the fore; a searching, a tentativeness with conventional life, and, maybe most of all, a solitude.

How do you share a solitude?

By recognizing and respecting each other's solitude, each other's searching, and taking comfort in the presence of a kindred spirit. We had questions stirring in us, but we didn't pretend to have answers.

We hugged again, people passing around us in the lane.

"I was looking for ice cream. I just got up from a nap," I said, still smiling with delight. "A great nap, and I had this craving. We found each other because of ice cream."

"Oh ice cream, very interesting. Yes. Let's have ice cream. I know a nice place."

While technically Lena and I had first met waiting for the train in Boo, with Ruo and Caroline, we finally figured out we had first seen each other in Deba. It was during check-in in that overwhelming *albergue* experience of mine. Another train station ironically, a place of connection.

It was a glance and I remember it clearly now. Her sea blue eyes and fair skin. Something youthful and hard at the same time. We held the glance for an extra instant, before the press of movement sent us in different directions.

What is it that accounts for such instances? Something working at a deeper level of consciousness, clearly. At some level we had known each other even before Deba. Maybe via my German ancestry, which I cannot trace beyond an orphaned great grandfather. Maybe we were bound through long past relationships.

For the next several days we mixed doing our own things with coming together. Lena liked to catch the local bus to different beaches – she loved water. I wandered the streets and markets. And I went for a massage, one of the best I've had, and way better than the shady foot massage I indulged in Paris – the matron there was clearly disappointed that no, really, all I want is my feet serviced.

The American *peregrina* had found the place and, as promised, texted me about the masseuse. The *peregrina* with the paining toes after Donostia, who'd joined the farewell table with the Germans in San Vicente de la Barquera, who was running out of time to reach Santiago. These are the random touches that gave continuity to the Camino in Spain, a kind of self-sustaining resonance that *peregrinos* shared. In contrast, *le Chemin* in Belgium and France was characterized more by external interaction, where Mia received and handed me to the Abbot, who sent me on to Jean & Jeanne, and on and on, sustained by those who gave me water, until Katie and Catherine ferried me across the frontier.

And here I am.

Here we are.

My one minor errand was to find cards to send to those who had taken in a stranger when he needed shelter: Jean & Jeanne, Seamus & Claire, M. et Mme Chenu, Isabelle, her mother and sisters. It was Michel Chenu who had put the idea in my head, that morning way back south of Paris, "Send a *carte postale* when you reach Santiago!"

But every postcard was uninspiring, even the ones of Santiago, especially the ones of Santiago. Most postcards are canned pictures aren't they, the precursor of the staged social media post – *Look, I'm here and you're not!*

Through the window of a quirky little shop I saw something promising, but the shop seemed forever on siesta. When I finally found it open, jackpot. Its postcards were in stacks, not racks, and I selected five by the same artist; saturated, semi-surrealist perspectives of Santiago.

Writing and sending these cards would give me great satisfaction. It is a simple act, of a few words, but it is an act done to acknowledge some of our very best qualities; our openness and kindness and generosity to strangers, all offered without asking for anything in return. Certainly my interactions could have been different were I another gender, race or nationality. That is not lost on me. Yet I have faith these qualities are robust. They distinguish our humanity. Yes, they can easily be buried by the day-to-day rush or suffocated by deeper prejudices. But without them we are lost.

One of the most delightful culinary discoveries Lena and I made in Ribadeo was *ortiguillas*. We had gone to a place on the recommendation of a nearby shopkeeper. I took the absence of the ubiquitous Trip Advisor seal of approval sticker in the window as a good sign. *Ortiguillas* was the one item on the menu we didn't recognize at all. When I asked the server, I couldn't make any sense of her explanation. We ordered it, the only way to find out what it was. I wrote down the word to look it up later. It turned out to be a kind of tempura of sea anemone. It had an underlying taste of fresh, cold seawater, and a hint of peppery, electric current. Odd description, I know, but it is offered in complete innocence because we had no idea what we were eating at the time.

I'd been taking *rabas, pulpo, sardinas, anchoas* and *pimientos de padrón* whenever I could. It was hard not to get an excellent plate so close to the source. There certainly are more elaborate regional dishes, but there was something very appealing about the simple freshness of these. All of it much more uplifting than the *saucisson âne* I'd chewed my last days in France. But with similar pangs of guilt, I can't say how much longer I'll order the extraordinarily clever octopus boiled alive and paprikaed for my *pulpo* plate.

The gulls hooted it up in the early mornings, their cries and chuckles bouncing off the buildings around the back of our *pensión*. I'd ended up in a room right next to Lena. The second night she had a dream on the other side of the wall; I was lying on her chest in the form of a black puppy, telling her, "Follow me if you know who I am."

As for me, mere meters away, perhaps at the same moment, I wake pressed into my bed by a great weight, not knowing where I am or what I am doing. What is this great force? was all I could muster in the disorienting instant of waking.

"It is the heart," Lena says later. "All people are connected. Some people they have doubts, but for me it is just normal. You and I, I don't know. We have a special connection."

We know each other, I am convinced, we are convinced, from long ago, but we don't know how.

Lena is not going to continue from Ribadeo.

"There is no point in me walking to Santiago. It would only be ritual. Or expectation for me now."

I want to argue, to convince her to keep going.

"For what, just the paper and stamp they give you at the end? To show people, to prove I have walked?"

"When I first saw you in Deba," I said to her, "when you were unguarded, I saw something rigid in you. I worry that if you don't allow some flexibility, it could break one day."

"Perhaps," she said. "But I don't think so."

Maybe all I'd seen in Lena was something I couldn't bend to my will.

I know she is right about not continuing. Too many of us are stuck in ritual, having lost the underlying meaning of what we are doing. But still, to have come this far.

"I cannot walk further. Even if I want to."

I didn't realize it, but Lena had injured her knee. She never mentioned it while we were walking together in our group.

"Yes, first time in my life I was injured. Very injured, so that it stopped me from walking. I had this pain in my knee from I guess it was on the fifth or sixth day when I started. And I walked and walked and walked with all the pain in my knee and I thought okay it will get better. But then there came the moment when I realized okay, this is for you Lena. Every time you want to do it and then you do it and do it and do it. You are going with the head. There is a German phrase, *mit dem Kopf durch die Wand*, which means something like, to be hell bent on getting your own way."

This reminded of the wall I'd run into outside of Aire-sur-l'Adour, when the determination in my head ran up against the reality of the Camino.

"And I know I'm a person like this. So the knee was a sign; Lena you can't do it like you want to do it. You have to give up."

I could tell these were difficult words for her, *you have to give up*. Lena was clearly someone who achieved things, who met expectations. Exceeded them.

"There are people they give up every time. They don't bring things to an end. And they have to learn other things. But for me, I have to learn that I have give up. Sometimes you just have to give up and say, okay, I tried, but can't do it. And you just have to feel all the pain that comes with this, that you lose. Feel all the humiliation. Thinking all the thoughts, when you lose, when you can't do something you really want to do, and you have to explain it to your friends and family."

She paused. "Yeah, and they maybe think you're a loser. And I have to accept it." Then laughed. "That's it!"

It took great courage, and wisdom, I thought, to come to this decision and accept it. And learn from it. At any point in the last month Lena could have cut out miles by taking a train or bus, lessened the load on her knee so she could walk the final 100km to Santiago for her *compostela* and the right to tell everybody at home she'd finished. But she didn't do this. She kept walking, kept walking until the Camino imparted its lesson. If there was a goal, this was it, the understanding. Not getting to the cathedral.

Ultimately there is no arrival.

"I still have one big question though," Lena said. "What do I want to do when I'm back in Germany!?" She tossed her head back and laughed. "My job was the problem and it still is the problem."

So, the Camino doesn't solve *everything*.

The final evening we stood in the passage outside our rooms, trying to say goodbye. There seemed to be no one else in the *pensión* besides the man behind the bar downstairs with the TV on.

The automatic timer of the corridor light kept turning off, pitching the scene into complete blackness. We talked, both a little awkward, both trying to draw out the moment, but neither wanting to appear too affected. I'd push the button to restore the light. She'd push the button. Sometimes we'd both reach, our fingers brushing.

"Okay then, goodnight."

"Yes, goodnight."

I left Ribadeo with a different mind than with which I'd entered. I was open and relaxed. My feet were flat, without padding, like the arms of an old sofa. They ached. But it didn't matter. I'd walk these miles to Santiago, not to get them over with, not to get the stamped *compostela*, but just to walk them. Whatever happened. Whether the miles offered me anything or not. There was only invitation, not expectation.

The land begins to heave and swell, as if it's taking a giant inbreath. Grey clouds low, pressing down. Dark green hills crouched. Mist rolling through vales with a life of its own. The softer limestones are left with the softer life of the coast. Now the unforgiving granites. Slabs heaved on edge by muscled backs for boundaries and fencing. Forested hillsides and stands of limp eucalyptus. Kitchen gardens overflowing with leaf, meant to sustain, not entertain. Women call their animals, both unseen. Brittle slate roofs, moss eaten. Fuelwood, in beehive stacks. Rough cut walls of sheds ripped from the same ancient log. Snippets of the A-8 motorway spanning undriven valleys, their towering concrete pylons like the legs of an alien machine stomping across the land. The *hórreos* now are rectangular, mostly of stone, mounted on mortared rock instead of staddles.

As the land tilted toward Galicia on the edge of Asturias I had stopped to ask a woman about the structure, still unsure what they were for.

"For corn, potatoes and meat."

And what are those pointed stones on top, like spikes?

She said a word I couldn't understand.

She searched for the English. "*Bruja, meiga*, witch."

They are to keep the witches from landing. At night.

A chuckle stuck in my throat. Of course there would be witches over this old land.

All the *hórreos* in Galicia I trod past had this deterrence, these menacing stone spikes. I couldn't help but check. And when some were broken or missing, I couldn't help but wonder.

Even the graveyards. Crosses towered from graves and crypts, bunched together, high and narrow, like spearpoints of a besieged troop. Holy fusillades ready for the night. Ready for the coming days of shadow.

The interior of Galicia felt more isolated than anything I'd passed through since stepping off with Rean & Jo. I'd read Galicia was one of Spain's poorest regions, if not the poorest. And it was the least densely populated of the regions I'd traversed in Spain. Galicia was also the home of Francisco Franco, Spain's dictator until 1975. Ironic that he could rule Spain for 36 years and leave his birth region so undeveloped. In contrast with Euskadi, there is virtually no heavy industry in Galicia. "Fish and shellfish," Ana told me, "and textile."

The language, Galego, is dense in my ears. I am completely lost and at first mistake it for something Eastern European, but it is the influence of Portuguese. On the Michelin 141, the definite articles *la* and *el* are replaced by *a* and *o*. It's hard for my eyes to process.

The Camino markers have flipped. It wasn't Asturias as I expected for some reason. It is here. The scallop shell indicates opposite to what it has done most of the rest of the Way. It now points with the curved ventral edge, the ribs fanning out in the direction of travel.

Walking down a remote road I encounter a sedan, which looks completely out of place on the rough track. It's coming slowly, as if scanning the surroundings. I move out of the way, wondering what errand he can be on out here. As he pulls alongside, me leaning on my trekking pole, he stops. His window rolls down and out floats cold air, cologne and a business card.

Galicia was the only area where people actively solicited for their *albergues*, like touts handing out menus in a tourist center. Approaching Mondoñedo the first afternoon a number of them waited, spaced out along the road. They weren't pushy. More hopeful than anything. To have to scrap for each *peregrino* hinted at tough competition, thin margins, and maybe a lack of other opportunities to pull together a decent living. Maybe *peregrinos* contribute proportionally more in this part of the Galician countryside than in others?

I wanted to patronize each.

But I was heading a few kilometers past town to a *donativo* I'd heard about. I liked the vibe of the *donativos*. I found them more joyful than the larger places, especially the municipal *albergues*. The *peregrinos* in them seemed less stressed, and the hosts more intimately involved. But there was something else drawing me to this particular place I couldn't quite articulate. It was a little far for a day, in fact approaching 40km again, but I couldn't resist.

I found O Bisonte on the quiet, uphill sweep of a one lane road. It was an old stone house with patchy exterior plaster. The *hórreo* stood tall and in sound condition, its witch defenses intact. The ridge on the roof of a shed was made of interlocking slates, without nails, instead of rounded tiles – I'd never seen the technique. Inside I found Carmen at an enormous cast iron stove which looked like it belonged in a museum. Pots bubbled away on top and nearby on a more modern apparatus. She seemed to be doing a dozen things at once.

The land sloped down and away from the back of the house and rolled up onto another ridge, more forest, field and pasture. Glimpses of other stone houses in the distance. It was great to be back in the countryside. The air had a stillness to it, and I knew the kind of night to expect; windless and silent, with only the calls of owls.

Heat adjusted and lids in place Carmen showed me around. Carmen was from somewhere else. She'd taken this house on rent a few years before and turned it into a unique stop along the Way. You could tell she put everything into it – it exhausted her but gave her inspiration. This was her home and she shared it.

Her *peregrino* bathroom was, I hazard to claim, the most chill along the Camino. Down around the side of the house, it was an expansive space with floor to ceiling windows. The pot faced the view. Stone floor, an elevated, wide open shower, prehistoric wall art reproduced on the remains of plaster, a plush sofa. It was a place to linger.

When she showed me the dining room, the large painting above the table caught my eye. A colored dreamscape of the cathedral in Santiago. It seemed incredibly familiar, recently familiar.

Was it one of the postcards I'd bought in Ribadeo?

"Where is this painting from?"

"Where do you think? I did it."

"No way!"

"You don't think I can paint?"

I dropped my pack and rummaged through the top compartment until I found the packet. "Look!"

Carmen laughed. She was delighted when I told her of my search for something special and for whom they were meant. I found these. And now, I end up in the house of the artist.

She'd converted the attic into an open bunk area. "But I think you will be more comfortable to share a room with another gentleman, more your age."

My age! I knew what that meant. I had to stop pretending I was in my 30s.

Through the door I could see the window wide open, the trees beyond. Yes, at least my roommate liked fresh air. Let the roving witches join us!

"His name is José. José, José?" she called.

I heard a grunt. No, it could only be.

"I'm not sharing a room with anyone called José," I said loudly and stepped through the door.

"Jerry!" José roused himself from the bed. "Mate! *¿Cómo estás?*"

It was a great mini-reunion and Carmen left us to it. It was good to see José. Though we'd only bumped into each other for a few days, then parted in Luarca, José had a good spirit about him. Kind of a mix of melancholy, gratitude, and easiness. I knew my peaceful night was right out the window though. José would snore like a bear. And he did, unremittingly. It was like sleeping in the engine room of the *Independent Pursuit*. The silicone earplugs were helpless.

Carmen laid out a vegetarian dinner more involved than the normal *donativo* spread, and it was plentiful, including the wine. I can't remember all the languages going around the table, but it was a convivial evening. Carmen's accounts of trying to fit into the tradition-bound countryside of Galicia as a single female were especially entertaining. "What, without a man I am nothing? Do you want me pregnant?"

One subject that riled her was the author of a popular German guidebook. He'd given her an unfavorable write-up, making criticisms she believed were baseless. And, given my experience with her, couldn't credit either.

She leaned forward from her chair at the head of the table, "He is Angela Merkel and I am the prime minister of Greece, he tells me how to run my house?" She pauses then exclaims, "Tell him to go fuck himself!"

More wine?

More wine!

The next evening I crowd into Plaza Santa María in Vilalba with hundreds of townsfolk and people from the surrounding countryside. Row upon row of open grills begin to flare with the drippings of roasting *sardinas*. A coven of witches barrels in from a side lane, hissing and calling, gesticulating and beckoning. They have red lips, green faces and flowers woven through their wild hair. For €2 you get a generous cup of *vino* shimmering at the rim – you choose the color – and a plate of fish. The lines begin to snake beyond the plaza, but Marie-Xose at the *albergue turístico* told me to go early, so I was one of the first. It's the festival of San Xoan, marking the summer solstice. A band is setting up on a stage for later, but in the meantime a folk group circulates among us in the plaza. They sing and play the *gaita* (traditional bagpipes), various drums, tambourines, scallop shells and something I can only describe as a small chest disk, struck up around the throat. The witches had been driven off.

It had been a good day walking from Carmen's O Bisonte, almost dreamy. More green mountains and valleys. The small road departing Carmen's headed up, up, up, and I think the land stayed somewhere around 500m above sea level. Lost in the walking a familiar sound from the day before penetrated, a rapid *scuff, scuff, scuff*. Stefan hove alongside, smiling and covered in a fine sheen of sweat. And just like the day before we exchanged pleasantries and he motored on.

It was quiet walking, largely away from roads. Time moved faster than I did. It's not that I felt slow, but more like I had detached from the normal tick-tock. Like a spacewalker casting free the tether. The special, high-pitched language of women calling their flocks mixed with the tinny tinkling of bells in the brush. I filled from gushing fountains with water so fresh from the depths of the Earth my metal bottle sweated, cold on my hip. Siamese cats appeared and disappeared here and there, like curious wood elves.

Blank of mind I wondered off the marked way. Slowly it dawned on me. Not because of the lack of markers, but because of the way the land had begun to bend. This is not the way to Santiago, something whispered to me. I stood for some time looking up at the surrounding hills and then turned around. I ran into José where I'd gone astray, and he put me back on the right path. José didn't come as far as Vilalba. I knew I wouldn't see him again on this Camino, but I suspected we'd find each other again, on another one.

You hear your story again and again, as you tell it, as you think it. And as interesting as other people's stories are, you realize they must find them just as tedious and repetitive, limiting and confining, as you find your own. I finally came to see it isn't my story measured against another, or other stories compared against others. It is all our stories together that are the story. This meta-story doesn't diminish the individual stories but makes them greater by placing them into a grander narrative. A narrative that has long been unfolding and will continue to roll on. Our solar system is around four billion years old. What was going on for the 10 billion years before that? What will go on for the next 10 billion? To feel a part of something so immense and mysterious, something so inconceivable, and yet we are living it...that will never feel stale or petty or pointless. If you can't stand in awe before such mystery, if you don't let go of your micro narrative at least a little bit, I feel sorry for you. You'll only end up choking on your bones. *Faith is patience with mystery.*

Back at the market in Ribadeo a vendor had returned a coin, wagging a finger at me, "No euro."

It looked like a euro to me, silvery center with a coppery rim. Same size and weight. At least in my hand. But not in the hand of a merchant whose fingers read coins like braille.

I looked more closely. *Real* on one side, *Brasil* on the other. Brazil? I'd never been to the country. Not even South America.

I was frosted. Someone had given me bum change somewhere, most likely deliberately. Damn it. Fine. I'll fob it off on someone else. Not one of these sharp-eyes in the market, but a busy clerk in a big store. Some kid.

I stewed like this for a little while, jingling the change in my pocket as I walked. What a dupe. I'd been taken advantage of. Laughed at. Made the fool.

Why was I so upset? Financially we're talking about a little more than a dollar, though you do tend to measure every euro as a pilgrim. I began to see the nature of my agitation. It wasn't the monetary value, it was the *I*, the little me, the stalking tyrant I'd spotted in Ermua Mendia on that forested ridge high above the Cantabrian Sea, the one I'd confidently dispatched on a cloud tumbling past on the wind. He'd snuck back, as he always does. And now I was choking on my bones.

So you'll feel better duping a pimply-faced cashier who'll have to explain to his manager why he wasn't paying attention? Will that make you feel clever, like a big man?

I move the *real* to a different pocket. No, you're coming with me. You've already passed on a bit of wisdom. I'll let you go at the right time, openly, not bitterly.

That time came my third night out of Ribadeo, at a little rural *albergue, muy tranquilo*. I'd been drawn by its odd name, Witericus. The interior walls of its tiny café were the exposed stone of the original structure. On nearly every lip and ledge were a variety of coins left by passing pilgrims. High up, barely within reach, I found a vacant spot for the *real*. You only get three tries to make it stick, and on the third it did. I don't know if there are any other *reais* on that wall, but I thought this *real*, having peeled back a little of my blindness, deserved some respite from being shuffled around unwanted in Ribadeo.

This morning, leaving Vilalba for Witericus, I thought of the fast-walking German. He must be long gone by now, no? Or maybe one more time? And sure enough, as if my thoughts had conjured him, there was Stefan, sheen of sweat and smile. But when he motored on this time, I was sure that was it, I wouldn't see him again. While it's almost impossible to remember where you stayed without checking your *credencial*, because the brain, or mine anyway, can't hold that much new stacked upon new. And the distinct colors of the days soon blend into one rainbow swirl. Immersing yourself in the Camino eventually clears a channel of intuition. It happened to me enough to notice.

You recall someone or think of something, and suddenly it manifests before you. It's in fact a little intimidating, this hidden power of foresight, for it is not firmly in our control. It summons us, rather than we do the summoning. And that is why I think most of us are more comfortable letting the power silt back over when we're back home. Losing something so unique reminded me of that metropolis of webs along the Loire, revealed in all its glory by the morning dew, but soon made invisible by the climbing sun. It was still there, even if we couldn't see it. I'd try to make a point of remembering.

The A-8 motorway was ending. I crossed over it for the last time. There was a sign. San Sebastián 568km.

In Baamonde, the quiet town at the motorway junction, who did I find having afternoon *cañas* (draft beers) waiting for the nice looking *albergue* to open? Anne Marie and Lizzy, the slow and steady Danes, exuding their characteristic good humor. This encounter I had not sensed beforehand. They would have passed while I recovered myself in Ribadeo. The perfect lesson in the value of slow and steady. Neither had suffered my tendinitis, flatfootedness, or fed-upedness.

I left them to find the Witericus, where I thanked and liberated the *real*, and shared an absolutely peaceful night of slumber. There were only six of us inside the high-ceilinged bunkroom, as many as there were kittens in the flowered bushes outside.

At this point I was no longer laboring in a particular direction. I was instead being carried along. I followed the markers across the countryside in the same way you follow a river downstream – the current takes you.

Orange pine needles were banked along the ragged asphalt of an empty lane approaching A Roxica. Sun rays freed their pungent scent. These visuals and smells were the same sensations I experienced as I cycled in the western Himalaya the previous year. And just as the sandy soil and aromatics had transported me from the French countryside near Vitry-aux-Loges to a summer afternoon at my grandmother's in South Carolina, now I was carried from Galicia to Uttarakhand, in northern India. But this time it wasn't being in one place and remembering another. It wasn't merely a jogging of dormant memories. I was in both places at once. Here and there.

It is a very different sensation. I feel unbounded.

I cross 700m. The highest point on the Camino del Norte I think. Perhaps the highest point the whole Way, unless I topped it somewhere along La Voie de Rocamadour.

The altitude is nothing for the Himalaya. Such elevation is not even considered the Himalaya proper.

But a burst of wind rushes through the pines along the road. It is the wind from that faraway range, blowing here from there, blowing there at the same instant as I feel it on my skin in Galicia.

The same wind that carries the great tits and hoopoes, that carries the cries of the women calling their animals, of the sound of an axe swing.

I look around our crowded world, at the irritating, the loathsome, the crude and pompous, myself included, and instead of judging them, I want to hold their hands and celebrate our solidarity. How interwoven *it* all is. To be a part of this tapestry, this interconnection, along with everyone else, how incomprehensibly marvelous, even if sometimes we can't stand each other.

I keep walking, utterly alone in the Galician landscape. Yet I know so many of us, even if unseen, are similarly underway. Aistė said something that resonates. *The people who I met walking the Camino are always with me. Their stories. And this keeps me going through life full-powered.*

When I get to Santiago, I think, I'll find Rean & Jo, give them a hug for embodying the kindness and generosity of the pilgrimage on my very first day. Setting me on the path. What I thought of as an exception, was really just the very special norm of the Way.

Ruo, she'd be relaxing in Porto by now. Or was she still walking, still searching, making her way to Lisbon?

And if I were with Michel of Braine-le-Château, he'd merely be approaching his halfway mark, readying to turn around and walk back.

I remembered the Abbot of Abdij Grimbergen, and the unseen monks. Yes, I kept you in my heart, thank you for keeping me in yours.

And I, *bien sûr*, had the *carte postal* for M. et Mme Chenu.

I was making for the monastery in Sobrado where I would spend the night in a crowded medieval dungeon and share the bunk bed with a milky-eyed German gnome who had feet as mine might have become if I had walked barefoot. Like a hobbit. It was a low-ceilinged torture chamber packed with sweaty pilgrims. I ran into Kemba, the Czech friends, and others. We broke bread and tipped a bit of wine.

"Before starting I thought walking the Camino would be a good break from alcohol," said Svatava as we paid the shopkeeper for a bottle, "but we've been drinking *every* night!"

Another night on the Camino.

My penultimate night.

The actual end was near.

But before the actual end, I had stumbled into something earlier in the day I'll call the metaphorical end. Or perhaps the metaphorical beginning. But definitely a different way of perceiving.

When I contemplated walking the Camino, part of my motivation was to get to know myself a little better, even if I didn't articulate this exactly. The Camino pulls you out of your routine, your comfort zone, and it is only in doing this that can you hope to develop fresh perspective. Whether you want to or not you'll get to know yourself a little better over the unfamiliar miles.

After some time underway, as I've noted, I began to sense that any insight was less about getting to know myself, and more about unknowing myself. It was more about stepping outside the small idea of myself and connecting with our shared meta-story. It was more about letting go of the guarded little narrative of who I thought I was for something greater, something more unitive. And I believe that happened, at least to some extent.

But ultimately, the Camino brought me even further, to the idea of going beyond the whole concept of a single self, whether that self be known or unknown. This is a difficult concept for me to hold on to, even though I experienced it directly.

To step back for a moment from the metaphysical evolutions on the Camino, let me note something more practical the Way impressed on me. That was for a safe place to sleep. This might sound unnoteworthy because a safe place to sleep is probably taken for granted by most of you who would be reading this account. But to be uncertain of how you will pass the night, day after day, it registers. I was, and am, immensely grateful for finding a secure and clean and comfortable place to fall asleep without fear of molestation every night along the Way, through Belgium, France and Spain. And on the container ship. Hard bed, soft bed, rubberized bed. Rustling, snoring, farting. Hooting owls or exploding plumbing. Swept or shabby. I am grateful for all the places I found and the people who kept them.

Now, returning to the concept of going beyond the idea of a single self, this developed most intensely in me through the experiences I had walking to Veix, dreaming in Gourdon, pausing near Ermita de Casquita, and this day along the road in Galicia. It was also present more generally in the walking, as I intuited in the idea of body consciousness that day walking to Tapia de Casariego. I guess I could term these experiences flow states. In each case I am unexpectedly taken beyond my conventional self and tap into states previously unimagined by me. In Veix, the deep well of poetry, in Gourdon the music and more poetry, at Ermita de Casquita, the unconditional contentment, and here, along the AC-934, a boundless upwelling of love.

But "flow state" as a term seems limiting, for it implies merely an enhanced state of mind. It is this, but also something wholly different. Maybe *flow awareness* or *flow consciousness* is a better way to put it. For it's not an enhanced state of mind as much as it is an alternative way of engagement, an alternative way of perceiving. A way of being. When it happens it's as if I've cracked the door on another realm, another dimension. But it is not a remote somewhere else, across the inconceivable distances of space-time, or beyond the mystery of death. It is here, right here, everywhere, all the time. Like the neutrinos flowing through us by the trillions right at this instant. Like the Holy Spirit. Like Liberation. I use the word *flow* very deliberately, because I *feel* the flow in every part of me. I can see it. I can hear it. I am it. The dam breaks between the conscious and the subconscious. The dam breaks between me and everything else.

I come down from that Himalayan ridge before A Roxica.

Approaching O Mesón, the polarity switches. Near kilometer 15 on the AC-934 to give a more precise location.

I was thinking about the great traveler of Güemes, and a famous priest, also in Cantabria I think, but neither of whom I met though they were sought out by those walking the Camino del Norte.

When I say the polarity switched, I mean the flow I felt inside me reversed. Like when Earth's magnetic field reverses.

I stop, slightly bewildered by the sensation. But it is a very clear feeling. Where normally my six senses take in stimulation and process it, now I feel a great flow leaving my body. Not in the sense that something finite is draining away to leave me empty. But in the sense that something infinite is flowing through me. Something boundless. Like love. Or God.

Standing there on the shoulder of the road I look at my hand. I look around. Everything appears normal. Bushes, bugs, sweat. But that this sensation, this current, has suddenly come to the fore is undeniable.

What is it?

Like with that sense of deep contentment that had come upon me almost two weeks earlier, at the junction by the Ermita de Casquita, I don't know exactly what to make of it.

It is as if I've tapped, or fallen into, a deep absorption, a *jhāna* as a Buddhist might say. Or ecstatic prayer as a Christian might. Or a Sufic trance. Where you are in union with something greater.

Its antecedent has to be the walking, I think. The type of walking I sensed that day on the way to Tapia de Casariego, where the walking is not a walk of arrival, or even rhythm, but a walk of flow.

In the same way that the cushion of meditation or prayer allows you to reach the roots of the mind, walking, long-distance walking in particular, can take you to the roots of the body, the roots of sensation and feeling. The roots of the body's consciousness. The repetitiveness of walking, like monks' chanting or the drone of Tibetan horns, it tunes you to deeper vibrations. And then, through this physical door also to the mind. For mind and body are only separate in our ignorance. And from this union, the flow.

I don't think all this exactly in the moment, but I know another way of perceiving has opened for me, at least temporarily. Right here on the roadside.

I think again of the traveler of Güemes, and the priest, who freely share what they have with passing pilgrims. Then the images of great political/spiritual figures flicker; the Dalai Lama, Jesus, Gandhi and Martin Luther King Jr. Immediately I see, I feel, the flow that comes through them. They channel it, in a boundless gush. They draw from a bottomless well, never taking from the multitudes who follow them, but only giving, sharing, transmitting. People with this kind of insight, this wisdom, they know there is no possibility of the source running dry. It is infinite, forever.

And then I imagine the worst of our popular figures. How they relentlessly suck the life force from their fans and followers. How we let them do this to us. They epitomize the neediness of our condition, where we are constantly in search of validation, grabbing at whatever we can from those around us. We are trapped by the idea of scarcity.

But it is, to use an important word of Rohr's, *abundance* I feel standing along this nondescript roadside, a powerful upwelling and outflowing. I have gone beyond the flow of walking, beyond the flow of everyday life. It shakes me, not physically, but existentially. I feel in the presence of God, whatever that might be, or maybe it's better to say in the presence of the truest sense of love. It is *unitive consciousness* mixed with *cosmic humility*, to use Rohr's terms again.

Whatever it is, it's an intense yet incredibly subtle vibration. I hear it in my head. And I think, if I can stumble upon this great cosmic flow, anyone can. That prospect brings with it a sense of hope and joy.

I feel like I should say the opening of this sensation in me was a shock. Or some kind of miraculous insight. But in the moment it was more like, oh, of course. It is only in reflecting that I have been able to give my thoughts any real coherence, begin to fully appreciate this moment.

But standing along the AC-934, in the sun, insects buzzing with the sound of the universe, I admit to being flatfooted, again. What am I supposed to do with this? The same thought I had at Ermita de Casquita. Even with the astonishment of Veix.

Sometimes I think that with more presence of mind (or maybe less presence!), more insight anyway, maybe I could have taken better advantage of these moments and harnessed the upwelling, the contentment, the flow. But somehow I doubt it works this way. This *flow consciousness*, or whatever it is, can't be quantified or captured, just like that quality of intuitiveness that comes with time on the Camino can't. Just like love. Like contentment. These states can only be realized. Realized and given space to manifest. If there is any answer or explanation to *all this*, it lies somewhere before the Big Bang. Not a place I expect to reach anytime soon. *Faith is patience with mystery.* I can be content with that.

I look at my thighs. They are smooth, my shorts having worn away all the hair as if waxed at the salon. I resume my steps along the AC-934, walking stick tapping rhythmically, water sloshing on my hip.

Santiago is another day and morning away. Ultimately there is no arrival.

Postscript

Ultimately, of course, I did walk into Santiago.

Sobrado sits along a secondary spur of the Camino Frances, from the city of Lugo. Setting out from the monastery in the morning was like merging into a highway from a country lane. It was a continuous parade of *peregrinos*. Lugo is at the 100km limit from Santiago, so many who want to do the minimum walking to qualify for a *compostela* start from there. The flow had the air of celebration. Groups far outnumbered solo pilgrims. Bursting with energy were the high school students. They laughed and talked and sang, surged together and broke apart and surged together again. I found myself among a bunch from Luarca and told them how much I had loved my brief stop in their town. We took some photos together then they raced on.

In Biomorto I stopped for a *café con leche* and a *tortilla* at a crowded café. Biomorto is about 10km short of Arzúa, where the main Camino Frances passes. I was resigned to joining the Camino Frances superhighway. It would only be for a night. I accepted it was finally time to leave the quiet spirit of the Camino del Norte.

Then I saw a sign.

A billboard really, pointing right as I was leaving Biomorto. A new way to Santiago. A new Way? But there was no one making the turn. The billboard looked so new I wondered if the route was actually open. Well, why not?

I veered off and left the carnival behind.

It turned out to be brand-new, only marked out a few months before. I walked for hours through rural countryside following markers, seeing very few people, replenishing my water where I could. There were no other pilgrims. There were no *albergues*. There were no establishments of any kind. No refreshment. It was like being back in rural France, except that I hadn't packed a lunch. I walked for 30km completely alone, enveloped in a solitary peace. This close to Santiago. I couldn't believe it. Finally, approaching a highway, the N-634 maybe, I came upon a woman selling cherries to passing motorists. I bought a half kilo bag. It's what got me through the final kilometers to A Labacolla. I chewed their juicy flesh, spitting the hard pits along the way. I couldn't have asked for a better final full day along the Camino de Santiago.

I said goodbye to my shoes and bought a bus ticket to Porto – I wouldn't be walking like Ruo. Taking off my backpack for the final time, at the *albergue* in Santiago, had been difficult. Like putting down a clinging child – *I don't want to put you down either, but I have to*. It was over, at least in the physical sense. But the string of beads my meditation group had given me, the one to which I'd attached a small scallop shell and tied to the shoulder strap? The one I touched at moments along the Way where I'd felt alone, a little lost? I had planned to "let it go", toss it ceremoniously over a cliff somewhere, or into the sea. I couldn't. I untied it and slipped it into my pocket.

Early morning, sitting on the back porch of the *albergue*, I watch a German drink one mini-can of *cerveza* Estrella Galicia after the other. Slurp, burp, crush, into the recycle bin then reach into the mini fridge. Bearded, youngish, he lights a cigarette. It's 7:00 a.m. What could his story be? Where had his Camino started? Where had it taken him?

The cathedral is shrouded in scaffolding.

I write Carmen's postcards.

In that packed *albergue* I sleep as deeply as I'd ever slept, sprawled on the bottom double bed the attendant had given me at a discount when he saw where I'd started. Yet through the fog of slumber and silicone earplugs, I can't help but be aware of the thunderous snoring of a fellow American. He snores so continuously and so violently, one suffering woman with a heavy Scandinavian accent finally cries, "Oh for God's sake!" Everyone's sentiments exactly. How can he not know? And his wife, in the upper bunk? The Camino. It imparts another lesson: in patience and tolerance, in connectedness and solidarity, in mutual respect and consideration. We are slow learners.

If my arrival in Santiago seems a little prosaic and anticlimactic, it's okay. I never considered Santiago the climax or even endpoint. Santiago was, is, just a place along a much longer Way.

A Way without end.

Looking Back

Tereza: *"I fell in love with walking and hiking. It is my way to freedom, and I can't imagine my life without it. I became a minimalist. I only need more kilometers, more mountain views, more long trails, more all day walking, more nights under the sky."*

Ruo: *"I am stronger than what I thought."*

Lena: *"Now I know the value of my just normal, normal life. Having a husband, having a baby, having a family, being healthy, having a hometown, living in a kind of freedom, living in peace. Struggling with all the daily things, yes, but happy about my just normal life."*

Aistė: *"I've learned to breathe life. Every inhalation is full of fullness, every exhalation is a release. At the end of the Camino de Santiago, one becomes completed, ready for the Camino de la Vida."*

INDEXES

Maps

Night Stays

North Atlantic
MV *Independent Pursuit*

Belgium
Antwerp, St. Julianus Gasthuys
Lier, gemeenshcap De Brug
Grimbergen, Abdij Grimbergen
Brussels, Sleep Well Youth Hostel
Braine-le-Château, home of Jean & Jeanne
Seneffe, La Désirade B&B
Croix-lez-Rouveroy, *gîte* Giselle

France
Aulnoye-Aymeries, Hôtel La Juste Place
Le Cateau-Cambrésis, *chambre d'hôte* Mireille
Saint-Quentin, Hôtel Vasco de Gama
Ham, Hôtel Le France
Abbaye d'Ourscamp, *refuge des pèlerins*

Compiègne, home of Seamus & Claire
Senlis, Monastère des Clarisses
Écouen, Hôtel Kyriad Paris Nord
Paris/Montreuil, friends' homes
Vauhallan, Abbaye Saint-Louis-du-Temple
Boissy-sous-Saint-Yon, home of M. et Mme Chenu
Étampes, *presbytère* Gîte Étape Notre Dame
Bazoches-les-Gallerandes, *presbytère* w/ Father Giuseppe
Vitry-aux-Loges, *presbytère* w/ Father Herman
Sully-sur-Loire, Hôtel Henri IV
Châtillon-sur-Loire, Le Relais de Mantelot
Saint-Thibault, Hôtel L'Auberge
La Charité-sur-Loire, *refuge des pèlerins*
Baugy, *refuge des pèlerins*
Bourges, Auberge de Jeunesse
Issoudun, Pèlerinage Issoudun
Châteauroux, Airbnb w/ Mona, Tania et Nil
Saint-Marcel, Hôtel Le Prieuré, w/ Mona, Tania et Nil
La Chapelle-Baloue, *gîte* Chez Elaine
Bénévent-l'Abbaye, *refuge des pèlerins* A dos d'Ânes
Bourganeuf, Hôtel Des Chevaliers
Eymoutiers, *presbytère*
Treignac, Chambre d'Hôte des Monédières
Corrèze, Auberge De La Tradition
Tulle, Hôtel Le Bon Accueil
Lanteuil, Hôtel Le Relais d'Auvergne
Martel, Les Trois Chats
Rocamadour, Refuge Lou Cantou de Nostro Damo
Gourdon, home of Pascale
Pomarède, Chambre d'Hôte Chez Jeanne
Montaigu-de-Quercy, Chambre d'Hôte Chez Bibi
Vignoble, w/ Hunt & Corinne
La Romieu, Le Refuge du Pèlerin
Éauze, Lou Parpalhou
Aire-sur-l'Adour, Hôtel de la Paix
Pigon, Vielle-Tursan, Chambre d'Hôte Philippe Labrouche
Hagetmau, *refuge des pèlerins* Relais de St-Jacques
Amou, Tailleur home
Sorde-l'Abbaye, *refuge des pèlerins*
Urt, Sarl House Auberge de l'Estanquet

Bayonne, Airbnb w/ Katie and Catherine
Saint-Jean-de-Luz, Hôtel Le Petit Trianon w/ Katie and Catherine

Spain
Hondarribia, Camping Faro de Higuer
Pasai Donibane, Hospital de Peregrinos
Donostia-San Sebastián, Pensión Aia
Zarautz, Pensión Txiki Polit
Deba, *albergue de peregrinos*
Lekeitio, Hostel Trinkete
Playa de Laida, Ibarrangelu, Camping Arketa
Bakio, Hostel La Parra
Plentzia, Pensión Arrarte
Portugalete, Pensión Santa María
Castro Urdiales, Hostería Villa de Castro
Liendo, *albergue de peregrinos*
San Miguel de Meruelo, Albergue de Meruelo
Boo de Piélagos, Albergue Piedad
Caborredondo, Albergue Izarra
San Vicente de la Barquera, *albergue de peregrinos* Galleon
Pendueles, Albergue Aves de Paso
Llanes, Pensión La Guia
Labacolla, Hotel Garcas
US, sister's home with nephews
Llanes, Pensión La Guia
Cuerres, Casa Belen
Colunga, Hotel Villa de Colunga
Peón, Karama Guest House
Avilés, *albergue de peregrinos*
Muros de Nalón, Albergue Casa Carmina
Santa Marina, Pensión Prada
Luarca, Albergue Villa de Luarca
Tapia de Casariego, *albergue de peregrinos*
Ribadeo, Mediante Hotel
Lugar Maariz, Mondoñedo, O Bisonte
Vilalba, Albergue As Pedreiras
Lugar Carballedo, Santa Leocadia, Albergue Witericus
Sobrado, Monasterio de Santa María
A Labacolla, Albergue Labacolla
Santiago de Compostela, Mundoalbergue

Illustrations, by chapter

1. Compostelagenootschap
Rean & Jo

2. Prelude at Sea
Royal Order of Atlantic Voyageurs
Escape pod
Navigation table
North Atlantic

3. Albert
Jeanne & Jean
Way marker, to Binche

4. Settling into France
Leaving St. Simon
Wind turbine at aerodrome
German and British war cemeteries, near Ham
Le Croix St. Elisabeth
Barge at Pont l'Eveque
Crossing the A1 before Senlis
Chapel of Monastère des Clarisses, Senlis
Rue Saint Jacques, Paris

5. M. et Mme Chenu
Colza field past Vauhallan

6. Father Giuseppe
Public knitting, Longpont-sur-Orge
Voie Romaine, from Étampes
Tractor tracks
Church, Faronville
Credencial stamps
Charolais cattle
Fresh cut timber, Domaniale d'Orleans
Château, Sully-sur-Loire

7. Over the Loire
Loire River near Gien
M. et Mme Chenu
Cycle path marking
Tania, Nil and Mona

9. Poetry of the Hills
Auburn cattle of the Creuse
Bénévent-l'Abbaye
Down from Corrèze
La Boucheur
Presidential candidates, Bannay
Entering Place Zola, Tulle
Wooden ladders, La Bitarelle
Stone outbuilding, La Bitarelle
Way to Rocamadour
Door handle, Gourdon
Pascale's lane, Gourdon
Road sign, past Saux

10. Fifty Days Past
Château de Chambert Floressas, above Dordogne River
Wood burner, Hunt & Corinne's, Vignoble
Pigeonnier, Hunt & Corinne's, Vignoble
Hunt & Corinne

11. Shadow of the Pyrenees
Garonne River
Signs on Voie du Puy-en-Velay
Colombage work, Caudecoste
Post box, Larroque-Engalin
Vineyard, Luppe Violles
Hôtel de la Paix, Aire-sur-l'Adour
WWI memorial, Le Bourg
WWI memorial and church, Vielle-Tursan
Farmhouse Philippe Labrouche, Pigon
Bunkroom, *refuge des pèlerins*, Hagetmau

12. Do You Like Rabbit?
Tailleurs; Isabelle, Cécile, Geneviève and Bernadette (seated)
Spectators, *course landaise*, Orthez
Coursière, course landaise, Orthez
Écarteur dodging *coursière, course landaise*, Orthez
Isabelle's great grandfather's house, Comblat
Lahontan
The knowing *âne*, Châteaux d'Aix, Saux
Golfe de Gascogne, Bay of Biscay, Bidart
Catherine with affogato and *coquille Saint-Jacques*, Ciboure

13. *Txotx!*
Barrels of *sagardoa*
Playa Zurriola, Gros
Surfers and mouse, Zarautz
Festival in Santa Marina, Zarautz
Lauburu on Hospital de Peregrinos, Pasai Donibane
Zumaia flysch

14. *Eskerrik Asko*
Ondarroa
Public fountain, Ispaster
Chapel of San Pedro de Atxarre Baseliza
GR signposts, cloud ridge above Bakio
Tiled building, Bakio
Beads from meditation group, Holy Cross

15. Cantabria
Hotel Arrarte, Plentzia
Liendo
Ferry boat, Laredo to Santoña
Playa de Langre
Ruo and Caroline exiting Santander
Carolina, Ruo and Lena, approaching Requejada
Tudancos
Bay at San Vicente de la Barquera

16. Scattering
Aistė's first tattoo
Communal meal, Albergue Aves de Paso, Pendueles
Hotel Garcas, A Labacolla
Prom King, Mac

17. Back in Asturias
Hórreo, Playa de la Huelga
Indiano home
Dairy cow, Santa Gedea
Sara y Aida, Casa Carmina, Muros de Nalón
Sunrise, Pensión Prada, Santa Marina
Bunk area, Albergue Villa de Luarca
11 o'clock, Pinera

18. Flow of the Road
Actual Michelin ZOOM 141 used for Galicia
Black puppy on way to San Xoan de Alba

Hórreo, nearing Galicia
Goiriz cemetery
Slate roof joinery, O Bisonte
Shed, O Bisonte
Through eucalyptus forest, heading to Lourenzá
The *FLOW*, AC 934

Postscript
Oboz shoes, finished in Santiago
Beads and shell covering O Mesón

Looking Back
The Way leaving Vilalba, Galicia

Map URLs, per d-maps.com Terms and Conditions

OVERALL ROUTE: https://d-maps.com/carte.php?num_car=2254&lang=en
FIRST DAYS: https://d-maps.com/carte.php?num_car=2090&lang=en
BRUSSELS TO PARIS: https://d-maps.com/carte.php?num_car=2976&lang=en
PARIS to Creuse River: https://d-maps.com/carte.php?num_car=2774&lang=en
La Voie de Rocamadour to VIGNOBLE: https://d-maps.com/m/europa/france/nouvelle-aquitaine/nouvelle-aquitaine05.pdf
VIGNOBLE to SPAIN: https://d-maps.com/carte.php?num_car=167730&lang=en
GIPUZKOA: https://d-maps.com/carte.php?num_car=242309&lang=en
BIZKAIA: https://d-maps.com/carte.php?num_car=242251&lang=en
CANTABRIA: https://d-maps.com/carte.php?num_car=13562&lang=en
ASTURIAS: https://d-maps.com/carte.php?num_car=13384&lang=en

ALSO BY AUTHOR

Narrative Nonfiction

No Center Stripe
A Thousand Flutterings

Poetry

Throat Filling with Sand

Made in the USA
Coppell, TX
13 February 2022

73542973R00187